**Rights and Responsibilities: Communitarian
Perspectives**
Series Editor: Amitai Etzioni

National Parks: Rights and the Common Good
    edited by Francis N. Lovett

Community Justice: An Emerging Field
    edited by David R. Karp

Civic Repentance
    edited by Amitai Etzioni

Civic Repentance

EDITED BY AMITAI ETZIONI

ROWMAN & LITTLEFIELD PUBLISHERS, INC.
Lanham • Boulder • New York • Oxford

ROWMAN & LITTLEFIELD PUBLISHERS, INC.

Published in the United States of America
by Rowman & Littlefield Publishers, Inc.
4720 Boston Way, Lanham, Maryland 20706
http://www.rowmanlittlefield.com

12 Hid's Copse Road
Cumnor Hill, Oxford OX2 9JJ, England

British Library Cataloguing in Publication Information Available

Library of Congress Cataloging-in-Publication Data

Civic repentance / edited by Amitai Etzioni.
    p.   cm. — (Rights and responsibilities)
    Includes bibliographical references and index.
    ISBN 0-8476-9234-5 (cloth : alk. paper). — ISBN 0-8476-9235-3
(pbk. : alk. paper)
    1. Communitarianism. 2. Community—Moral and ethical aspects.
3. Social ethics. 4. Social values. 5. Reparation. 6. Repentance.
7. Reconciliation. I. Etzioni, Amitai. II. Series: Rights and responsibilities
(Lanham, Md.)
HM216.C56   1999
303.3'72—dc21   98-30411
                                     CIP

Printed in the United States of America

♾™ The paper used in this publication meets the minimum requirements of American
National Standard for Information Sciences—Permanence of Paper for Printed Library
Materials, ANSI/NISO Z39.48–1992.

Contents

Preface

Civic Repentance

Amitai Etzioni

The essays collected here arose from a desire to study the lack of repentance in our civic culture, the consequences of this void, and how it might be filled. One may wonder why one would expect in the first place to find a conception such as repentance in our civic culture, which is mainly a secular one. Repentance, it has been correctly suggested, is a religious concept.[1] But one must first note that there are several important concepts that made their way from religion into our civic culture, and civic culture is clearly better for it. One such concept is stewardship, an idea many environmentalists employ when they discuss our obligations to Mother Earth. Another is reconciliation, which I shall discuss further. Repentance is not currently a concept often employed in civic dialogue, although it is occasionally loosely batted about.[2]

The absence of a well-grounded and well-developed concept of civic repentance causes considerable injustice and negative social consequences for various communities. Before I can justify this statement, I need to briefly indicate the key elements of the concept of repentance that one finds when one studies it as a religious concept. Most important, it has two elements that often come to mind and one that is overlooked surprisingly often and that may well be the most important of the three.

One element is that the person who has violated his or her religious beliefs is expected to show true remorse. The second element is that the person is supposed to do penance: pay his or her dues. Numerous discussions of repentance stop at this point. However, if this were all there is to repentance, a person could sin all week, show remorse on Sunday morning, do his or her penance by reciting a prayer fifty times, and start all over again, sinning, on Monday, possibly repeating the cycle—if not every week, all too often. Full repentance thus entails a third element: that of restructuring one's life. The loan shark helps form a mutual savings association; the drug dealer finds a legitimate job and holds on to it; the accountant who embezzled not only returns the funds but carefully guards the integrity of the accounts entrusted to him.

In the world of religion, or at least in many of the religions we are most familiar with, repentance is a key element. But this notion of repentance is far from accepted in our civic culture. A young person can show true remorse, serve whatever term is meted out to him by the judge, and lead an exemplary life for years to come, and he is still an "ex-con." Many of his civil rights are not restored. He cannot join several professions. There is a lacuna in his résumé that potential employers can freely ask about and use to deny him employment. And those in the know often treat him as an ex-con, not as a person who repented in full.

My main thesis is that we should adopt the religious concept of repentance into our civic culture. The details are complex and less pivotal. We could, for instance, seal the police files of those who stayed out of trouble for at least ten years (longer if the offense was a severe one). Such files would not be reopened until after a person was convicted of a new crime (but before sentencing). Or, we could allow past offenders to "fill the gaps" in their résumé, and not consider it an offense if they claimed to have been in a learning phase, in an adult education program, when actually they were locked behind bars. (After all, some rather important learning does take place.) As I said, details need to be worked out, but people should have opportunities to be restored to as full a membership in the community as possible.

There are two basic reasons to proceed in this way. First, it is grossly unfair to treat people who have met the full requirements of repentance as if they were no different from repeat offenders. Second, the lack of opportunities for full restoration exacts social costs. Closed doors are a major reason ex-cons hang around ex-cons, reinforcing one another's criminal tendencies, and why they do not find full repentance particularly rewarding or spiritually fulfilling. They continue to be treated as outsiders.

The essays collected here speak directly to this issue. The first, by Jeffrey Harrison, discusses the mechanisms through which offenders can regain their memberships in economic or political institutions. The article is predicated on the hypothesis that, at least in certain professions and states, repentance and redemption play a role in decisions regarding offending individuals' economic rights and the right to vote. The discussion therefore serves as a means of assessing this hypothesis. To begin, Harrison discusses current laws and rules governing the treatment of those who have acted outside of what is considered socially acceptable behavior. Examining thirty professions chosen from a 1976 American Civil Liberties Union study, he finds that those professions requiring the greatest degree of formal education often are most heavily subject to character regulation. The status of voting rights for ex-convicts varies from state to state, though more states appear to disenfranchise ex-cons today than twenty years ago.

Harrison then argues that at least in some states and for some professions, mechanisms do exist through which ex-offenders can regain their former status. Particularly, he argues that of crucial importance to this redemption is an unconditional demonstration of repentance and reparation on the part of the offender. Review boards and courts seek to assess the authenticity of repentance, and are likely to grant full readmission into some professions if the offender's repentant attitude is thought to represent a genuine moral transformation. On the other hand, Harrison notes that there is little correlation between repentance and the restoration of voting rights for ex-convicts. Rather, in those states that do restore voting rights, restoration occurs when the offender completes his sentence. Little or no effort is made to determine whether the offender has repented for his act by the time he has completed his sentence.

The masterful work by Gordon Bazemore lays out in great detail the elements of a particular form of civic repentance, restorative justice. For Bazemore, restorative justice holds that crimes harm both individuals and communities. For justice to be achieved, more than punishment is required. Instead, responses to crime must balance the needs of victims, communities, and offenders. Restorative justice is far from widely practiced. Indeed, it might be said to be a rather innovative idea, although in one form or another it has been with us, and with Native Americans and members of other cultures, for centuries. The idea raises many skeptical eyebrows in our repentanceless civic culture, which is much more punitively minded. Readers of Bazemore's essay will find a carefully laid out discussion of what restorative justice entails, references to previous works in this growing area of thought and study and an extensive and powerful review of the literature. Readers will then be able to form their own judgments of whether restorative justice should play a much larger role in our future, at least for first-time and for non-violent offenders.

Central to restorative justice is the repentance of the offender, embodied in Bazemore's term "earned redemption." While the goal of reintegrative justice is to restore the offender to membership in community, this can occur only if the offender repents for his crime and makes reparations to his victims. In this way, an offender must earn his return to society by admitting and apologizing for his act and repairing the harm he has caused both his victims and the community. Bazemore reports that the social process for achieving such repentance is the conference in which friends and family of the victim and the offender meet under the supervision of a mediator. The offender is confronted directly with the harm he has caused, as well as with the disapprobation of his family and friends. Once the offender realizes and admits his guilt, a suitable punishment is agreed upon, usually including some act of reparation. The process ideally leads to the eventual reintegration of the offender into the community. Finally, Bazemore concludes by reporting the success of experimental reintegrative justice programs in this country as evidence that such an approach to crime holds promise in the United States.

John Haley's outstanding study takes us into a civic culture that is very much given to restoring offenders into the community. He discusses the criminal justice system in Japan, a country in which repentance and redemption, in the form of apology and pardon, play a vital cultural role. Haley argues that this cultural phenomenon, largely lacking in other industrialized countries such as the United States, helps to explain the startlingly low crime rates Japan has enjoyed since World War II. As is so often the case in strong cross-cultural comparisons, the difference between the ways Americans and Japanese treat the same offenses and offenders is remarkably illuminating. Of particular interest is the incorporation of apology and repentance in the formal criminal justice system. Haley shows that if criminals in Japan admit their crimes, display remorse, and offer to make reparations to their victims, they are often released with little more than a slap on the wrist. However, offenders who fail to follow these steps are severely punished for their crimes. Indeed, it appears that Japanese authorities care more about an offender's recognition of authority and the communal values broken than retributive punishment. But despite the apparently unique role of apology and repentance in Japanese culture, Haley argues that these concepts, though perhaps more readily evident in Japan, are also present to a degree in American communities. He believes that, through a consideration of Japan, we can learn to build upon these concepts in this country and incorporate them into American criminal justice. Finally, Haley points out the preliminary success of experimental programs in the United States that seek to incorporate the ideas of apology and pardon.

Although the context and approach are quite different, Haley, like Bazemore, directly addresses the question: What does civic repentance entail? Both Bazemore and Haley highlight the importance of the community for repentance. Repentance is not merely or even largely a personal endeavor; it involves the other members of the community, including the victims of the offense, as well as the core values of the community. It might be an exaggeration to suggest that full civic repentance may not be possible outside community, but surely such a claim is not too far from the sociological facts and insights these two authors share with us.

Estelle Frankel discusses important connections between the notion of repentance, particularly as conceived in Jewish religious thought, and the role of repentance in psychotherapy. Though they are not identical, she argues that the Jewish notion of repentance, or *teshuvah*, is given secular expression through psychotherapy, although in a modified form. She writes that teshuvah provides a path of return to one's true spiritual nature, a path that reunites the individual with a larger spiritual community. In comparison, psychotherapy provides a secular path towards a sense of individual psychic wholeness. Through psychotherapy, individuals can come to an understanding of their past mistakes, accept responsibility for them, and work to restructure their lives. Frankel proceeds to investigate the steps involved in teshuvah and the psychological importance and implications of these steps.

An additional, important question Frankel raises is to what extent psychotherapy, however similar in process to repentance, is value free. That is, is psychotherapy a process that can be geared to numerous if not all values, or does it contain a value agenda all its own? This issue is of crucial importance because repentance, civic or otherwise, is not merely a process through which those who have been punished and have reconstructed their lives are reintegrated into the community, but also a process through which they become recommitted to a set of core values. But these values are not random. We would not accept that someone had repented if he strayed from and then recommitted himself to the values of the Ku Klux Klan or those promoted by the Nazis. This leaves open the question of how one distinguishes the values of a good society from errant values, a subject not tackled here. It is both interesting and important to note, however, that psychotherapy need not be limited to those who are sick or suffering from mental disorders. Psychotherapy can be and is used by many "healthy" people to improve their lives through the insights that the analytic process provides.

In his fine essay, Patrick Glynn calls attention to a phenomenon rarely studied that deserves much more attention, and not just by those interested in repentance: reconciliation. Whereas the preceding chapters discuss personal repentance and reintegration into the community, this one focuses on the relations among major social groups. A major religious group, a whole race, even a nation can repent, and in the process make amends and be reconciled with others that were its victims (for example, Germany and Israel). Social science has surprisingly little to tell us about the conditions under which group repentance and reconciliation work rather than fail, and what might be done to make them more authentic and compelling. Glynn's observations and insights open the doors to much better understanding of the opportunities, processes, and limitations of intergroup reconciliation.

Glynn's chapter discusses the importance of repentance rituals for one difficult and persistent social problem: race relations. Specifically, Glynn contends that Evangelical approaches to "racial reconciliation" have important advantages over secular approaches such as multiculturalism or conflict resolution theory. He contends that religious groups, such as the Southern Baptist Convention, the National Association of Evangelicals, and the Promise Keepers, possess a greater capacity for collective apology than secular organizations, particularly government. As evidence, Glynn cites the recent controversy over a proposed national apology for slavery, as opposed to the comparative success enjoyed by religious rituals aimed at racial reconciliation. The essay asks us to consider whether, at least for some issues, repentance ought to retain its religious context if it is to result in genuine social change.

David Carney's contribution examines the extent to which a particular class of people—politicians and high-profile government officials such as Charles Colson, Oliver North, Lee Atwater, Bob Packwood, and Marion Barry—demonstrate repentance for transgressing societal norms. The chapter examines the histories behind the activities of particular individuals, and assesses the level of repentance for each. He finds that most of the figures studied exhibit no or only rather limited and tentative repentant attitudes, though the degree of repentance varies from person to person. The article raises several important concerns. Most notably, we are forced to ask whether the general lack of contrition among this group of people reflects the absence of specific mechanisms for repentance and redemption, or whether public leaders are less able to accept responsibility for wrongdoing than other groups of people in society.

In his brief chapter, Dr. Stanley Platman, noting that the religious concepts of redemption and repentance have rarely influenced American secular life, discusses one arena in which mechanisms for repentance and redemption exist: a physician rehabilitation program in Maryland. What distinguishes this program's approach to repentance from the mechanisms discussed by Jeffrey Harrison is that it offers doctors who abuse drugs or alcohol a chance to straighten out their lives before losing their license to practice medicine. By committing themselves to this program, doctors demonstrate their repentance for their transgressions, and their desire to change their lives for the better. Successful completion of the program allows doctors to keep their license without the strict penalties that drug and alcohol abuse normally entail. However, should a doctor renege on his or her commitment and so signal a lack of repentance, disciplinary boards impose severe punishments.

Notes

Tim Bloser greatly helped me in bringing these essays to closure for this publication. Jessica Mayer worked diligently on this project before Tim Bloser joined us. I would like to thank the Lilly Foundation for making this study possible. I am especially indebted to the guidance of Sister Jeanne Knoerle.

1. For detailed discussions concerning the conception of repentance in several religions, see Amitai Etzioni, ed., *Repentance: A Comparative Perspective* (Lanham, MD: Rowman & Littlefield, 1997). That volume reflects the first part of this project.

2. For a detailed discussion, see Amitai Etzioni, *The New Golden Rule* (New York: Basic Books, 1996), chapter 8.

PART ONE

Chapter One

Repentance, Redemption, and Transformation in the Context of Economic and Civil Rights

Jeffrey L. Harrison

A. Introduction

Individuals who have been excluded in some manner from society as a result of violating its laws or norms are often required to repent and to undergo redemption[1] in order to be readmitted. In a practical sense, *readmission* means being permitted to participate in critical institutions in that society. Two of the more important formal institutions are those in which one exercises economic and political autonomy. For example, admission to a profession means one can wield a certain degree of economic power. Similarly, being permitted to vote permits one to express preferences and possibly influence public policy.[2]

This chapter is devoted to the role of repentance and redemption in qualifying one for admission to these two institutions. It focuses not on what is required to exercise these types of rights in the first place, but on the role of repentance when one has violated community norms in such a manner that he or she has had these rights removed.[3] The linkage between the loss of these rights and community norms is fairly obvious. Criminal conduct by an individual raises the issue of whether that person is likely to act in a manner consistent with the public interest when engaged in a profession.[4] Similarly, disenfranchisement is sometimes justified by the reference to the fact that the felon has breached the social contract.[5] Thus, as Judge Friendly has written, "A man who breaks the laws he has authorized his agent to make for his own governance could fairly have been thought to have abandoned the right to participate in further administration of the compact."[6]

In section B the analysis begins with a summary of current laws governing moral character and criminal conduct as they relate to economic rights and the civil right of voting. It does so by summarizing state laws regarding such matters.[7] It is offered in part as a means of comparing similar sanctions described in a 1976 study prepared by David Rudenstine and the ACLU.[8] Section C is a more focused discussion of the importance of repentance and redemption in the context of formal and informal community norms. It suggests that under ideal circumstances the relevant authorities would like to determine whether the person seeking readmission has undergone a moral transformation.[9] Section D is devoted to interpreting judicial opinions that discuss the factors that determine whether one will qualify for readmission to a variety of economic spheres. The research suggests that the question of repentance is dealt with by reference to a number of specific measures of moral development including restitution, contrition, and altruism. Finally, in section E, the role of repentance and redemption in the context of the restoration of voting rights is discussed.

With respect to the latter discussion, one caveat is in order to avoid some inferences from the discussion that follows. The undertaking of this project was predicated on the idea that repentance and redemption play a role in decisions about economic rights and the right to vote. In fact, it could be viewed as part of an overall hypothesis. The result of the study confirms this hypothesis with respect to economic rights. On the other hand, in the context of voting rights, repentance and redemption seem to have little importance independent of the way they may coincide with the conventional objectives of punishment. This will be discussed more fully in section E.

B. Current Regulations Regarding the Loss of Economic and Voting Rights

Although the focus of this research is repentance and redemption, it is useful to examine the following tables as a baseline measure of the initial approach of courts and legislatures to those who have acted outside what is deemed to be allowable behavior. Table 1.1 contains the results of a study of twenty professions in all fifty states and the District of Columbia. The twenty professions were chosen from a list of three hundred found in the 1976 ACLU study. This sample was chosen in an effort to include a range with respect to educational requirements and the importance of public trust to the effective functioning of the profession. Following the lead of the 1976 study, each jurisdiction and profession was put into one of four categories.

In the table, an X indicates that no requirement was found with respect to the moral character or prior criminal record of an applicant in that state. The number 1 indicates that the applicant must not have a criminal record. The number 2 indicates that the applicant must be of good moral character. Finally, a number 3 indicates that the applicant must be of good moral character and not have a criminal past.[10]

A comparison of the results of this 1997 study with the 1976 study suggests

Table 1.1
Selected State Regulated Professions
Concerning Felonies and Moral Character

PROFESSION   STATE

	AL	AK	AZ	AR	CA
Accountant	2	2	3	2	X
Architect	1	X	2	X	X
Attorney	3	3	2	2	2
Barber	2	X	X	2	X
Day/Child Care Operator	X	X	3	2	2
Driving Instructor	2	2	2	2	1
Electrician	X	X	X	X	X
Engineer	1	X	2	2	X
Exterminator	X	X	2	X	X
Hearing Aid Salesperson	2	1	2	2	X
Insurance Adjustor	2	3	3	3	X
Midwife	2	X	X	X	X
Mine Inspector	X	X	X	2	X
Motor Vehicle Salesperson	X	X	2	X	2
Optician	X	X	3	X	X
Pawnbroker	X	X	1	X	X
Podiatrist	2	X	X	2	X
School Bus Driver	2	2	2	2	1
Tattoo Artist	X	X	X	X	X
Teacher	2	1	X	X	3

KEY: **1**=Felony
            2=Moral Character
            3=Felony & Moral Character
            X=Not Regulated as to Either Felony or Moral Character

Table 1.1

PROFESSION	STATE				
	CO	CT	DE	DC	FL
Accountant	X	X	3	2	2
Architect	2	X	3	3	2
Attorney	2	2	2	2	2
Barber	X	X	X	X	X
Day/Child Care Operator	X	2	X	2	2
Driving Instructor	3	3	2	X	X
Electrician	X	X	X	X	X
Engineer	X	X	X	3	2
Exterminator	X	X	X	X	X
Hearing Aid Salesperson	X	X	3	X	2
Insurance Adjustor	2	X	X	1	2
Midwife	X	X	X	2	2
Mine Inspector	X	X	X	X	2
Motor Vehicle Salesperson	X	2	X	X	X
Optician	X	2	X	X	X
Pawnbroker	2	X	X	2	2
Podiatrist	X	2	X	X	2
School Bus Driver	X	X	X	1	2
Tattoo Artist	X	X	X	X	X
Teacher	2	X	X	X	2

Table 1.1

PROFESSION	STATE				
	GA	**HI**	**ID**	**IL**	**IN**
Accountant	2	X	3	1	X
Architect	1	X	3	2	X
Attorney	2	2	2	2	2
Barber	X	X	X	X	X
Day/Child Care Operator	X	X	X	X	X
Driving Instructor	2	X	X	2	2
Electrician	X	X	X	X	X
Engineer	1	X	X	2	X
Exterminator	X	2	X	X	X
Hearing Aid Salesperson	2	X	2	X	X
Insurance Adjustor	X	X	1	X	1
Midwife	1	X	1	2	X
Mine Inspector	X	X	X	X	X
Motor Vehicle Salesperson	X	2	2	X	X
Optician	2	3	X	X	X
Pawnbroker	1	X	X	X	X
Podiatrist	1	X	2	3	X
School Bus Driver	X	X	2	X	2
Tattoo Artist	X	2	X	X	X
Teacher	X	X	X	2	X

Table 1.1

PROFESSION	STATE				
	IA	KS	KY	LA	ME
Accountant	2	1	2	2	1
Architect	2	X	2	2	X
Attorney	2	2	2	2	2
Barber	X	2	2	2	X
Day/Child Care Operator	X	X	X	X	X
Driving Instructor	X	2	2	X	X
Electrician	X	X	X	1	X
Engineer	X	X	1	X	X
Exterminator	X	X	X	X	X
Hearing Aid Salesperson	X	X	1	2	X
Insurance Adjustor	X	X	X	X	X
Midwife	1	X	X	2	X
Mine Inspector	X	X	2	X	X
Motor Vehicle Salesperson	X	1	X	1	X
Optician	X	X	X	X	X
Pawnbroker	X	1	X	X	X
Podiatrist	X	X	2	2	2
School Bus Driver	2	X	X	X	X
Tattoo Artist	X	X	X	X	X
Teacher	1	X	2	X	2

Table 1.1

PROFESSION	STATE				
	MD	**MA**	**MI**	**MN**	**MS**
Accountant	1	2	2	2	2
Architect	1	2	2	2	3
Attorney	2	2	2	1	2
Barber	X	X	2	X	3
Day/Child Care Operator	X	X	2	X	1
Driving Instructor	X	X	X	2	X
Electrician	X	X	X	X	X
Engineer	1	1	2	2	2
Exterminator	X	X	X	X	X
Hearing Aid Salesperson	2	X	2	2	X
Insurance Adjustor	X	X	1	X	2
Midwife	2	2	X	X	X
Mine Inspector	X	X	X	2	X
Motor Vehicle Salesperson	X	X	X	X	X
Optician	1	1	X	X	X
Pawnbroker	2	X	X	2	1
Podiatrist	X	2	1	2	2
School Bus Driver	X	2	X	X	X
Tattoo Artist	X	X	X	X	X
Teacher	X	2	X	X	1

Table 1.1

PROFESSION	STATE				
	MO	MT	NE	NV	NH
Accountant	2	2	3	2	3
Architect	2	X	2	2	3
Attorney	2	2	2	2	2
Barber	2	2	2	2	2
Day/Child Care Operator	X	2	X	1	1
Driving Instructor	X	X	X	2	X
Electrician	X	X	X	X	X
Engineer	2	2	2	2	3
Exterminator	X	X	X	X	X
Hearing Aid Salesperson	X	2	2	X	X
Insurance Adjustor	X	X	2	3	X
Midwife	X	2	X	2	3
Mine Inspector	X	X	X	X	X
Motor Vehicle Salesperson	2	X	X	X	X
Optician	X	X	X	2	X
Pawnbroker	2	X	1	X	2
Podiatrist	2	2	2	2	2
School Bus Driver	X	2	X	2	1
Tattoo Artist	X	X	X	X	X
Teacher	2	3	2	3	1

Table 1.1

PROFESSION	STATE				
	NJ	NM	NY	NC	ND
Accountant	2	2	2	2	3
Architect	2	2	2	3	3
Attorney	2	2	3	2	2
Barber	X	3	2	1	2
Day/Child Care Operator	2	2	1	2	1
Driving Instructor	2	X	X	X	X
Electrician	X	X	X	X	X
Engineer	2	2	2	2	2
Exterminator	X	X	X	2	X
Hearing Aid Salesperson	2	1	2	2	2
Insurance Adjustor	1	3	3	3	X
Midwife	1	X	2	X	1
Mine Inspector	X	X	X	X	X
Motor Vehicle Salesperson	X	2	X	X	X
Optician	X	X	X	X	X
Pawnbroker	X	X	2	3	X
Podiatrist	3	2	2	2	2
School Bus Driver	1	X	1	X	2
Tattoo Artist	X	X	X	X	X
Teacher	1	X	2	2	2

Table 1.1

PROFESSION	STATE				
	OH	OK	OR	PA	RI
Accountant	2	2	X	2	2
Architect	2	2	X	2	2
Attorney	2	2	2	2	2
Barber	2	X	X	X	2
Day/Child Care Operator	1	2	1	1	X
Driving Instructor	X	1	2	2	X
Electrician	X	X	X	2	1
Engineer	2	3	X	2	3
Exterminator	X	X	X	X	X
Hearing Aid Salesperson	2	2	1	3	2
Insurance Adjustor	1	2	1	1	2
Midwife	3	1	2	2	2
Mine Inspector	2	X	X	2	X
Motor Vehicle Salesperson	X	1	X	X	X
Optician	2	X	X	X	2
Pawnbroker	2	2	1	1	X
Podiatrist	3	1	2	3	2
School Bus Driver	2	2	3	1	2
Tattoo Artist	X	X	1	X	X
Teacher	2	3	3	2	2

Table 1.1

PROFESSION	STATE				
	S C	**S D**	**TN**	**TX**	**UT**
Accountant	2	3	1	2	2
Architect	2	2	1	2	2
Attorney	2	2	2	3	2
Barber	X	2	1	1	2
Day/Child Care Operator	1	1	1	1	X
Driving Instructor	X	X	X	X	X
Electrician	X	X	X	X	2
Engineer	2	3	1	2	2
Exterminator	X	X	X	X	X
Hearing Aid Salesperson	2	2	X	1	X
Insurance Adjustor	2	X	X	X	X
Midwife	X	3	3	1	2
Mine Inspector	X	X	X	X	X
Motor Vehicle Salesperson	X	X	1	X	1
Optician	3	2	2	X	X
Pawnbroker	1	X	3	3	X
Podiatrist	3	2	2	2	X
School Bus Driver	2	1	1	1	1
Tattoo Artist	X	X	X	X	X
Teacher	1	3	3	2	1

Table 1.1

PROFESSION	STATE					
	VT	VA	WA	WV	WI	WY
Accountant	3	3	2	2	1	1
Architect	1	X	2	2	1	1
Attorney	2	3	2	3	2	2
Barber	X	2	X	2	1	2
Day/Child Care Operator	X	1	X	1	X	X
Driving Instructor	2	1	X	X	1	X
Electrician	X	X	X	X	X	X
Engineer	1	2	2	2	1	2
Exterminator	X	X	X	X	X	X
Hearing Aid Salesperson	1	2	X	3	1	1
Insurance Adjustor	2	X	1	X	X	1
Midwife	1	2	2	3	1	1
Mine Inspector	X	2	X	2	X	X
Motor Vehicle Salesperson	2	X	X	X	X	X
Optician	X	2	2	X	X	X
Pawnbroker	X	2	X	X	X	X
Podiatrist	1	2	1	3	X	2
School Bus Driver	X	3	X	1	X	X
Tattoo Artist	X	X	X	X	1	X
Teacher	1	1	X	2	2	X

that there have been few if any major changes in the underlying philosophy of when an individual should be excluded from a profession. There are, however, predictable changes in overall regulatory patterns as different professions increase in the level of public interest they are afforded. For example, childcare workers and those involved in casino gambling are scrutinized more closely in the late 1990s than in previous years, while barbers and cosmetologists are scrutinized less.

The table reveals a number of interesting patterns. First, all states had in place some form of "character" regulation in the case of attorneys. Health care professionals and accountants were treated similarly. In all likelihood, this can be traced to two factors. The first is the specialized nature of the knowledge used by those categories of professionals. The second is that the relationship between the professionals and their clients can involve highly personal information. Of the twenty professions examined, the least regulated were tattoo artists and pest control providers. This makes for an interesting comparison. In both these instances there is an obvious risk of danger to the customer and specialized knowledge held by the practitioner. On the other hand, unlike the case of health care professionals, there is little need for these professionals to have intimate knowledge of the clients' personal affairs. Of course, in the case of some of the professional categories, the low level of regulation may simply indicate that not all states have a need for a specific kind of professional service. Thus, there may be a discernible geographic distribution of mine inspectors or even tattoo artists.

What appears to be a correlation between specialized knowledge and the level of regulation can probably be more precisely stated as a correlation between knowledge gained as a result of formal education and regulation. For example, in the table, attorneys, accountants, engineers, podiatrists, and teachers were all more regulated than electricians, motor vehicle salespeople, and driving instructors. A number of interpretations could be offered for this. One, as suggested above, is that the issue of character is of greater importance when the knowledge is specialized. A second is that professions made up of people who have made considerable investments in acquiring specialized information may also have an interest in protecting the public image of that profession.

State-by-state comparisons are also interesting. In this survey of twenty professions, the heaviest regulations were found in Ohio, Pennsylvania, and Virginia. In these states, fifteen of twenty professions selected were subject to some form of character regulation. The lowest level of regulation was found in Indiana, Maine, Delaware, and Hawaii. In these four states, only five of the professions surveyed were regulated as to the character of the applicant. Except for the fact that all four regulated attorneys, there was little similarity in the other professions regulated. Perhaps two cautionary reminders are in order. First, the patterns presented here may be a function of the sample of the twenty professions chosen. It would be speculation to suggest that the same patterns would emerge if all three hundred professions of the 1976 study were reexamined. Second, the regulation addressed here has to do with character and admission or readmission to a profession. One should not conclude that the presence or absence of this type of regulation is a good indicator of an individual state's overall regulatory policy.

Table 1.2 reports on the voting rights status of ex-convicts as reported in 1996 by the Federal Elections Commission.[11] The table indicates a fair amount of variety among the states, ranging from those in which convicts are permitted to vote while incarcerated to those in which conviction means permanent disenfranchisement.[12] In addition, as the table suggests, treatment for crimes involving treason or elections may be treated differently than other felonies. This 1996 report of voting rights can be compared with another 1996 survey by Kathleen M. Olivares, Velmer S. Burton and Francis Cullen,[13] a 1986 study by Velmer S. Burton, Francis Cullen, and Lawrence F. Travis,[14] and the 1976 ACLU report. What these comparisons suggest is that there has been only a slight increase over the past twenty years in the voting restrictions experienced by those convicted of serious crimes. For example, the 1996 study by Olivares, et al. reports that fourteen states disenfranchise those who commit felonies or other serious crimes and do not offer automatic restoration when the individual's sentence or probationary period is complete.[15] In 1986, the study by Burton et al. put the number at eleven.[16] In 1976, the number was seventeen.[17] There is some evidence of a mild trend during the past ten years toward greater restriction of the civil rights generally of those convicted of crimes.[18] Additional interpretation of these tables is found in section E.

C. Repentance, Redemption, and Self-Interest

The Roles of Repentance and Redemption

The issue of repentance and redemption in the context of efforts to gain or regain economic or political empowerment can arise in a virtually unlimited number of ways. For example, a law student may apply for bar admission after being initially rejected when it is revealed that he or she violated the school's honor code.[19] An attorney may seek readmission to the bar after being disbarred for committing a felony.[20] A dentist may have his license suspended after sexually assaulting a patient.[21] An individual convicted of a felony in any one of several states may permanently lose the right to vote.[22]

These are all instances in which actual or aspirational community norms are violated. And, as a consequence there are varied reasons for formal and informal community sanctions. For example, imprisonment for a felony or suspension of a professional license most likely is motivated by a desire to deter future conduct by similarly tempted individuals. It can also be explained by reference to the other standard rationales for punishment — rehabilitation and retribution.[23] In a broader sense, the effort may be not to punish the individual but to protect the public by incapacitating or isolating those who have exhibited a propensity to step outside

Table 1.2

| STATE | CONVICTS DISENFRANCHISED FOR: | | | AND WHILE ON: | |
	FELONY	ELECTION	TREASON	PAROLE	PROBATION
Alabama	*Defined in AL constitution*	X	X	X	
Alaska	X	X	X	X	X
Arizona	X	X	X	X	X
Arkansas	X	X	X	X	X
California	X			X	
Colorado	X			X	X
Connecticut	X			X	X
Delaware	X	X	X	X	X
Dist. of Columbia	*If incarcerated*				
Florida	X			X	X
Georgia	*Case by case*			X	X
Hawaii	X		X		
Idaho	X		X	X	X
Illinois	X	X			
Indiana	X				

Table 1.2

CONVICTS DISENFRANCHISED FOR: AND:

STATE	FELONY	ELECTION	TREASON	ON PAROLE	ON PROBATION
Iowa	X			X	X
Kansas	X	X	X	X	X
Kentucky	X	*Bribery only*	X		
Louisiana	X			X	X
Maine				*N/A*	*N/A*
Maryland					
Massachusetts		X		X	X
Michigan	X				
Minnesota	X	X	X	X	X
Mississippi	*Certain crimes*			X	X
Missouri	X	X	X	X	X
Montana	*If incarcerated*				
Nebraska	X			X	X
Nevada	X		X	X	X
New Hampshire	X	X	X		

Table 1.2

CONVICTS DISENFRANCHISED FOR: **AND:**

STATE	FELONY	ELECTION	TREASON	ON PAROLE	ON PROBATION
New Jersey	X	X		X	X
New Mexico	X			X	X
New York	X	X		X	
North Carolina	X			X	X
North Dakota	X		X		
Ohio	X	X	X		
Oklahoma	X			X	X
Oregon	X				
Pennsylvania	*If incarcerated*	X			
Rhode Island	X			X	X
South Carolina	X	X	X	X	X
South Dakota	X			X	X
Tennessee	X		X	X	X
Texas	X			X	X
Utah		X	X		

Table 1.2

AND:

CONVICTS DISENFRANCHISED FOR:

STATE	FELONY	ELECTION	TREASON	ON PAROLE	ON PROBATION
Vermont		X			
Virginia	X	*If a felony*	X	X	X
Washington	X			X	X
West Virginia	X	*Bribery only*	X	X	X
Wisconsin	X		X	X	X
Wyoming	X	*If a felony*		X	

the norms.[24] For example, the cheating student may be more likely than noncheaters to abscond with a client's funds. In addition, some reasons for excluding these people may be a pretense; professional associations generally are motivated to retard new entry as a means of limiting competition.[25] Similarly, the fear that those convicted of criminal offenses would, if permitted to vote, seek to control the content of criminal law seems farfetched.[26]

The issues of repentance and redemption do not arise with respect to why rule-breakers should be subject to an excluding action. Instead, the issues center around when the sanctions should end and the more affirming action of permitting the person to reenter the community and its critical institutions begins. At its most basic level, the decision to permit reentry is one that calls on the community to place its trust in the individual. This willingness to place that trust in someone is likely to be greater if the person has repented—has recognized and rejected the values or beliefs that led to his or her actions.

Obviously, the notion of rehabilitation is closely linked to the idea of repentance, and some courts seem to view them as synonymous. In these instances, a person who has been rehabilitated has recognized the seriousness of his or her wrongdoing. It is possible, however, to distinguish these outcomes. A person who has been conditioned to change his or her behavior may be rehabilitated but not have repented in the sense of having undergone a moral transformation. It is also clear that repentance does not necessarily lead to reinclusion. For example, with respect to both economic rights and voting rights, the interest of competitors may be to exclude others who may dilute their influence as incumbents.[27] In addition, in a number of states, voting rights are restored when an individual's sentence is complete. Whether the end of the sentence is correlated with the point of repentance is doubtful. Repentance may occur when the sentence begins or not at all. Indeed, in some states, once one is disenfranchised, he or she cannot regain these rights.[28] Finally, in the case of economic rights alone, the belief that one is now a good risk and unlikely to cause further harm may be offset by the sense that the profession itself will lose its integrity in the eyes of the public by readmitting some individuals.[29]

Self-Interest and Community Interests

Before addressing the specifics of repentance and redemption in the context of economic rights, it is useful to examine in greater detail how these phenomena relate to the existence of a social structure generally. One thing that seems clear is that groups of humans and other species tend to undergo formal and informal processes in which rules and sanctions for violating those rules evolve.[30] This appears to be the case even if one accepts the conventional economic assumption that individuals are rational maximizers of self-interest. In the terms economists use, individuals begin to "internalize" the negative consequences—externalities—of their actions.

Whether termed moral development[31] or broadening one's sense of self,[32] this empirical observation does not explain how the actual internalization process, or at least the appearance of internalization, occurs. The possibilities range from genetic factors[33] that "require" a member of a species to sacrifice all for the benefit of the species, to learning to play the prisoner's dilemma game in which one "pretends" not to be narrowly self-interested as a means of maximizing gain.[34] In between are various combinations of effects and outcomes resulting in more community-mindedness than one might expect from the rational-maximizers typically envisioned in conventional economic models.

One starting point for investigating the development of norms is to envision narrowly self-interested individuals involved in the prisoner's dilemma game. These are circumstances in which individuals learn that it is not in their self-interest to act in a wholly self-interested manner. Even in this situation in which the strategy is to "cooperate," there must be some means of assuring others that one will cooperate. This is an especially critical issue, because in the case of both economic rights and voting rights the people involved have already demonstrated what others regard as a lack of trustworthiness. In other words, having already violated certain norms, one is not likely to be given unconditional trust by society or its representatives.

In this context, the emphasis in the repentance/redemption duality may be seen as falling on redemption because the question is whether a party is able to demonstrate his or her repentance to the satisfaction of those who can grant redemption. This is markedly short of the idea, as the more meaningful question is one of actual repentance. Nonetheless, as in solving the prisoner's dilemma, the action that seems most likely to be persuasive as a means of demonstrating repentance is an unconditional act suggesting that one *does* value the norms of the community. In more technical terms, the strategy would be to "cooperate" and to make oneself vulnerable.[35]

Thus, if one were stating an informal hypothesis, it might be that redemption (and readmission) is more likely to follow when there is an *unconditional* demonstration of commitment to the norms of the institution. An example may be useful here. Suppose, as often happens, an attorney is disbarred for unethical conduct, or a law school graduate with a criminal past is refused admission to the bar. A range of responses could be and have been used. One end of the spectrum might be to permit automatic readmission when a predetermined amount of time has passed.[36] Good behavior during this period suggests very little about repentance and trustworthiness. Another possibility is to provide the applicant with a series of steps that must be followed before readmission. This might include a specified number of hours of community service. This too tells very little about the person's repentance. Finally, at the other end of the spectrum is an unconditional approach. In other words, there are no predetermined steps that the candidate must take and no assurance that any specific steps will result in reinstatement. This involves a case-by-case analysis with the emphasis on discovering whether the person has indeed internalized the desired values independent of a focus on self-interest. Or, as one court has put it in denying the application of a bar applicant, "the applicant's determination to conclude his criminal activity apparently did not flow from an 'inborn' resolve to change his moral character."[37]

In one way, the last approach is the least desirable because it invites arbitrary action and abuse of power. In a context in which the individuals deciding on readmission are also motivated by economic concerns, the mix of a case-by-case value analysis approach and a more preconditioned approach seems desirable. As the analysis in section D illustrates, this middle position seems to be what has evolved.

This examination for cooperativeness or community-mindedness is really an inquiry is into the individual's current level of moral development. When viewed in these terms, it is useful to consider Lawrence Kohlberg's studies of moral development.[38] Kohlberg identifies three levels of moral development, each containing two stages. The three levels are labeled preconventional, conventional, and postconventional. At the preconventional level, the individual responds to "good and bad, right or wrong, but interprets these labels in terms of either the physical or hedonistic consequences of action (punishment, reward, exchange of favors) or in terms of the physical power of those who enunciate the rules and labels."[39] This level of moral reasoning is comparable to the basic neoclassical behavioral assumption that individuals are rational maximizers of self-interest and rely on a relatively primitive cost-benefit analysis.[40]

At Kohlberg's conventional level, "maintaining the expectations of the individual's family, group or nation is perceived as valuable in its own right regardless of immediate and obvious consequences."[41] The post conventional level involves "a clear effort to define moral values and principles that have validity and application apart from the authority of groups or people holding these principles and apart from the individual's own identification with these groups."[42]

The hypothesis might thus be modified and the issue addressed as to whether courts rely on unconditional community-minded acts to ascertain a Kohlberg-like moral development. What the research suggests is that courts are uniformly in search of an indication that an individual is willing to forgo a personal cost-benefit analysis in favor of a perspective in which the interest of the group (for example, the public, the profession) takes precedence. This is consistent with Kohlberg's conventional level. Obviously, a great deal of this behavior takes place in a context in which the individual is striving for redemption, and thus whether acts are unconditional is always a question. Consequently, rather than rely exclusively on unconditional actions, courts rely on a variety of things to determine whether the individual has earned redemption.

Having laid out this model as a general hypothesis, a slight refinement is necessary. Most of what has been suggested is consistent with individuals moving between different levels of moral development. And, as the discussion in section D indicates, this analysis is at the heart of what many authorities do when addressing economic rights. On the other hand, it is equally clear that one may have the requisite fundamental moral values and that the offending activity is an aberration. In these instances, the inquiry is not focused on a major change but on factors that might account for conduct that is out of character .

D. Values, Actions, and Symbols and Readmission to the Professions

The determination of whether repentance has occurred can, obviously, be based only on observable evidence. Thus, practical considerations require courts to examine many of the following:

- restitution
- specific statements or actions that indicate contrition
- character testimony from individuals in the community and the profession
- participation in community service activities; express acknowledgment of wrongdoing
- the time that has passed since the offending conduct
- whether the offense represents a pattern of conduct or an aberration
- personal characteristics

This catalogue of items tends to simplify the nature of the analysis.[43] There are a number of qualifications to be kept in mind. First, readmission may be granted when (1) the excluded individual is found to have undergone a moral transformation, or (2) when the individual already possesses the necessary level of moral competence and has acted out of character. Second, the analysis is, for the most part, a substantive one as opposed to one that is merely formalistic. For example, in a 1997 case,[44] the owner of a general store at which lottery tickets were sold sought to have her father's name added to her lottery agent's license. The father had been convicted of bookmaking, bribery, and receipt of stolen goods and had been pardoned. Although the pardon meant that his voting rights and right to serve on a jury were restored, the court held that the pardon could not be equated with a determination that the father was morally fit to serve as a lottery agent.[45]

Third, the factors are weighed, and an unremarkable showing on one is often offset by a superior showing on the others. Fourth, the weight afforded all of these factors is in part a function of the seriousness of the violative action and how closely it is associated with the profession. Thus, a convicted arsonist[46] may find it easier to be admitted to the practice of law than someone who, in a position of trust, has embezzled funds.[47] Fifth, some courts require that the evidence of repentance be related to the wrong that has been done. For example, in 1990 the Supreme Court of California was unpersuaded that an attorney who was criminally liable for stealing funds from clients could establish his good moral character by overcoming alcohol and drug abuse problems.[48] On the other hand, a convicted counterfeiter who then operates without incident in a context of enormous financial responsibility has a more compelling case.[49] Finally, as already noted, a finding that a party is repentant and worthy of rejoining a professional community does not mean he or she will do so. In addition to the fitness of an individual to rejoin a professional community, courts typically view the decision of readmission as dependent on whether readmission would be consistent with maintaining the confidence of the pubic in the profession.[50]

The importance of a number of these factors is discussed below in the context of specific representative cases.

Restitution

In many cases, the fact that the applicant for readmission has paid restitution to those injured by the conduct is pivotal. Sometimes restitution is required, and in other instances it is not formally required although it is so compelling that it is tantamount to being required.[51] The function of restitution has been recognized by the U.S. Supreme Court, which has observed, "Restitution is an effective rehabilitative penalty because it forces the defendant to confront, in concrete terms, the harm his actions have caused."[52]

If anything, the Supreme Court's view of restitution serves to highlight the difficulty of placing restitution within the analysis of whether repentance has occurred. In other words, how, if at all, is restitution related to development of a "new person" sufficient to warrant readmission? In two respects, it works more like traditional punishment. It can have a deterrent effect in that it does create in unreformed actors a need to engage in a cost-benefit analysis before repeating the violation. It may also have a more subtle effect of behavior modification in that the actor's actual preferences for some types of conduct can become less appealing. In the first instance, it would be incorrect to say that restitution is a signal of any meaningful reform. In the second instance, the issue is much more difficult but can hardly be equated with some spontaneous or even self-generated reform. On the other hand, as one California court has observed, the failure to make restitution suggests "a nonchalance about . . . financial obligations"[53] that would be inconsistent with repentance.

Precisely this quandary was addressed in *The Matter of Alfred Morris Miller*, a 1993 California case.[54] Mr. Miller, after thirty-seven years of legal practice without incident of misconduct, become the executor of an estate and evidently treated the assets as though they were his own. Eventually he was ordered by the probate court to repay $232,955 to the estate, which he did. He was found in contempt of court and voluntarily tendered his resignation to the bar.

Nine years after the incident, Miller applied for readmission. The lower-level tribunal recommended that he be readmitted, relying in part on Miller's "restitution." This analysis was the subject of appeal based on the argument that whether or not "restitution constitutes significant evidence of rehabilitation depends on whether the payment was spontaneous."[55] In this case, restitution was not explained by reformation but by "external pressure."

The court rejected the argument, stating that restitution still deserved "significant weight." The court supported this assertion by noting than once it was clear that restitution was required, Miller's "behavior was exemplary." In order to secure payment of restitution, he provided his own house and other property as collateral. Within two years he had paid the total amount due, reflecting what the court termed "an appropriate willingness, earnestness and sincerity."[56]

It is important to view the court's assessment of Miller's attitude in the context of the other weight factors listed above. For example, as noted, the behavior seemed to be an aberration. In addition, Miller showed contrition by admitting his wrongdoing and submitting his resignation to the bar; engaged in pro bono public service; provided letters from attorneys, a judge, and employers attesting to his moral character; and held positions of trust without incident during the nearly ten-year period of inactivity.

The contextual nature of restitution and its importance to the process of making an accurate assessment of the wrongdoer is vividly obvious in a South Dakota case.[57] An attorney, Pier, embezzled $45,000 from his client. Five years later he requested and received reinstatement. The court saw its goal as one of assuring that the attorney could not "inflict wrongs on society." Critical to the court's opinion was the fact that the attorney had repaid the $45,000 within days after he admitted his wrongdoing. The court noted, "Repayment alone will not establish rehabilitation, but certainly restitution expresses the sincerest form of atonement and is the surest mark of accountability."[58]

Pier was able to supply much of the same kind of evidence as Miller—community service, single offense, letters attesting to high moral character. Beyond this evidence, however, the court seemed to weigh a number of more specific personal factors. For example, the court considered the type of stress Pier was under at the time. His family was in a financial crisis, his marriage was severely strained, and both he and his wife were on medication for depression.[59] Although *Pier* and *Miller* both indicate that restitution is important, they also suggest that it is assessed along with other corroborating factors. *Miller* and *Pier* are also indicative of the relatively forgiving analysis that is applied when the event appears to be outside the individual's normal pattern of behavior.

The importance of restitution as an indicator of personal change can be further appreciated by comparing *Miller* and *Pier* with *Hippard v. State Bar of California*.[60] Hippard's violation consisted of numerous occasions of misappropriating funds from his legal clients as well as writing bad checks. He resigned from the bar in 1976 and sought readmission in 1987. In the interim he held several different jobs, was divorced, and underwent therapy for what was described as a "me-first" attitude.[61] His petition for readmission included twenty-seven letters from a variety of individuals, including attorneys, former clients, a superior court judge, and his former therapist.

Although the court noted that the violations had occurred in the relatively distant past, that he had been reliable with child support payments, and that he had made "substantial progress," it denied the request for readmission. Despite the assertion that the presence or absence of restitution was not to be determinative, the absence of restitution was in fact the sticking point. One of the requirements for reinstatement was the return to clients of any property to which they were entitled. Hippard argued that he was simply financially unable to make restitution, and the court accepted the theory that full restitution was not required as long as a showing could be made that the effort was sufficient to support an inference that Hippard was rehabilitated. On the other hand, by assessing Hippard's financial records, the court concluded that he may have been in a better position to make restitution than he claimed and that some of the restitution efforts occurred only after the petition for reinstatement.[62]

As already suggested, it is difficult to separate the various motives behind the focus on restitution. To some extent it is purely punitive in nature, perhaps appealing only to the self-interest of the applicant. In other cases, there is an obvious link between making restitution and realizing one's wrongdoing in the sense of having betrayed the community. In these instances, the making of restitution is closely linked to the concept of contrition.

Contrition

The element of contrition is described by a Kansas court as "the demonstrated consciousness of the wrongful conduct and disrepute which the conduct has brought on the profession."[63] A number of problems can arise here. For example, there is a difference between actually being contrite and demonstrating contrition. In addition, it is possible to be unable to make the necessary demonstration because of a firmly held belief that one has done no wrong. In these instances, the individual is put to the hard choice of standing by his or her convictions and suffering further exclusion or *demonstrating* contrition at the expense of a loss of personal integrity.

A rather stark example of the consequences of the failure to be contrite is *Viloria v. Sobol*.[64] Viloria, a physician, lost his license to practice medicine after alleged sexual misconduct involving a fourteen-year-old patient. In his effort to be readmitted, Viloria admitted to having "faulty judgment,"[65] but he also blamed the police and the accuser by presenting evidence of her character and actions. Ultimately, his application for readmission failed due to a failure to "fully understand . . . the harm his conduct could cause."[66]

Only slightly less subtle is *Francois v. State Board of Registration for the Heal-*

ing Arts, a 1994 Missouri case.[67] Francois was a physician who pleaded guilty to fourteen counts of falsely applying for Medicare payments. His license to practice medicine was revoked in 1988. In 1990, Francois's application for readmission was denied based on a conclusion that he had failed to present evidence of good moral character. More specifically, he had not demonstrated that he "understood the wrongfulness of his acts or had embraced a new moral code."[68] What seemed most troubling to the administrative agency involved and to the appellate court were two aspects of Francois's statements associated with his application. First, he seemed to suggest that somehow in the process it was he who had been "wronged." Second, he stated that "he was 'trying to endure the shame and humiliation that all of these circumstances have caused me in front of my peers, family and friends.'"[69] This language suggested that the crux of Francois's argument was not that he had changed but simply that he had suffered enough. Again, this fell short of the transformation that is critical to restatement. Language that was similarly damning was offered by a former high school teacher who was convicted of sexually assaulting his student and later applied to join the bar. According to the committee reviewing the case, the applicant was "too articulate, glib and adept at explaining away his past behavior."[70]

Whether an individual is contrite can also be communicated through his or her assertions. A good example is *Office of Disciplinary Counsel v. Lau.*[71] Lau was suspended from the practice of law as a result of numerous ethical violations. During the period of suspension, Lau continued to represent clients, and readmission was denied.[72] This pattern repeated itself, eventually resulting in a five-year suspension. Lau argued that a number of factors should militate against the extended suspension, including his remorse. To this the court replied, perhaps aptly, "given the *many* expressions of [remorse] in Lau's multiple disciplinary actions, it is a factor that cannot be accorded much weight."[73]

Demonstrations of Moral Development: Actions and Testimonials

Aside from restitution and contrition, a number of other observable factors are associated with the "new person."[74] In some instances, these are actions that signify a deviation from the simple pursuit of self-interest. In other instances, an extended period of hard work and dedication that is not necessarily related to altruism is also persuasive. A standard case is *Florida Board of Bar Examiners re D.M.J.,*[75] in which an alleged cocaine trafficker sought to join the Florida bar. Although acquitted on the criminal charge, the Board of Bar Examiners found that D.M.J. had willingly participated in the criminal activity, had lied to investigators, and had falsified information on his application to law school.[76] Against this history, the applicant was able to present numerous testimonials as to his moral character, including ones from judges, attorneys, and law professors. In addition, he had been active in charitable work with the Civil Air Patrol and the Kiwanis Club.

The Florida Supreme Court ordered that D.M.J. be admitted to the bar. Similarly, in an Oregon case, the bar applicant was convicted of growing marijuana. Crucial to his admission to the bar was his work on behalf of the "disadvantaged and afflicted," including those suffering from AIDS. On the other hand, the probative value of good deeds can be undercut it they seem to be "required" or clearly taken on with the aim of making a compelling case for readmission.[77]

Less an emphasis on good deeds than on hard work is a Florida case involving a bar applicant who had served prison terms for the sale of cocaine while an undergraduate.[78] He continued his education and six years after his arrest earned a law degree. Two years later he received a graduate degree in law. The court reasoned that the applicant's educational efforts were evidence of a "resolve to chart a new course for his life."[79] Primarily, the court focused not on good deeds per se, but on his lawful efforts and diligence over an eight-year period.[80]

Other Factors

In addition, the actual repentance/redemption decision involves a weighing of a number of other factors. One of these—the time since the violation—is weighed in the anticipated fashion—all other factors remaining constant, a longer period of time since the offense means that the required transformation is more likely to have occurred.[81] Two other areas of inquiry relate primarily to the issue of whether the offending conduct was an aberration. The first is the individual's overall behavioral pattern. A long period of acceptable behavior interrupted by a single bad act suggests a temporary fall from grace. Second, personal circumstances that may have resulted in extraordinary pressure may also indicate that the desired core moral values are present.

Behavioral Patterns

One test of the development of a "new person" is a concern for a pattern of behavior as opposed to a single incident. Thus, in a Maryland case,[82] a court considered the bar application of an individual (K. B.) who had entered into a bigamous marriage at age twenty-one and by the time he graduated from law school, in his late twenties, had acquired several credit cards by using fictitious names, Social Security numbers, and employment information. The applicant had served eighty-nine days in a federal detention center, provided misleading testimony at various hearings, and made only a partial effort at restitution that seemed more motivated by a desire to be admitted to the bar than by moral concerns.[83]

If anything, the case of K. B. must be a leading example of the ultimate con man or of a true split personality. For although the court considered the above, it was also confronted with evidence that K. B. had been the president of his student body at his undergraduate college, was president of the student bar association while in law school, had been presented with an award at graduation by the faculty in recognition of his outstanding qualities of "leadership and character," was deeply involved in church activities, including acting as a trustee, and was able to provide letters from attorneys and judges attesting to his rehabilitation.[84] In denying admission, the court reasoned that K. B.'s conduct was consistent with a "perceived necessity to maintain a desired level of social prestige . . . and a willingness to risk violating serious criminal laws in order to so."[85]

The case of K. B. can be compared with that of Max Allen.[86] Allen graduated from Harvard Law School in 1949. He had served in the Navy and practiced law for nearly thirty years before being convicted, in 1978, of arson and then serving time in prison. During these thirty years he had what the court described as an unblemished record. He was indefinitely suspended from the practice of law and applied for readmission five years later. The Massachusetts Board of Bar Overseers rejected his request but was reversed by the Supreme Judicial Court of Massachusetts. Clearly, the one-time "error," as evidenced by the passage of thirty years before the incident and ten years after it, seemed to convince the court that "time and experience may mend the flaws of character which allowed a mature man to err."[87]

Sometimes the objectionable behavioral pattern is confined to a shorter period of time and involves the actual effort to regain admission. For example, in *Margolis v. Wisconsin Board of Medical Examiners*,[88] Margolis sought restoration of his license to practice medicine, which had been revoked as the result of convictions relating to tax evasion. In his effort, however, to regain admission, it was discovered that his testimony differed from that offered at his criminal trial and that he had offered incomplete information to other states to which he had applied for a license. In effect, the deceit that was part of the criminal convictions seemed to extend even to efforts to be relicensed.[89]

Personal Circumstances

A number of the details often found in opinions about readmission are not always clearly relevant. Opinion writing is often characterized by the selective inclusion of facts that make the outcome of the case more acceptable. At the same time, the facts that courts seem, at least implicitly, to view as relevant may also be important to the substantive analysis. For example, in the case of Steven Pier, described above,[90] the court goes to unusual lengths to describe a personal situation—divorce, his wife's infidelity—and financial situation that would be consistent with the behavior's being an aberration.[91] Similarly, in a decision reinstating an attorney who had written bad checks, one of the first factual findings was that she was "thirty-three years old, married and the mother of two children ages seven and five."[92] In yet another case, the fact that the applicant for readmission, who had been convicted of manufacturing a controlled substance, had undergone the trauma of his wife's murder and a period of clinical depression also seemed relevant.[93] Still another opinion begins with the statement that the individual "was born in 1947, the son of immigrants" and follows with the information that he "owned a $400,000 apartment in Paris, where he met and married his wife."[94] Needless to say, this individual was not admitted.

Discussion

At the outset, it was suggested that officials considering the reinstatement or readmission of an individual could be seen as seeking to answer two related questions. First, is the applicant a person who has undergone the type of moral development that results in the subordination of narrow self-interest to community interests? Second, is the applicant a person who has always acted consistently with community goals but has, possibly due to personal circumstances, temporarily strayed? In both cases, the question is whether the individual's conduct will likely be consistent with the desired norms.

Obviously, no matter how painstaking the inquiry, it is impossible to determine whether a person has internalized community values or has, during the period of scrutiny, experienced a "jailhouse conversion." If the latter is the case, there is no repentance, and the redemption is based on a false premise. Moreover, after readmission there is no guarantee that the offending conduct will not be repeated as the individual may play the odds that he or she will avoid detection. Finally, even if his or her post reinstatement behavior is exemplary, there is no assurance that it is not the result of the simple deterrent effect of the sanctions, with the self-interested person simply calculating that the expected gains from violations are less than the expected costs of detection.

Although there is no sure way of distinguishing the truly repentant person from one adhering to the rules in order to further his or her self-interest, the variables that are deemed relevant by public officials leave little doubt that their goals are not simply to punish or to use sanctions for deterrence. All of the elements from restitution to personal circumstances suggest broader goals than those typically associated with traditional criminal law objectives. Indeed, the preceding analysis makes it clear that the objective is not simply to avoid further harm but to address the question of one's positive commitment to the community.

E. Disenfranchisement and Franchisement

As indicated in Table 1.2, the vast majority of states disenfranchise those who have been convicted of felonies. The overall data with respect to the restoration of the right to vote is found in Table 1.3. Taken from the 1996 report of the Federal Election Commission,[95] the table indicates that voting rights are restored as a matter of course in all but fourteen states. In those states, executive or legislative action[96] is required for voting rights to be restored. Two aspects of this data are particularly noteworthy. First, the same criminal conduct may have drastically different consequences as far as voting depending upon the state in which the crime is committed. Obviously, there is no consensus view as to disenfranchising those who have

Table 1.3

PROVISIONS FOR RESTORATION OF VOTING RIGHTS

STATE	DISCHARGE OF SENTENCE	RELEASE FROM CONFINEMENT	OTHER PROVISIONS	EXECUTIVE PARDON
Alabama			X [1]	
Alaska		X		X
Arizona			X [2]	X
Arkansas	X			X
California	X			
Colorado		X		X
Connecticut	X			X
Delaware			X [3]	
District of Columbia	X			
Florida	X			X
Georgia	X			
Hawaii	X			X
Idaho	X			X
Illinois		X		X

Table 1.3

PROVISIONS FOR RESTORATION OF VOTING RIGHTS

STATE	DISCHARGE OF SENTENCE	RELEASE FROM CONFINEMENT	OTHER PROVISIONS	EXECUTIVE PARDON
Indiana		X		
Iowa				X [4]
Kansas	X			X
Kentucky				X
Louisiana		X		
Maine	N/A			
Maryland	X			X [5]
Massachusetts				X [6]
Michigan		X		
Minnesota	X			
Mississippi	X		X [7]	
Missouri	X			X
Montana		X		
Nebraska	X			X

Table 1.3

PROVISIONS FOR RESTORATION OF VOTING RIGHTS

STATE	DISCHARGE OF SENTENCE	RELEASE FROM CONFINEMENT	OTHER PROVISIONS	EXECUTIVE PARDON
Nevada	X			X [8]
New Hampshire	X			X [9]
New Jersey	X			X
New Mexico	X			X
New York	X			X [10]
North Carolina	X			X
North Dakota		X	X [11]	
Ohio	X			X
Oklahoma	X			X
Oregon			X [12]	X
Pennsylvania	N/A			
Rhode Island	X			X
South Carolina	X			X
South Dakota	X			X

Table 1.3

PROVISIONS FOR RESTORATION OF VOTING RIGHTS

STATE	DISCHARGE OF SENTENCE	RELEASE FROM CONFINEMENT	OTHER PROVISIONS	EXECUTIVE PARDON
Tennessee	X			X [13]
Texas	X [14]			X
Utah	N/A			
Vermont	N/A			
Virginia			X [15]	
Washington	X			X
West Virginia	X			
Wisconsin	X			X
Wyoming				X

Table 1.3 continued

1.	Pardoned by state board of pardons and paroles
2.	Restoration of civil rights
3.	Legislation pending for restoration after five years
4.	Governor or parole board recommendation may restore rights
5.	Must receive executive pardon after second felony
6.	Rights restored three years from date of final conviction
7.	Two-thirds vote of both houses of state legislature
8.	Application can be made after five years
9.	State Supreme Court pardon
10.	Or parole board
11.	State pardon board
12.	Discharged, paroled, or conviction set aside
13.	No restoration for first-degree murder, aggravated rape, voter fraud, or treason
14.	Two years from completion of sentence
15.	Governor may restore rights

Note: This table is compiled from data in Brian J. Hancock, "The Voting Rights of Convicted Felons," *Journal of Election Administration* 17 (1996): 35.

committed crimes. Second, there is very little indication that repentance is a factor other than what level of repentance, if any, may be inferred from the person's completion of his or her sentence. There is little sign of a case-by-case analysis devoted to determining whether the crucial conduct was an aberration or whether the person involved has undergone a moral transformation.

It is useful in analyzing the restoration of voting rights to review the reasons for denying the right to vote to those convicted of crimes in the first place. In all, four rationales of varying legitimacy seem to have been offered.[97] First, as noted in the introduction, is the "social contract" justification recognized by Judge Friendly in *Green v. Board of Elections*.[98] Second, the proposition has been advanced that the person violating the law is morally unable to vote in a way that is consistent with the common good.[99] Third, a rather weak argument has been made that those who have violated the law would vote—evidently in concert—to change the scope and enforcement of criminal law.[100] Finally, it has been suggested that those who have engaged in criminal conduct are more likely to engage in election fraud.[101]

The later two rationales seem fanciful if not simply impractical.[102] The first two rationales fit squarely into the general area of the individual's moral development and commitment to a larger self than one narrowly defined. Precisely how this issue is related to the length of a prison sentence or any predetermined standard is not obvious, which suggests that the linkage of the right to vote to incarceration is something of a non sequitur. This is manifested in two ways. Restoration of the right to vote is denied to those who are morally qualified. In addition, under current law, even the least repentant criminal is automatically restored in time in most states.

This questionable linkage can be examined further by comparing the rationales for disenfranchisement with the purposes of punishment. Punishment has the purposes of rehabilitation, deterrence, retribution, and incapacitation. In the case of voting, the social-contract rationale—the most compelling of the four rationales for disenfranchisement—would seem to have as its purpose only the eventual assurance that, as a voter, the individual would have an interest in society's well-being. Put differently, it is difficult to see disenfranchisement as realistically achieving any of the usual goals of punishment. Ideally, the same analysis that characterizes the restoration of economic rights would seem to be called for in the case of voting rights. But actual practice is quite different.

Given disconnectedness between voting rights restoration and repentance, only a few general observations are possible. First, the data suggests, albeit weakly, that it is possible to view the attitude of states toward the restoration of voting rights as changing along with attitudes toward the purposes of punishment. More specifically, as rehabilitation as a purpose of punishment rises and wanes so too does the likelihood that voting rights will be restored. As the tables indicate, there was a slight decline from 1976 to 1986 in the number of states in which voting rights were permanently removed. Since 1986, the number has increased. This trend is roughly consistent with a period during which rehabilitation was looked upon with favor compared to one during which there was a call for harsher treatment of criminals.[103]

Second, although the number of states permanently disenfranchising those convicted of serious crimes has varied with the overall variation in views of the purposes of punishment, southern states have traditionally been the most reluctant to restore voting rights. For example, in Mississippi, restoration occurs only by a two-thirds vote of both houses of the legislature. Although it is dangerous to generalize, this seems consistent with the conventional view of the South as more conservative and less concerned with rehabilitation than with the other purposes of punishment. It has also been linked to conscious efforts at racial discrimination.[104] A third factor to be noted, and not just with reference to the South, is the disproportionate impact disenfranchisement has on blacks. It has been estimated that one in seven black men are currently disenfranchised as a result of criminal conviction.[105]

These data suggest that those who are convicted of crimes either have little political clout or are not motivated very strongly to have their voting rights restored. In actuality, both of these are probably true. On the issue of political influence, those who are incarcerated are from traditionally relatively powerless groups. In addition, nationwide voter apathy supports an argument that restoration of the right to vote may not be a high priority. This can be contrasted with economic rights—a context in which the individual is highly motivated to achieve restoration and in which there is a fair amount of political influence.

The powerlessness of those disenfranchised does not mean that other segments of society should not evidence greater concern about voting rights. The input of the repentant convict or ex-convict may be extremely valuable in determining policy. On the other hand, the current absence of attention to this issue suggests that this input is not valued by those who are in positions to restore voting rights.[106] Moreover, there is an ambivalence characterized by some generalized belief in the "right to vote" being offset by a more practical concern about defining the electorate in a way that maintains the status quo. This lack of attention also may be traced to another distinction between voting rights and economic rights. A person who is denied economic rights may not be able to earn a livelihood and may become a "cost" to society. Deprivation of voting rights, on the other hand, is relatively inexpensive in a monetary sense, and the losses are hardly tangible.

F. Conclusion

This analysis has focused on the roles of repentance and redemption in the context of decisions to readmit individuals to economic and political institutions. The specific contexts examined are the right to professional licensure and the right to vote. Surprisingly, the role of repentance and redemption in these two contexts is quite different. When it comes to licensure, the issue of repentance is expressly addressed. Courts and administrative agencies focus on the question of trust. More specifically, does the person who violated community standards now possess the moral competency or community-mindedness to justify renewed trust? Factors such as restitution, contrition, altruistic acts and behavioral patterns all play a role in case-by-case analysis.

Paradoxically, the justifications for disenfranchising those who have committed crimes are similar to those offered for denying economic access. Yet the roles of repentance and redemption are quite different. There is virtually no analysis of the moral competence of the disenfranchised. Instead, disenfranchisement is treated as a form of punishment. This is something of a conceptual mismatch, as disenfranchisement would seem not to serve or only marginally to serve any of the typically offered rationales for criminal sanctions. The lack of a substantive analysis of the moral competence of those who have committed serious crimes can be traced in part to the impracticality of such an analysis. It is more likely a function of the relative political powerlessness of those who are convicted of crimes and a general ambivalence about how inclusive a democracy can or should be.

Notes

1. In this chapter, these terms will often be used together. The concept of repentance refers to one's internal change, whereas redemption is the societal response to that change.

2. Voting is just one of a host of civil or political rights including the right to serve on juries, hold public office, etc.

3. In some instances, individuals will lose already existing rights such as the right to vote or the right to practice medicine. In others, they will not have qualified for these rights in the first place but become disqualified. This discussion focuses on regaining existing rights and gaining forfeited but not yet enjoyed rights.

4. The public-interest rationale can be a justification for what is in reality a policy of protecting the financial interests of a profession or a ruling elite. Here, however, it means the protection of the public, generally, from a harm caused by one who has violated community norms.

5. *Green v. Board of Education*, 380 F.2d 445 (2nd Cir. 1967), *cert. denied* 389 U.S. 1048 (1968). Also see Note, "The Disenfranchisement of Ex-Felons: Citizenship, Criminality, and 'The Purity of the Ballot Box,'" 102 *Harvard Law Review* 1300 (1989). In addition to the social-contract rationale, other rationales are (1) to avoid the influence of convicts on the criminal law; (2) to reduce the likelihood of election fraud; and (3) to exclude those with doubtful "moral competence." See "The Disenfranchisement of Ex-Felons," 1300.

6. *Green v. Board of Education*.

7. David Rudenstine, *The Rights of Ex-Offenders* (New York: Avon Books, 1979).

8. In addition, the results of a 1986 study on civil rights generally, including voting rights, is used for comparison purposes. Velmer S. Burton, Jr., Francis T. Cullen, and L. F. Travis III, "The Collateral Consequences of a Felony Conviction: A National Study of State Statutes," *Federal Probation* 51 (1987): 52.

9. As the following materials indicate, the issue is also sometimes viewed as whether an individual who already possesses the "right" values has behaved out of character.

10. Rudenstine, *Rights of Ex-Offenders*, 171.

11. Brian J. Hancock, "The Voting Rights of Convicted Felons," *Journal of Election Administration* 17 (1996): 35.

12. Subject to reinstatement by executive or legislative action.

13. "The Collateral Consequences of a Felony Conviction: A National Study of States Legal Codes 10 Years Later," *Federal Probation* 60 (September 1996): 10 [hereinafter "1996 Study"]. This article was done for the purpose of comparing its results with those found in a 1986 report. In addition to voting rights, the authors also examine the right to serve on a jury, the right to hold public employment, the right to hold public office, and the right to own a firearm, among others. What the comparative aspect of their studies reveals is that the position of convicted felons has changed little when it comes to the right to vote, the right to serve on a jury, and the right to own a firearm. There was, however, a dramatic increase, from eight to forty-six, in the number of jurisdictions requiring felons to register with state law enforcement officials.

14. "The Collateral Consequences of a Felony Conviction: A National Study of State Statutes," *Federal Probation* 51 (1987): 52 [hereinafter "1986 Study"].

15. 1996 Study.

16. 1986 Study.

17. Rudenstine, *Rights of Ex-Offenders*. There appears to be some discrepancy between recent studies. For example, 1996 Study lists fourteen states as permanently restricting the right to vote. It compares this number with 1986 Study, which lists eleven states in the same category and concludes that there has been a modest increase in voting rights restrictions. On the other hand, the Hancock study, upon which Table 2 is based, seems to list nine to twelve states in this category.

18. See Richard Dawkins, *The Selfish Gene* (New York: Oxford University Press, 1976).

19. *In re Petition of John A. Zbiegien for Review of the State Board of Law Examiners' Decision*, 433 N.W.2d 871 (Minn. 1988).

20. See, e.g., *In the Matter of Max J. Allen*, 509 N.E.2d 1158 (Mass. 1987).

21. See, e.g., *Melone v. New York Education Department*, 581 N.Y.S.2d 894 (N.Y. 1992).

22. See Table 1.2.

23. See generally Wayne R. LaFave and Austin W. Scott, Jr., *Criminal Law*, 2nd

ed. (St. Paul, Minn.: West Publishing, 1986), 22-27.

24. LaFave and Scott, *Criminal Law*.

25. See generally Jeffrey L. Harrison, Thomas D. Morgan, and Paul R. Verkuil, *Regulation and Deregulation* (St. Paul, Minn.: West Publishing, 1996), 34-5.

26. Note, "The Disenfranchisement of Ex-Felons," 1302-3.

27. This is more obvious in the case of economic rights, but, given the disproportionate number of blacks who are imprisoned and are disenfranchised, a case can be made that there is an impact on electoral outcomes. See generally Andrew L. Shapiro, "Challenging Criminal Disenfranchisement Under the Voting Rights Act: A New Strategy," *Yale Law Journal* 103 (1993): 538-39.

28. Conversely, most states restore voting rights automatically upon completion of the sentence or parole. Given the high rates of recidivism, there hardly seems to be much of a connection between voting rights and rehabilitation or moral development. See discussion in section E.

29. See, e.g., *In the Matter of the Reinstatement of William M. Page to Membership in the Oklahoma Bar Association and to the Roll of Attorneys*, 866 P.2d 1207 (Okla. 1993); *In the Matter of the Petition of Steven L. Pier for Reinstatement to the Practice of Law*, 561 N.W.2d 297 (S.D., 1997).

30. See, e.g., Robert D. Cooter, "Decentralized Law for a Complex Economy: The Structural Approach to Adjudicating the New Law Merchant," *University of Pennsylvania Law Review* 144 (1996): 1643; Richard H. McAdams, "Group Norms, Gossip and Blackmail," *University of Pennsylvania Law Review* 144 (1996): 2237; Michael Reisman, "Lining-up: The Microlegal System of Queues," *University of Cinncinati Law Review* 417 (1985).

31. Lawrence Kohlberg, "Moral Stages and Moralization," in *Moral Development and Behavior*, ed. T. Likona (New York: Holt, Rinehart, and Winston, 1976).

32. See, e.g., Amitai Etzioni, *The Moral Dimension* (New York: The Free Press, 1988), 26-29; H. Margolis, *Selfishness, Altruism and Morality* (New York: Cambridge University Press, 1982); Jeffrey L. Harrison, "Egoism, Altruism and Market Illusions: The Limits of Law and Economics" *UCLA Law Review* 33 (1986): 1338-54.

33. Dawkins, *The Selfish Gene* .

34. Robert Axelrod, *The Evolution of Cooperation* (New York: Basic Books, 1984).

35. The prisoner's dilemma is "won," or at least "solved," when each player adopts a strategy that appears not to be in his or her short-term self-interest.

36. In the case of bar membership, some states do in fact set a minimum time, but unconditional readmission does not follow.

37. *In re Application of David H.*, 392 A.2d 83 (Md. 1978).

38. A. Colby, L. Kohlberg, J. Gibbs, and M. Lieberman, "A Longitudinal Study of Moral Judgment," *Monograph of the Society for Research in Child Development* 48, nos. 1-2 (1983).

39. Lawrence Kohlberg, *The Philosophy of Moral Development* (San Francisco:

Harper and Row, 1981), 17.

40. Harrison, "Egoism, Altruism and Market Illusions," 1324.

41. Kohlberg, *Philosophy of Moral Development*, 17.

42. Kohlberg, *Philosophy of Moral Development*, 18.

43. Deborah Rhode, "Moral Character as a Professional Credential," *Yale Law Journal* 94 (1985): 543-46; Maureen M. Carr, "The Effect of Prior Criminal Conduct on the Admission to Practice Law: The Move to More Flexible Admission Standards," *Georgetown Journal of Legal Ethics* 8 (1995): 367.

44. *Storcella v. Department of Treasury, Division of State Lottery*, 686 A.2d 789 (N.J. 1997).

45. For similar reasoning but a different result, see *Petition of John B. Harrington*, 367 A.2d 161 (Vt. 1976).

46. *Matter of Max J. Allen.*

47. *Office of Disciplinary Counsel v. K. S. Lau* 1997 WL 292801 (Ha. 1997).

48. *Stanley v. State Bar of California*, 788 P.2d 697 (Cal. 1990). A similar point is made in *In the Matter of the Application of Donald G. Mathews for Admission to the Bar of New Jersey*, 462 A.2d 165 (N.J. 1983). On the other hand, the South Dakota Supreme Court has ruled that recovery from alcoholism may warrant reinstatement when the misconduct was proximately caused by the alcoholism. *In the Matter of the Discipline of Herman B. Walker*, 254 N.W.2d 452 (S.D. 1977). See also *Florida Board of Bar Examiners re J.A.S.*, 658 So.2d 515 (1995).

49. *In the Matter of Jerry D. Rudman*, 1993 WL 404095 (Cal. 1993).

50. See, e.g. *Reinstatement of William M. Page*; *Petition of Steven L. Pier.*

51. *In re Petition of Donald W. Medley*, 687 So.2d 1219 (Miss. 1997); *Brookman v. State Bar of California*, 760 P.2d 1023 (Cal. 1988)

52. *Kelly v. Robinson*, 479 U.S. 36, 49, n.10 (1986).

53. *Harrington v. Department of Real Estate, State of California*, 263 Cal. App.3d 394 (Cal. 1989).

54. 1993 WL 156082 (Cal. 1993)

55. 1993 WL 156082 (Cal. 1993), 2-3.

56. 1993 WL 156082 (Cal. 1993), 3.

57. *Petition of Steven L. Pier.*

58. *Petition of Steven L. Pier.*

59. *Petition of Steven L. Pier.*

60. *Hippard v. State Bar of California*, 782 P.2d 1140 (Cal. 1989).

61. *Hippard*, 782 P.2d 1140 (Cal. 1989).

62. *Hippard*, 1146.

63. *Varkas v. Kansas State Board of Healing Arts*, 833 P.2d 949, (Ka. App. 1997).

64. 597 N.Y.S.2d 218 (N.Y. 1993).

65. 597 N.Y.S.2d 218 (N.Y. 1993), 218.

66. 597 N.Y.S.2d 218 (N.Y. 1993), 219.

67. 880 S.W. 2d 601 (Mo. 1994).

68. 880 S.W. 2d 601 (Mo. 1994), 603.

69. 880 S.W. 2d 601 (Mo. 1994).

70. *Application of T.J.S.*, 1997 WL 151417 (N.H. 1997).

71. 1997 WL 292801 (Ha. 1997).

72. For a similar pattern in the context of a reapplication of a dentist, see *C.O. Wedeberg v. Department of Registration and Education*, 237 N.E.2d 557 (Ill. 1968). See also *In the Matter of the Application for the Reinstatement of Gordon Clinton Peterson*, 274 N.W.2d 922 (S.Ct. Minn., 1979).

73. *Lau*, 5 (emphasis added). Of a similar nature are cases in which the applicant has not completed conditions specified for readmission or has behaved in a less than fully candid manner during the period of reapplication. This casual attitude also speaks of a lack of contrition. See, e.g., *Cogan v. Board of Osteopathic Medicine*, 505 N.W. 2d 1 (1993) and *In the Matter of the Application of Charles M. for Admission to the Bar of Maryland*, 545 A.2d 7 (Court of Appeals, Md., 1988).

74. See, e.g., *In re Cason*, 294 S.E.2d 520 (Ga. 1982).

75. 586 So.2d 1049 (1991).

76. 586 So.2d 1049 (1991), 1050.

77. *In the Matter of Harvey Prager*, 661 N.E.2d 84 (Mass. 1996).

78. *In re Petition of Jose Agustine Diez-Arguelles*, 401 So.2d 1347 (S.Ct. Fla., 1981).

79. *Petition of Jose Agustine Diez-Arguelles*, 1349.

80. Work toward the doctorate in clinical psychology played a role in the readmission of another disbarred attorney. *In re Elaine W. Kerr*, 675 A.2d 59 (D.C. 1996). On the other hand, for an older case suggesting that years of work and evidence of "honesty and integrity in business dealings" is not sufficient evidence to permit readmission, see *Roth v. State Bar*, 253 P.2d 969 (Cal. 1953).

81. See, e.g., *In the Matter of the Application of John Curtis Dortch for Admission to the Bar of Maryland*, 687 A.2d 245 (Md. 1996); *In re Application of Bernard F. Avcollie*, 637 A.2d 409 (Conn. 1993); *Pharr v. Standing Committee on Recommendations to the Bar*, 346 A.2d 115 (Conn. 1975).

82. *In re Application of K. B. for Admission to the Bar of Maryland*, 434 A.2d 541 (Md. 1981).

83. *In re Application of K. B*, 541-46.

84. *In re Application of K. B.*

85. *In re Application of K. B*, 546.

86. *Matter of Max J. Allen.*

87. *Matter of Max J. Allen*, 1162. For an example of a single incident of plagiarism by a law student not establishing a pattern of behavior, see, *In re Petition of John A. Zbiegien for Review of the State Board of Law Examiner's Decision*, 433 N.W. 871 (Minn. 1988).

88. 177 N.W.2d 353 (Wisc. 1970).

89. Giving misleading information on bar applications with regard to prior misconduct often undermines an individual's claim to have been rehabilitated. See, e.g., *In the Matter of Albert Lee Willis*, 215 S.E.2d 771 (N.Ca. 1975).

90. *Harrington v. Department.*

91. *Harrington v. Department,* 298.

92. *The Florida Bar, re Ana Hernandez-Yanks*, 690 So.2d 1270 (Fla. 1997).

93. *In the Matter of the Application of Kenneth Miles Jaffee, for Admission to the Bar of the State of Oregon*, 874 P.2d 1299 (Ore. 1994).

94. *Matter of Harvey Prager.*

95. 1996 Study.

96. For example, in Mississippi a two-thirds vote of both houses of the legislature is necessary in order to regain one's right to vote.

97. Note, "The Disenfranchisement of Ex-Felons," 1300. See also Jesse Furman, "Political Illiberalism: The Paradox of Disenfranchisement and the Ambivalences of Rawlsian Justice," *Yale Law Journal* 106 (1997): 1221-2.

98. 380 F.2d 445.

99. Note, "The Disenfranchisement of Ex-Felons," 1307-9.

100. Judge Friendly, in *Green,* also seems to endorse this justification. 390 F.2d at 451.

101. *Kronlund v. Honstein*, 327 F.Supp. 71 (N.D. Ga. 1971).

102. Furman, "Political Illiberalism," 1221.

103. 1996 Study, 15. This is best exemplified by the increase in the number of states passing criminal registration laws.

104. Shapiro, "Challenging Criminal Disenfranchisement," 539-41.

105. Andrew Shapiro, "Voting Rights Are for Ex-Felons Too," *Sacramento Bee*, 15 January 1998, B7.

106. The ambivalence felt about assuring the "right to vote" to all and protecting the "democratic" process of those who are not morally "qualified" is discussed by the commentator cited in notes 5 and 98.

Chapter Two

Communities, Victims, and Offender Reintegration: Restorative Justice and Earned Redemption

Gordon Bazemore

Currently, when a crime is committed, two primary questions are asked: Who did it? and What should be done to the offender? The latter question is generally followed with another question about the most appropriate punishment and/or, at least in the case of a juvenile offense, most appropriate treatment or service to promote rehabilitation. The question of punishment or treatment has been a primary preoccupation of criminal justice dialogue for the past four decades.

Indeed, modern criminal justice ideologies—conservative, liberal, libertarian, "just desserts"—can be easily grouped into general categories based on different views of how this question of intervention should be addressed.[1] In the past two decades, several of these ideologies appear to have coalesced at the policy level around a broad framework that gives priority to punishment and lesser emphasis to rehabilitative goals, places central focus on "desert" as the primary rationale for decision making, and expands the use of incarceration at all levels of criminal and juvenile justice in the United States.[2] Despite a continuing failure to find clear empirical evidence in support of the deterrent value of incarceration, this *retributive justice* framework[3] or *punitive paradigm*[4] has attained dominant influence in national and state policy.[5] In response, many corrections professionals and their allies continue to promote an individual treatment model of rehabilitation and have emphasized the need for treatment and services, which, they argue, if adequately funded and administered with regard to "what works" best for specific populations of offenders, can reduce crime by rehabilitating offenders.[6] Other critics of the new punitiveness in criminal justice point to both the expense and the injustice of these policies, especially as they have impacted minority communities.[7]

But the retributive paradigm has become popular not because of the efficiency of punishment but because, in the minds of policymakers and the public, punitive sanctions serve to affirm community disapproval of proscribed behavior, denounce crime, and provide consequences to the lawbreaker.[8] The treatment model, on the other hand, clearly fails to accomplish these functions. Rather, treatment appears to be unrelated to the offense, related solely to the needs of lawbreakers, and to require nothing of offenders beyond participation in counseling or remedial services. It is difficult to convince most citizens that treatment programs provide anything other than benefits to offenders (for example, services, educational and recreational activities), and there is little in the message of the treatment response that attempts to communicate to an offender that he or she has harmed someone and should take action to repair damages wreaked upon the victim(s).

Increasingly, critics from a variety of different perspectives are beginning to view the obsession with offender punishment and treatment in the current response to crime as one-dimensional and insular. Too often the treatment and punishment intervention paradigms reduce the justice function and process to a simplistic choice between helping or hurting offenders, and hence fail to address and balance the multiple justice needs of communities. In addition, these approaches share a "closed-system" focus on the offender that ignores the needs of crime victims and other citizens and fails to engage them effectively in the response to crime. Moreover, with the exception of libertarian perspectives,[9] all promote expanding the reach and responsibility of the criminal justice system, while in some cases undercutting the role of communities in the response to crime.

In recent years, advocates of a "third way" have begun to insist that it is possible to ask very different questions about crime. Viewed through the lens of *restorative justice,*[10] crime is important because it causes harm to individuals and their communities. If crime is in fact about harm, "justice" cannot be achieved simply by punishing or treating offenders. Rather, justice processes must promote repair, or an attempt to "heal the wound" crime causes.[11] In contrast to the one-dimensional focus on punishment or treatment, restorative justice is based on the principle that justice is best served when there is a balanced response to the needs of citizens, offenders and victims. It is based on the assumption that basic multiple community expectations—to feel safe and secure, to ensure that crime is condemned, and to allow for offenders to be reintegrated—cannot be effectively achieved by a narrow focus on the needs and risks presented by offenders. Rather, to meet these needs and repair the harm crime causes, victim, community, and offender must be viewed as clients of the justice system and must be involved meaningfully as coparticipants in a holistic justice process.[12]

In repairing the harm caused by crime, restorative responses necessarily elevate the role of crime victims in the justice process. Because victims have been neglected as a client of criminal justice systems,[13] much of the literature and practice of restorative justice in the past decade have focused on victim reparation and involvement.[14] But restorative justice does not set "victims rights" against the rights of offenders. Nor does it view advocacy for victims' needs and involvement as a zero-sum game that is incompatible with a concern for the needs and risks presented by offenders and for the general justice needs of communities.[15] To date, however, there has been little specific discussion of the role of offenders in restorative justice once they have been held accountable by repairing harm to the victim and victimized community.

Is there a "restorative" approach to offender reintegration, or would offenders simply be punished and/or provided with standard correctional treatment? I will argue that restorative justice principles imply a unique approach to offender rehabilitation that necessarily involves victim and community, symbolically if not always actively, in the reintegrative process. This process, which I will refer to here as "earned redemption,"[16] requires an approach involving sanctions that allows offenders to "make amends" to those they have harmed in order to earn their way back into the trust of the community.[17] To be effective, reintegration ceremonies focused on earned redemption would also require that rehabilitative efforts work in close harmony with these sanction processes, with efforts to promote safer communities, and with efforts to meet the needs of crime victims. Finally, a process of earned redemption must be built upon naturalistic rather than expert-driven processes of maturation and reintegration in communities.

The primary purpose of this chapter is to explore prospects for expansion of earned redemption as a restorative justice model of offender reintegration. I first attempt to place the reintegration issue in the larger context of restorative justice as an evolving, emerging movement and paradigm for criminal and community justice that is primarily distinguished by an emphasis on the role of victims and communities in the justice process. I then describe three general components of a restorative justice model of reintegration that give primary emphasis to refocusing criminal justice sanctions and the sanction process. The discussion and conclusion outlines structural and cultural obstacles to implementing such an approach in the United States. and considers a basic strategy for linking what have thus far been micro-level responses to crime to the larger task of systemic criminal justice reform.

What Is Restorative Justice?

The restorative justice response to crime can be best described as a three-dimensional collaborative process. As Table 2.1 illustrates, this vision is best understood by examining what restorative justice might "look like" for victim, community, and offender as coparticipants in this process. For the victim, restorative justice offers the hope of restitution or other forms of reparation, information about the case, the opportunity to be heard, and input into the case as well as expanded opportunities for involvement and influence. For the community, there is the promise of reduced fear and safer neighborhoods, a more accessible justice process, and

Table 2.1
What Does a Restorative Justice System Look Like?

Crime Victims:
➤ Receive support, assistance, compensation, information, and services.
➤ Receive restitution and/or other reparation from the offender.
➤ Are involved and are encouraged to give input at all points in the system and direct input into how the offender will repair the harm done.
➤ Have the opportunity to face the offenders and tell their story to offenders and others if they so desire.
➤ Feel satisfied with the justice process.
➤ Provide guidance and consultation to justice professionals on planning and advisory groups.

Offenders:
➤ Complete restitution to their victims.
➤ Provide meaningful service to repay the debt to their communities.
➤ Must face the personal harm caused by their crimes by participating in victim-offender mediation if the victim is willing or through other victim awareness processes.
➤ Complete work experience and active and productive tasks that increase skills and improve the community.
➤ Are monitored and supported by community adults as well as justice professionals and are supervised to the greatest extent possible in the community.
➤ Improve decision-making skills and have opportunities to help others.

Citizens, Families, and Community Groups:
➤ Are involved to the greatest extent possible in holding offenders accountable, rehabilitation, and community safety initiatives.
➤ Work with offenders on local community service projects.
➤ Provide support to victims.
➤ Provide support to offenders as mentors, employers, and advocates.
➤ Provide work for offenders to pay restitution to victims and service opportunities that provide skills and also allow offenders to make meaningful contributions to the quality of community life.
➤ Community groups assist families to support the offender in obligation to repair the harm and increase competencies.
➤ Play an advisory role to courts and corrections and/or play an active role in disposition through one or more neighborhood sanction processes.

accountability, as well as the obligation for involvement and participation in condemning crime, reintegrating offenders, and preventing and controlling crime. Because crime is viewed as a result of a breakdown in social bonds that link individuals and communities and is, in addition, a cause of a further weakening in these bonds, the "justice" response to crime at the community level must also involve citizens and community groups in repairing damaged relationships or building new relationships.[18] For the offender, restorative justice requires accountability in the form of obligations to repair the harm to individual victims and victimized communities, and the opportunity to develop new competencies, social skills, and the capacity to avoid future crime.[19]

By the standards suggested in Table 2.1, restorative justice is a work in progress; no community or justice system is fully "restorative." While there are many examples of restorative justice practices, adoption of restorative justice as a systemic philosophy has been rare. Moreover, there are already multiple tendencies and priorities within what might be called a restorative justice movement and several competing philosophical, ideological, and theoretical themes in the restorative justice literature.[20] However, many apparently new initiatives are actually modern adaptations of ancient settlement and dispute resolution practices.

Historical Overview

The principles and approaches now being referred to as restorative justice are grounded in ancient codes of conduct and practices that have been at the core of many religious and ethical traditions.[21] In fact, prestate societies appear to have made use of two primary responses to crime. The first, based primarily on vengeance, was associated with repayment of harm *with harm*.[22] In addition, there were, as Weitekamp argues, in virtually all acephalous societies a variety of settlement and dispute resolution practices that typically included some effort to repair the harm and might today be called restorative.[23] Generally, these practices focused on some form of repayment or restitution to the victim or his or her family, and indeed such reparative practices were formalized and detailed in a variety of ancient justice documents:

- The Babylonian Code of Hammurabi (c. 1700 B.C.) prescribed restitution in property offense cases.

- The Sumerian Code of UrNammu (c. 2060 B.C.) required restitution even in the case of violent offenses.

- The Roman Law of the Twelve Tables (449 B.C.) required convicted thieves to pay double the value of stolen goods, and more if the thief had concealed the stolen goods in his or her home. The earliest surviving collection of Germanic tribal laws (the *Lex Salica* promulgated by King Clovis soon after his conversion to Christianity in A.D. 496) includes restitutionary sanctions for offenses ranging from homicides to assaults to theft.

- Ethelbert the Anglo-Saxon ruler of Kent, England, issued the Law of Ethelbert (c. A.D. 600) containing detailed restitution schedules. For example, the laws differentiated the value of the four front teeth from those next to them, and those teeth from all the rest.

- The Hebrews, perhaps more than any other ancient people, understood the importance of peace (*shalom*) in the community. Shalom meant much more than "absence of conflict," as many Westerners understand peace today. Shalom meant completeness, fulfillment, wholeness—the existence of right relationship among individuals, the community, and God. Shalom described the ideal state in which a community should function.[24]

Acephalous societies generally preferred reparative and often ritualistic responses to crime that sought to restore community peace and harmony to crime as an alternative to blood feuds, which generally had devastating consequences for community life.[25] The emphasis on vengeance later became more formalized and more predominant, and also moderated somewhat in the late Middle Ages as feudal lords and kings consolidated the response to crime and social control through the power of the state. Van Ness et al. argue that the Norman invasion of Britain marked the beginning of a paradigm shift, a turning away from the understanding of crime as a victim-offender conflict within the context of community toward the concept of crime as an offense against the state.[26] William the Conqueror (1066) and his descendants saw the legal process as one effective tool for centralizing their own political authority. Eventually, anything that violated the "king's peace" was interpreted as an offense against the king, and offenders were thus subject to royal authority. Under this new approach, the king, and gradually "the state," became the paramount victim, while the actual victim was denied any meaningful place in the justice process. As this occurred, the emphasis on reparation to crime victims was gradually replaced with the emphasis on punishment of the wrongdoer by the state, now referred to as retributive justice.[27]

Although reparation in the form of restitution and community service had been used occasionally by U.S. courts in this century,[28] these sanctions did not become widely popular as sentencing options until the 1970s. Restitution and community service, and to a lesser extent victim-offender mediation, have been used since the 1970s with some regularity in U.S. criminal and juvenile courts and are often administered by probation and community diversion programs.[29]

The "New" Restorative Justice Movement

In the 1990s, these and other reparative sanctions and processes are again receiving a high level of interest as part of a broader movement alternatively labeled restorative justice,[30] community justice,[31] and restorative community justice.[32] In the United States, a series of high-level discussion work group meetings were recently held within the Office of Justice Programs (U.S. Department of Justice) at the request of the attorney general, and restorative justice has sparked national and international discussion and debate in the United States, Canada, New Zealand, Australia, and several European countries.[33] Restorative justice policies and practices are clearly "on the ground" in local communities, states, provinces, and even entire countries. In some cases, such as New Zealand—where disposition of all delinquency cases with the exception of murder and rape are handled in community family group conferences—and the state of Vermont—where most nonviolent felons and misdemeanors are sentenced by community boards to make reparation to the victims—restorative justice plays a dominant role in criminal justice policy.[34] Significant state and local impact can also be seen, for example, in Minnesota, Maine, and other states that have adopted restorative justice as the mission for their corrections departments. State juvenile justice systems in Pennsylvania, Florida, New Mexico, Idaho, and Montana, among others, have adopted restorative justice principles in policy or statute.[35]

There are no easy explanations for this rise in interest in restorative justice at a time when criminal justice systems in most states appear to be embracing a punitive model. However, much of this interest seems to have emerged during a unique period of convergence between diverse justice philosophies and political, social, and cultural movements. Specifically, modern restorative justice appears to have been directly influenced by new developments in the victims' rights movement and an expanded role for victims in a community justice process;[36] the community and problem- oriented policing philosophy and movement;[37] and renewed interest in indigenous dispute resolution, settlement processes, and associated political efforts (especially in Canada) to "devolve" criminal justice responsibilities to local communities.[38] In addition, the women's movement and feminist critique of patriarchal justice[39] and the growing critique of both "just desserts" and rights-based, adversarial perspectives, as well as of social welfare models, in criminal and juvenile justice[40] have also affected the evolution of the new restorative justice movement.[41]

Despite these divergent political and cultural influences, restorative justice seems to be uniting a growing number of community leaders and justice professionals around an emerging consensus that neither punitive nor rehabilitation-focused models are meeting the needs of communities, victims, and offenders. Those familiar with criminal justice systems know that programs such as restitution and community service and related reparative sanctions that could be considered the core of restorative justice intervention are now in common use by court and correctional agencies throughout the country. In addition, today a wider "menu" of practices and programs including family group conferencing (FGC), victim impact panels, and community sanctioning boards has been added to the core restitution, community service, and victim-offender mediation options.[42]

What's "New"? Programmatic, Systemic, and Holistic Reform

Whereas any justice agency can add new programs, programmatic reform in the absence of a change in values and priorities is unlikely to lead to restorative outcomes. If only 10 percent of offenders are referred to a court's restitution program, for example, and similar proportions complete meaningful community service, or meet with their victims, the jurisdiction can hardly be said to be "restorative." Although the restorative justice framework has been developed and refined based on a process of examining innovative programs and processes such as restitution, community service, victim-offender mediation, and FGC rather than through a more deductive process,[43] programs are not ends in themselves but simply a means to achieve outcomes that should flow from a clear understanding of community and other client needs.[44] In most criminal and juvenile justice systems, staff roles and management imperatives are seldom examined to ensure that they are driven by these needs and expectations.

The reality, unfortunately, is that in justice systems more concerned with incapacitation, deterrence, and offender-focused interventions, restorative practices and programs remain on the margins and generally receive low priority. Although criminal justice reform is nothing new, as closed-system initiatives, few if any modern reforms have been spurred by community input but have instead been system-driven, and often top-down and reactive, responses to crisis and abuse. Closed-systems are insulated from input from their environments, including their communites. They are also hierarchical and reactive. Like the treatment and punishment paradigm on which they are based, modern reform efforts have been insular and one-dimensional; although system-driven, no reform has been truly *systemic*. Though many modern reforms have brought about well-intended improvements, whether focused on diversion, deinstitutionalization, case management, detention crowding, or due process concerns, these reforms share a piecemeal quality in their focus on one component or system function. Most criminal justice reforms have sought to rationalize and improve the structure, process, and techniques by which offenders are treated and punished, but have not questioned *why* things are done this way or the *nature* of the intervention enterprise. At the end of most reform initiatives, paid professionals continue to administer treatment, punishment, and offender surveillance outside the context of the offender's and victim's community. As they fail to address other community concerns that crime raises, it is little wonder that these interventions often do not mean much to offenders, victims, and other citizens.

Currently, as the left column of Figure 2.1 suggests, systemic reform in criminal justice is difficult because decisions about staff roles—what it is that justice professionals "do" in the response to crime—as well as resource allocation and management approaches are based primarily on tradition and the needs of criminal justice bureaucracies (for police officers, guards, caseworkers) and on the current skills and role definitions of criminal justice professionals. Innovation, when it occurs, is often based on the addition of specialized units or programs, and often seems to be driven by the need to be in step with the program trend of the month.

What is most "new" and different about restorative justice theory and practice,

Figure 2.1
New Paradigms and Systemic Reform

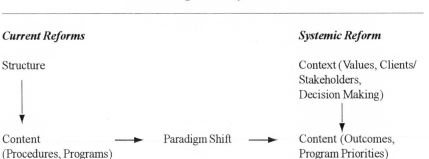

however, is its three-part agenda for systemic reform in the response to crime based on the priority given to repairing harm, by involving victim, community, and offender in the justice response and attempting to address the diverse justice needs of communities. First, restorative justice advocates propose broad changes in the justice process itself, which ultimately shifts the focus more toward community rather than criminal justice system solutions, and seeks to build capacity in communities to sanction crime, reintegrate offenders, repair harm to victims, and promote genuine public safety. In this regard, genuine systemic reform makes possible a questioning of basic values and assumptions about crime, as well as the ends and means of the response to it. Systemic reform initiatives therefore first raise questions about the *context* of intervention: what values, principles, and assumptions define the essence of crime and what should be done about it; whom the system should serve as "clients" and who should be involved in the response to crime and in making decisions about intervention, and by what process these decisions should be made (see Figure 2.1).

Second, as the right side of Figure 2.1 suggests, based on the answers to these questions and an effort to develop intervention aimed at meeting community needs and expectations, systemic reform would then seek change in the mission of criminal justice. Such change would focus on the *content* of intervention: what goals and performance outcomes are sought as the justice system seeks to address the needs of its clients, what messages are to be communicated, and what changes in clients are to be brought about as a result of intervention; what methods—programs and intervention practices—will be used to accomplish these goals. While current policy is often program-driven, systemic reform would ensure that program priorities are *values-driven* and that practices are selected based on their capacity to accomplish mission outcomes.

Finally, the choice of intervention priorities should then dictate the *structure* of the criminal justice system and thus determine what staffing patterns, resources, and professional roles are required to carry out these interventions and accomplish system goals. Hence, while current policy and reform *begins* with the current structure and seeks to make changes in procedures and programs, systemic reform ends with questions about structure after holistic change in content and context has been addressed (see Figure 2.1).

Restorative justice theory[45] and practice[46] thus provides a new vision for a future community justice response to crime based on a different set of values and principles, focused on the needs of a different set of clients who are also involved as stakeholders in a range of decisions about the most appropriate response to crime. These new values in turn form the basis for a new mission for management of criminal justice agencies and systems that articulates a different set of performance outcomes that gauge the success of an intervention based on the extent to which measurable changes are brought about in the status of victim, offender, and community as system clients. These outcomes thus provide the basis for establishing intervention priorities and initiating new programs (or discontinuing old ones). Intervention priorities in turn prescribe new roles and responsibilities for criminal justice professionals in assisting communities in meeting sanction, rehabilitation, public safety, and victim reparation needs. Differences between these performance outcomes, program priorities, and system roles and responsibilities as components of the current and restorative justice missions can be briefly described as follows:

- *Different Outcomes*: While the ultimate, long-term intervention goal of most criminal justice systems is reduced recidivism, short-term objectives are often elusive or limited to incapacitation and provision of services. In restorative justice, intervention outcomes seek change not just in offenders, but in each of three clients focused on healing, repair, reintegration, safety, and sense of community. These outcomes move beyond efforts to punish offenders or deliver treatment in the traditional sense and are designed to address multiple justice needs/expectations based on restorative principles. Examples include: proportion of victims involved in and satisfied with the justice process; proportion of offenders completing restitution and community service agreements; number of citizens involved in crime prevention, sanctions, offender mentoring and victim services; reductions in fear of crime and in school violence; and number of offenders completing work and service experiences and increasing attachment to conventional groups.

- *Different Program Priorities*: While there is no single restorative justice practice or program, accomplishing these objectives assumes that several programs and practices focused on repairing harm to the victim, holding offenders accountable, and enhancing public safety and peacemaking, would get priority under restorative justice. Restorative programs and practices include a range of interventions aimed at meeting public safety, sanction, and rehabilitative as well as victim restoration objectives (see Table 2.2).

- *Different Roles for Criminal Justice Professionals and New Organizational Structures*: To ensure that intervention practice is focused on restorative outcomes and serves and involves three clients in an effort to repair the harm

Table 2.2
Some Restorative Sanction Practices

Restitution to Crime Victims: It is important that payment be clearly linked to the victim, even if it is processed through the court and that young offenders be provided opportunities to earn funds to repay victims (e.g., through employment programs).

Victim-Offender Mediation: Offenders meet with victims and a third-party mediator to allow the victim to obtain information about the crime and express feelings to the offender, to develop a reparative agreement, and to increase offender awareness of the physical, emotional, and material impact of crime.

Direct Service to Victims: At the victim's request (usually through mediation or other process), offenders are required to perform direct service.

Service to Surrogate Victims: Offender work crews (crime repair crews) repair homes and businesses damaged by break-ins and vandalism.

Restorative Community Service: Work that is valued by the community and often suggested by neighborhood groups or by crime victims; such service often helps the disadvantaged, promotes economic development, or improves the general quality of life.

Service Chosen by the Victim: Victims recommend service projects for offenders as part of a mediation agreement.

Payment to Victim Service Fund: Offenders pay to support victims' services when restitution to their specific victim is not needed.

Victim Impact Statements: With approval from the victim, young offenders can read victims' impact statements or listen to and view audio/video statements that tell how the crime detrimentally affected the victim and his or her loved ones.

Victim-Offender Mediation: A well-planned constructive dialogue facilitated by a mediator trained in both juvenile justice and victimology tenets can increase victim satisfaction and develop mutually agreed-upon plans that hold the offender accountable for his or her actions.

Victim Awareness Programs: Incorporate an educational model that helps youthful offenders understand the impact their crimes have on their victims, their communities, their families, and themselves, and include crime victims as guest speakers.

caused by crime, the role of criminal justice professionals must change. Rather than simply administer sanctions and services, the role of professionals in a restorative justice model would focus primarily on facilitating active citizen involvement in community justice processes (see Table 2.3).

Criminal justice professionals cannot begin to change their missions (outcomes, practices, and management protocols) without a clear understanding of restorative values, the role of clients/coparticipants, and the new decision-making process needed to gain their input and participation. These values, participants, and processes form the *context* for restorative justice reform and are discussed briefly below before consideration of the specific issue of offender reintegration.

The Context of Restorative Justice

Viewed through the restorative lens, crime is understood in a broader context

Table 2.3
New Roles in Restorative Justice

Stakeholder Roles

Victim	Participate in defining the harm of the crime and shaping the obligations placed on the offender.
Community	Responsible for supporting and assisting victims, holding offenders accountable, and ensuring opportunities for offenders to make amends and strengthen relationships.
Offender	Active participant in decisionmaking and in reparation to victim and community and competency development.

Professional Roles

Sanctions	Facilitate mediation; ensure that restoration occurs (by providing ways for offenders to earn funds for restitution); develop creative and/or restorative community service options; engage community members in the process; educate community on its role.
Rehabilitation	Develop new roles for young offenders to allow them to practice and demonstrate competency; assess and build on youth and community strengths; develop partnerships.
Public Safety	Develop range of incentives and consequences to ensure offender compliance with supervision objectives; assist school and family in their efforts to control and maintain offenders in the community; develop prevention capacity of local organizations.

than what is suggested by the questions of guilt and what should be done to punish or treat the offender. Howard Zehr argues that in restorative justice, three very different questions receive primary emphasis.[47] First, what is the nature of the harm resulting from the crime? Second, what needs to be done to "make it right" or repair the harm? Third, who is responsible?

As will be illustrated in the case examples below, the first two questions are best answered with input from crime victims, citizens, and offenders in a decisionmaking process that maximizes their input into the case. Answering the third question focuses attention on the *future* rather than the past and also sets up a different configuration of obligations in the response to crime.[48] No longer simply the object of punishment, the offender is now primarily responsible for repairing the harm caused by his or her crime. A restorative criminal justice *system* would, in turn, be responsible for ensuring that the offender is held accountable for the damage and suffering caused to victims and victimized communities by supporting, facilitating, and enforcing reparative agreements. But, most importantly, the community plays a critical role in setting the terms of accountability.[49]

The need to engage and involve communities in the response to crime is based on an implicit, and sometimes explicit, critique of the ability of the formal justice system and the capacity of criminal justice professionals to address the needs of those most adversely affected by crime. As Judge Barry Stuart notes:

> Crime [control and prevention] should never be the sole, or even primary business of the State if *real differences* are sought in the well being of individuals, families and communities. The structure, procedures, and evidentiary rules of the formal criminal justice process coupled with most justice officials' lack of knowledge and connection to [the parties] effected by crime, preclude the state from acting alone to achieve transformative changes.[50] (Emphasis in original)

This assumed incompetence of the formal justice system and the need for a different set values, a different sense of the coparticipants in the justice process, and better ways to involve them in decision-making processes is best seen by examining the experience of these coparticipants in two cases.

Two Cases

Recently, in a large city, a thirty-two- year-old man entered the home of a neighbor, and walked upstairs into the bedroom of her fourteen-year-old daughter. For almost an hour, the man made lewd and offensive comments while sitting on the girl's bed. After the man had been arrested and charged, the young woman and her mother were asked by the court to complete a victim impact statement. Except for a brief moment when the man had lightly stroked her hair, she had not been physically molested by the intruder. Yet the young girl had felt traumatized and "dirtied" by the fact that the man had sat on her bed. After talking at length, the girl and her mother decided that what the girl most needed was a new bed. The victim impact statement submitted asked for $500 in restitution from the offender to cover the cost of the bed, an apology, and a recommendation for a year of therapy and other assistance for the offender. The judge ordered twelve months' jail time and a $500 fine payable not to the girl's family but to the court.

In a small town in the same state, a fourteen-year-old male, after pointing a loaded gun (which was actually a BB rifle) at a neighbor, was arrested, charged with second-degree assault with a deadly weapon, and taken to juvenile court in his town. The neighbor, a man of about thirty-five who had been so frightened and upset by the incident that he insisted the case be fully prosecuted, was reluctantly persuaded to participate with the offender in a victim-offender mediation session. At the session, after venting his anger and frustration at being startled with the loaded weapon, the victim learned that the boy liked to hunt. When he asked in the mediation session whom the boy hunted with and learned that it was the boy's grandfather, an idea emerged that he would later propose when it was time to discuss an appropriate sanction. The outcome of the mediation was that, at the victim's request, the boy would be required to tell his grandfather what he had done. After several days of reluctant hesitation, the boy told his grandfather and so informed the victim.

Retributive and Restorative Justice

The experiences in each case were dramatically different for the offender, the victim, and even the community. Most audiences who have heard the young man's story believe that he learned an important lesson (and did not get off easy) and that the victim was satisfied. Moreover, some have observed that the small community may have witnessed an important example of how a dispute that might otherwise have created a serious offense record for the youth, wasted court time, provided little relief to the victim, and created fear in the community of "armed and danger-ous" juveniles could be effectively resolved. In the first case, most agree that the victim was ignored and again victimized, that the offender got no treatment and might even have been more dangerous at the completion of his jail time, and that the community paid the cost of the jail term while receiving little in return.

Most who hear the young girl's story are also upset with the judge for ignoring the victim's request. But while the conversion of the victim's request for restitution into a court fine seems especially insensitive, the judge was merely operating on the basis of the assumptions of the current system of justice decision making. Referred to by some as a *retributive justice* paradigm,[51] these assumptions result in the exclusion and disempowerment of victims, offenders, and other citizens and are responsible in part for the general absence in most criminal justice systems of the coparticipant involvement depicted in Table 2.1. Although these cases are not necessarily typical, the experiences of victim, offender, and community parallel those that occur daily in criminal justice agencies everywhere. In addition, the contrast between them provides a useful illustration of how client needs are not addressed effectively by an approach to dispositional decision making that is limited by rigid, rule-driven, impersonal procedures focused on defining "winners and losers" and fixing blame[52] (see Table 2.4).

New Coparticipants and Restorative Processes

Crime victim needs are especially likely to be overlooked unless victims are given a direct voice in decision making. What is most unique about the restorative justice value base, and most difficult for many criminal justice professionals to accept, is its expansion of the role of crime victims in the justice process. Although victims' *rights* have received increased attention throughout criminal justice sys-

Table 2.4
Paradigms of Justice: Old and New *

Crime and Reaction

Retributive Justice	Restorative Justice
Crime is an act against state, a violation of a law, community, or an abstract idea.	Crime is an act against another person.
Punishment is effective.	Punishment alone is not effective in changing behavior disruptive to community relationships.
a. The threat of punishment deters crime. b. Punishment changes behavior.	Crime control lies primarily in the community.
The criminal justice system controls crime.	

Victims and Community

Retributive Justice	Restorative Justice
Victims are peripheral to the process.	Victims are central to the process.
Community on sideline, represented abstractly by state.	Community as facilitator in restorative process.
Imposition of pain to punish and deter/prevent.	Restitution as a means of restoring both parties; goal of reconciliation/restoration.

The Offender

Retributive Justice	Restorative Justice
Offender accountability defined as taking punishment.	Accountability defined as taking responsibility and taking action to repair harm.
The offender is defined by deficits.	The offender is defined by the capacity to make reparation.
No encouragement for repentance and forgiveness.	Possibilities for forgiveness.

*Adapted from H. Zehr, *Changing Lenses: A New Focus for Crime and Justice* (Scottsdale, PA: Herald Press, 1990).

tems in most states, victims' *needs* are often addressed only after the needs of police, judges, prosecutors, and corrections staff (in winning cases, processing offenders, or managing resources) have been considered. Despite frequent complaints about the inability of offenders to pay victim restitution, for example, many jurisdictions that do a poor job of enforcing restitution orders have been highly successful in the collection of offender fines and fees.[53] Indeed, in many probation and parole agencies, victim compensation and restitution have taken a backseat to the collection of money used to support criminal justice agency functions.[54] Moreover, while prosecutors appear to spare no expense and effort to gain victim input for efforts to increase the probability of conviction and length of sentence, time and resources for providing victim services, mediation, and reparative programs seem always in short supply.[55] Because years of focus on the needs and risks of offenders mean that victims do not start from a level playing field, justice professionals and citizens moving toward a restorative justice approach are giving primary attention to victims' needs for physical and material reparation and emotional healing.[56] When actively engaged, victims often express unique concerns and interests that are frequently unrelated to offender punishment or even to the need for material reparation:

> I can tell you that what most victims want most is quite unrelated to the law. It amounts more than anything else to three things: victims need to have people recognize how much trauma they've been through . . . they need to express that, and have it expressed to them; they want to find out what kind of person could have done such a thing, and why to them; and it really helps to hear that the offender is sorry—or that someone is sorry on his or her behalf.[57]

Even as it places central emphasis on victim needs and the requirement that offenders are held accountable to victims, the restorative justice paradigm also responds to the "mutual powerlessness" of offenders *and* victims in the current system and assumes the need for communities to provide opportunities for offender repentance and forgiveness following appropriate sanctioning.[58] Restorative processes, whose potential benefits to each coparticipant are illustrated by the first case, work best with the active participation of victim, offender, and community. They therefore demand opportunities for such participation that are sensitive to and supportive of victim and citizen needs. Although court proceedings with some flexible discretion by judges and other court decision makers could accommodate some of the changes needed to increase such active involvement, critics of the formal, retributive justice structure agree that minor changes in the court process will be insufficient to alter the current focus of these insular systems that have proved themselves inadequate to the task.[59] Achieving restorative goals and the general vision of restorative justice is therefore likely to require expanded use of nonadversarial and less formal community decision-making alternatives that allow for greater and more meaningful involvement of citizens and victims in decisions about the response to those who commit crimes and rely heavily on informal conflict resolution based on dialogue and negotiation. Table 2.5 suggests some promising existing models for victim and citizen participation in decision making. In the past five years, an explosion of interest in these new models has been a major catalyst behind support for restorative justice.

Restorative Justice, Reintegration, and Earned Redemption

- In inner-city Pittsburgh, young offenders in an intensive day treatment program solicit input from community organizations about service projects the organizations would like to see completed in the neighborhood. The offenders then work with community residents on projects that include home repair and gardening for the elderly, voter registration drives, painting homes and public buildings, and planting and cultivating community gardens.

- In South Florida, youthful offenders, sponsored by the Florida Department of Juvenile Justice and supervised by The 100 Black Men of Palm Beach County, Inc., plan and execute projects that serve a shelter for the care and treatment of abused, abandoned, and HIV positive/AIDS-infected infants and children.

- In cities and towns in Pennsylvania, Montana and Minnesota—as well as in Australia, New Zealand, and Pennsylvania—family members and other citizens acquainted with an offender or victim of a juvenile crime gather to determine

Table 2.5
Some Restorative Decision-Making Processes

➢ *Victim-Offender Mediation.* Trained mediators facilitate face-to-face discussion between offender and victim to allow for expression of feelings and discussion of harm and obligation, and arrive at agreement with offender to repair the harm.

➢ *Family Group Conferencing.* Allows for community, victim, and family input into the development of a restorative sanction for juvenile offenders in a process initiated by a trained facilitator.

➢ *Circle Sentencing.* A sentencing and problem-solving process currently being implemented in Canada facilitated by a judge or community member and attended by victim, offender, and a variety of local citizens who support both and wish to develop a local resolution of the crime.

➢ *Community Reparative Boards.* Currently being implemented in Vermont, these citizen sentencing panels develop agreements with nonfelony offenders that focus their probation on victim and community reparation, understanding of harm caused by their crime, and avoiding future offending behavior.

➢ *Reparative Court Hearings.* Though these are best implemented in an informal community setting, some judges hold special hearings to determine victim reparation as a separate part of the dispositional process in court.

what should be done in response to the offense. Often held in schools, churches, or other community-based facilities, these family group conferences (FGCs) are facilitated by a community justice coordinator or police officer and are aimed at ensuring that offenders are made to hear community disapproval of their behavior, that an agreement for repairing the damage to victim and community is developed, and that a plan for reintegrating the offender is designed and executed.

- In Cleveland, ex-offenders mentoring young offenders in juvenile justice programs work with chores and faith communities to provide shopping and support services for the home-bound elderly.

- In Minnesota, department of corrections staff collaborate with local police and citizens groups to establish FGC programs and ways to inform the community about and involve them in offender monitoring and victim support. In Dakota County, a Minneapolis suburb, local retailers and senior citizens whose businesses and homes have been damaged by burglary or vandalism call a crime repair hotline to request a work crew of probationers to repair the damage.

- In secure facilities for young offenders operated by the California Youth Authority, crime victims organize victim awareness training and crime impact panels designed to sensitize offenders to the personal harm resulting from their crimes.

- In Deschutes County, Oregon, juvenile offender work crews cut and deliver firewood to senior citizens and recently worked with a local contractor to build a homeless shelter.

- In the city of Whitehorse, Yukon, and other Canadian towns and villages, First Nation as well as nonaboriginal citizens sit sometimes for hours in a circle listening to offenders, victims, their advocates, and other community members speak about the impact of crimes. When the feather or "talking stick" is passed to them and it is their turn to speak without being interrupted, they may comment favorably on rehabilitative efforts already begun by the offender, who may be a chronic and sometimes violent perpetrator well known to the community. Speakers in these circle sentencing (CS) sessions also express concerns for the victim or the continuing threat posed by the offender and, at the end of the session, attempt to come to consensus about a rehabilitative plan for the offender and an approach to healing the victim and the community.

- In several Montana cities, college students and other young adult "core members" in the Montana Conservation Corps supervise juvenile offenders on environmental restoration, trail-building, and other community service projects and also serve as mentors to one or more of the young offenders.

What do these examples have to do with reintegration or rehabilitation? Very little, if the reference is to most treatment programs in most criminal justice systems in the United States. Although it is possible to find similar activities in various locations around the world, those interventions are viewed by many justice professionals—and most correctional program staff—as "side shows." They are clearly not seen as part of the rehabilitative agenda of most courts and corrections agencies.

Yet these case studies contain at least some of the seeds of a new way of thinking about rehabilitation and reintegration that is focused less on treating offenders than on building communities; less on new treatment programs and more on institutional reform to promote youth development; less on counseling to improve self-image and more on changing the *public* image of people in trouble who have earned their way back into the community; less on criminal justice "experts" and more on building connections between offenders and community residents. The value of restorative justice to victims and communities goes well beyond this chapter's primary concern with meaningful offender reintegration. In addition, the current climate of "get tough" responses to crime provides few opportunities for meaningful discussion of offender reintegration and acceptance, whether or not it is earned. The principles of restorative justice, however, provide some hope for promoting a new way of thinking about both sanctions and reintegration that make possible, and even encourage, offender repentance and begin to create cultural prototypes for community reacceptance of offenders who have made amends for the harm they have caused.

Forgiveness has been an important concept implicit in much restorative writing and explicit in some.[60] However, forgiveness has become an unpopular term in the crime victims' movement because it has been identified with an overt or implied coercion of victims to forgive the offender and a suggestion that those who do not or cannot are less worthy of the justice system's concern and support.[61] But while reintegration through earned redemption does not imply any obligation on the part of victims, it does imply some tradition of *societal* mercy and some basic level of *community* capacity to forgive, if not to forget, the actions of offenders once they have made reparation to individual victims and victimized publics.[62] Hence, rather than look to correctional programs or treatment models, this concern with "earned redemption" suggests that it is more important to look to community dynamics and the link between communities, crime, sanctions, and public safety.

Partly because of the emphasis in restorative justice practice and literature on the victim-offender dyad,[63] the community role as coparticipant in restorative processes has been the least well developed. The role of the community in offender reintegration, and in a sanction process consistent with reintegrative efforts, is the cornerstone of a theory of restorative rehabilitation. Increasing the capacity of community groups and institutions to demonstrate collective mercy and develop strategies to reintegrate offenders who have earned their way back into the good graces of the community is thus a major agenda for restorative justice advocates.

Crime, Social Relationships, and Theories of Reintegration

Because restorative justice ideas have in fact emerged "from the field," it has been said that the restorative framework is largely practice in search of a theory of crime. But while restorative practice is not associated with a specific etiological perspective, restorative justice principles are consistent with several traditions in criminological theory.[64] At the macro level, ecological theories of community and crime focus on the relationship between structure and culture as manifested in social disorganization and the inability of informal controls to limit deviant behavior.[65] At the micro level, social control perspectives[66] emphasize the importance of the "bond" individuals have with conventional groups. This bond can in turn be viewed as culturally and structurally fixed in the roles individuals assume in the context of socializing institutions (family, work, school) which thereby account for informal constraints on deviant behavior based on affective ties to significant others (teachers, parents), as well as on a more rational "stake in conformity" that limits individual involvement in crime by the risk criminal behavior poses to the offender's future legitimate opportunities.[67]

For those concerned with correctional intervention to rehabilitate offenders, a focus on strengthening this bond can also inform a reintegrative strategy. At a more intermediate, interactional level of analysis, consistent with social learning theories such as differential association,[68] the restorative justice response to crime seeks to mobilize intimates and "communities of concern"[69] around the offender to promote resolution, restitution, or other informal settlement. Such informal processes may be the first step in what some have labeled "reintegration ceremonies."[70] Such ceremonies are clearly distinguished from the "status degradation ceremonies" of the formal court process and the isolation experienced by offenders in retributive processes,[71] which, consistent with the insights of societal reaction and labeling perspectives, are often said to be criminogenic.[72]

Against this theoretical backdrop, the restorative view of crime and community can be understood with reference to a familiar cycle of crime, fear, withdrawal, isolation, weakened community bonds, and more crime.[73] This sequence provides an important key to thinking about patterns of crime, community dynamics, and the reaction to offenders[74] and about the capacity of community norms and tolerance limits to control harmful behavior and to reinforce law-abiding behavior. The more connected community members are, the more likely they are to restrain criminal impulses. As community bonds are weakened, the power of community disapproval as a force restraining crime is reduced.

Crime harms victims, communities, offenders, and other citizens and in essence damages the social fabric and peace of communities.[75] While it is impossible to say which comes first, citizens, crime victims, and offenders are caught up in a cycle in which crime is both a cause of breakdowns in individual and community relationships and a result of these breakdowns. One of the most basic themes in restorative justice is the need to strengthen or rebuild social and community relationships.[76] Restorative justice responses to crime attempt to break into the cycle of crime, fear, and weakened relationships, and in so doing offer a holistic approach to addressing the sanction, safety, preventive, peacemaking, and rehabilitative needs of communities.

At the community level, a restorative response to crime seeks first to build and strengthen relationships by increasing the nature and quality of participation in problem solving and the response to crime and conflict. From this perspective, the general health of a community—and its crime rate—is directly related to the extent to which citizens participate in the community:

> When citizens fail to assume responsibility for decisions affecting the community, community life will be characterized by the absence of a collective sense of caring, a lack of respect for diverse values, and ultimately a lack of any sense of belonging. Conflict, if resolved through a process that constructively engages the parties involved, can be a fundamental building ingredient in any relationship.[77]

Since the root of crime is community conflict and disharmony, "justice" cannot be achieved by a government "war on crime" but rather by *peacemaking and dispute resolution*.[78] In this sense, crime—or any conflict—is viewed as an opportunity because it calls attention to social conditions that cause conflict and provides a chance for the community to affirm its values and tolerance limits.[79] Implicit in restorative justice is the assumption that as communities practice resolving disputes creatively, their capacity to do so also increases. The *process* of resolving conflict is therefore as important as the specific outcome in each case because, through this process, community members are believed to learn new skills and to increase confidence in their ability to manage conflict and to control/prevent crime in the future. For their part, when they facilitate or contribute to these processes, justice professionals get closer to the root causes of crime *and* are less likely to reach beyond their competence.[80]

Relational Rehabilitation

If communities and justice professionals can learn how to resolve conflict, they can also learn how to reintegrate offenders. As is the case with conflict resolution, a restorative approach to rehabilitation is based on the general idea of building or rebuilding relationships. At the individual level, if crime is viewed as the result of weak bonds, a *relational rehabilitation* must be focused primarily on strengthening the offender's ties or bonds to conventional adults and peers, and on changing the offender's view of law-abiding citizens and the community. At the community level, intervention to strengthen bonds must focus on changing citizens' views of offenders and on increasing the willingness and capacity of community groups to take responsibility for integration and reintegration, as well as for informal sanctions and social control.[81]

In the case of delinquent young people, the intervention approach to achieve rehabilitation, integration, and habilitation would have the primary objective of strengthening bonds to conventional groups and would, as in conventional maturation processes, be centered around developing and enhancing youth/adult relationships. From a restorative perspective, this would begin with the small "communities of concern"[82] around the offender and branch outward as the offender increases his or her ability to build and manage relationships and strengthen both affective and rational ties to conventional adults and adult institutions. The broader relational rehabilitation "project" would then be focused on a community and institutional learning process by which members practice, create, and replicate models of offender reintegration.

It goes almost without saying that the criminal and juvenile justice systems were not set up to support or enhance this kind of relationship building. Rather than strengthen bonds between offenders and community groups, correctional treatment programs are individualistic interventions designed to "cure" psychological problems or remediate presumed deficits. Based on an individual treatment paradigm, or "medical model," that generally locates the cause of crime and delinquency in individual offenders, this approach is theoretically and practically insular and one-dimensional.

At best, treatment programs may seek to influence family dynamics—but often with little or no theoretical guidance about how and why the family intervention effort is in any way related to the offender's behavior.[83] For the most part, treatment programs are decontextualized attempts to address the offender's thinking and behavior in settings isolated from crime victims and victimized communities, in which the real harm that resulted in the offender's criminal justice involvement is no longer viewed as relevant. Juvenile justice interventions, for example, target individual youth rather than adults and adult institutions for change and fail to address the role of relationships, group conflict, and institutional and community processes in crime causation.[84] Moreover, such interventions do not take account of how these factors may either promote or hinder rehabilitation. By promoting an implicit view of habilitation and rehabilitation as something that happens *in treatment programs*, the treatment model also fails to build on naturally occurring supports that may enhance positive relationships and bonds with conventional community adults.[85] The narrow focus on offender deficits and disturbances also supports a closed system of intervention outcomes that are effectively limited to successful adjustment and accommodation to the regime of treatment programs[86] and that define success almost exclusively in terms of process measures (for example, number of clients served, number of program graduates, successful program completion), rather than outcomes relevant to reintegration.[87] Finally, treatment programs have increasingly taken responsibility away from communities and the socializing institutions (such as schools and work) that serve them. In reinforcing the value of treatment "experts" and highly specialized services, while downplaying the role of nonprofessionals, treatment programs distance the rehabilitative enterprise from communities and the real people in them.

The one-dimensionality of treatment results from divorcing rehabilitation from the context of other essential functions of criminal justice and from the justice expectations and needs of communities. Although, according to recent surveys, communities and most citizens support a rehabilitative agenda,[88] they also expect "justice" systems and agencies to do more than treat offenders. Though juvenile justice professionals in particular speak in great detail about the treatment needs of offenders and about programs that allegedly meet these needs, they are seldom able to articulate what sanctions are being imposed on the offender and what is being done to protect the community. Should communities be expected to support interventions that appear to provide only a *benefit* to the offender, especially when sanctions and public safety issues seem to be ignored?[89] As Braithwaite and Mugford suggest:

> Worse still, we fear that even when something does work, it is seen to do so only in the eyes of certain professionals, while "outside" the system ordinary citizens are left without a role or voice in the criminal justice process.[90]

In moving beyond the closed-system approach to rehabilitation, a relational approach would need to challenge the insularity and one-dimensionality of both the retributive and the individual treatment/social welfare model of correctional programs. While there are also broader social and economic justice, youth advocacy, and institutional reform issues that would need to be addressed in a complete model of offender rehabilitation,[91] criminal justice issues from a restorative perspective focus on the immediate need to build or rebuild relationships between offenders and their communities. This requires attention to three theoretical projects and collateral policy initiatives that flow rather naturally from restorative justice principles. These principles present a potential challenge to current rehabilitation models and form the basic components of a new approach to reintegration.[92]

Toward Integration and Resonance

First, if there is to be a restorative justice "theory" of reintegration, it must therefore include a concern with the extent to which community and victim are meaningfully engaged in a more integrated justice process and the extent to which key community needs *other than* the need for offender rehabilitation are addressed. An underlying premise of restorative justice is the idea that offenders are not well served when the needs of victims and community are neglected and when these two coparticipants are not in some way involved in the process. More than this, the logical and theoretical assumptions of restorative justice suggest that it is difficult to effectively address the needs of any one juvenile justice client without involving and addressing the needs of the other two. For example, from a restorative perspective, important first steps in an offender's rehabilitative or reintegrative process include a feeling of shame or remorse and an effort to make amends;[93] the voluntary involvement of victims and community to the greatest extent possible in holding the offender accountable is an important component of this process. Similarly, to make progress toward healing and restoration, many victims rely on the reparative actions of offenders and the community, to provide restitution, acknowledge their suffering, provide information and support, and express apology and remorse. When justice is viewed as repairing the harm and rebuilding damaged relationships, the response to crime must attend to all of those damaged by the crime.

Second, neither treating nor punishing offenders will make communities safe. Nor do these responses meet public demands to censure crime, affirm and enforce tolerance limits, provide consequences for crime, and effectively reintegrate lawbreakers. Practically speaking, citizens are less likely to support the idea of reintegration and rehabilitation until sanction needs and public safety concerns have been addressed. When these needs are addressed in an integrated way, efforts to sanction crime, manage risks, and reintegrate offenders become mutually interdependent, and they may be viewed as means toward the ends of repairing harm to victims, offenders, and communities and hopefully facilitating transformative changes in each.[94] For example, when offenders are censured by repairing harm to victims, they stand a better chance of preserving and enhancing their own human dignity, a necessary prerequisite for rehabilitation. Sanctions that degrade and isolate the offender, on the other hand, weaken bonds that foster reintegration and ultimately heighten risks to public safety. Similarly, efforts to reintegrate or censure offenders that do not explicitly attend to public safety concerns of the community can never win public support or create a climate in which victim needs can be meaningfully addressed. At a minimum, in restorative justice there should be compatibility or "resonance" between sometimes disparate efforts to address these primary justice needs of communities.[95]

Third, to effectively meet the needs of the three coparticipants in crime and give them a voice and role in the response to crime, restorative justice calls for a more informal, naturalistic response that emphasizes the role of citizens, community groups, and socializing institutions.[96] A relational approach to rehabilitation cannot be clinical in its focus, but must instead emphasize community socialization networks and naturally occurring processes in its analysis of how most delinquents grow up to be normal, productive adults. Young people in the juvenile and criminal justice systems share with many other young people a lack of a sense of usefulness and belonging, or connectedness. Because they, unlike most adults, do not hold positions of responsibility in work, community, or family groups that allow them to make meaningful contributions, many young people become marginal commodities, or even liabilities, in a society where status is largely determined by one's productive participation in the economy. Those youth who lack the clear promise of *future* access to meaningful adult roles that success in school may provide have little to lose by delinquent and other forms of deviant behavior; the stake in conventional behavior is low, and bonds to conventional social groups are weak.[97]

Completing treatment programs does not solve these problems of connectedness and lack of legitimate identity of young offenders. While treatment programs may be helpful, being drug free, for example, does not give young offenders the skills needed for access to those roles (in work, family, and community) that provide law-abiding adults with a stake in conformity. A restorative approach to rehabilitation would seek to enhance those competencies that help young offenders develop positive relationships with conventional adults and would seek to increase the capacity of adults and adult organizations to allow young offenders to demonstrate competency by creating new roles for youth to contribute productively to their communities. Increasing vocational, educational, social, and interpersonal and decision-making competencies, for example, is best accomplished through an effort to provide young offenders access to roles that engage them experientially in productive activities including work, community service, and conflict resolution. Policy and intervention strategy must then build upon and seek to enhance the capacity of socializing institutions such as school and work as well as informal networks and processes to support reintegration.

Elsewhere I have addressed this third component of an approach to offender reintegration based on restorative justice and youth development principles in a more comprehensive way.[98] The remainder of this chapter therefore focuses primarily on the first and second theoretical projects. To do so, I address the need for a new approach to sanctions, and an integration of sanctions and rehabilitation functions as a means of improving the prospects for "earned redemption." Because censuring offenders has so commonly been thought of only in terms of the narrow objectives of "just punishment,"—or as Christie suggests, causing pain to the offender,[99]—it is especially important to think about the resonance, or lack of it, between sanctions and rehabilitative interventions. "Project One," the focus on the needs and involvement of victims, offenders, and community in all interventions, is incorporated in this discussion.

Rethinking Sanctions

Punishment, by stigmatizing, humiliating, and isolating the offender, may have a counterdeterrent effect by minimizing prospects that the offender may gain or regain self-respect and the respect of the community.[100] Ironically, punishment often encourages lawbreakers to focus on themselves rather than the person they harmed as the victim[101] and may undermine self-restraint by attenuating natural feelings of shame and a sense of morality[102] while weakening community bonds by damaging family, peer, and other adult relationships.[103] Although the current trend in most of the world (and certainly in the United States) seems to be in the direction of punitive sanctions that maximize harm to the offender,[104] the continuum of possible sanctions ranges from those intended primarily to threaten or harm offenders (and would-be offenders), which generally emphasize incarceration, to other approaches that may build community solidarity and commitment and ultimately strengthen the bonds between offenders and community members.

As Herbert Packer argued in his now classic discussion of this topic, depending on *intent* sanctions can be directed toward compensatory, deterrent, regulatory, and rehabilitative ends, as well as retributive punishment.[105] Although few question the inevitability of some punishment or deny that any sanction may be experienced by the *offender* as punitive, it is possible to consider and give priority to different censuring objectives in the response to crime. In recent years, a number of scholars have challenged the effectiveness of retributive punishment and argued that sanctions may also serve important expressive, educative, and symbolic functions.[106] Quoting Durkheim, for example, Braithwaite highlights the role of sanctions in moral education and underscores the limitations of punishment aimed only at threats and offender suffering:

> Since punishment is reproaching, the best punishment is that which puts the blame . . . in the most expressive but least expensive way possible. . . . It is not a matter of making him suffer . . . or as if the essential thing were to intimidate and terrorize. Rather it is a matter of reaffirming the obligation at the moment when it is violated, in order to strengthen the sense of duty, both for the guilty party and for those witnessing the offense—those whom the offense tends to demoralize.[107]

From this perspective, expressive sanctions aimed at communicating value-based messages to offenders and the community and affirming obligations and accountability should be more effective in regulating conduct and more likely to promote community solidarity and peaceful dispute resolution.[108] Although punitive sanctions may detract from the accomplishment of both reparative and rehabilitative goals, if intended to educate, sanctions can, as Durkheim pointed out, reinforce obligation and responsibility and provide an understanding of the suffering caused to other individuals that resulted from an offender's crime.[109] Such a sense of obligation, as modern communitarians would argue, can strengthen bonds and reinforce a sense of justice.[110] From a restorative perspective, sanctions should be first focused on repairing the harm to victims and the community and thereby allowing communities an outlet for symbolic, collective denunciation of crime as well as the affirmation of tolerance limits.[111] But while sanctions are intrusive and coercive and should not be disguised as "treatment," the sanction process has important implications for any rehabilitative approach. When carried out based on restorative principles, sanctions may themselves have rehabilitative impact.

The Rehabilitative Potential of Sanctions

A growing body of empirical research is supportive of the rehabilitative value of reparative restitution, community service, and other restorative sanctions and processes.[112] Some studies suggest that the rehabilitative impact is increased when reparative sanctions are viewed by the offender as fair and when they are truly victim-focused.[113] Restitution, community service, and related reparative requirements such as victim awareness training, especially when reinforced with victim-offender mediation, can be high on the educative scale.[114] According to one study, completing restitution and community service was found to be associated with enhanced feelings of citizenship and community commitment.[115] At the end of a continuum from least to most educative sanction responses are settlement or dispute resolution processes in which the offender also learns important competencies that are transferable to a variety of settings. Such learning is heightened and the rehabilitative power of sanctions enhanced, according to "affect" theorists,[116] in processes that allow for emotional content and expression. Though too infrequently utilized in Western societies, such processes may enhance offender relationships in employment and other roles while also providing essential competencies needed to prevent violent resolution of future conflicts.[117]

Unfortunately, reparative sanctions have been criticized unfairly by a group of treatment researchers[118] who have for the most part ignored, misread, or misinterpreted positive (or at least encouraging) findings from experimental and other empirical studies of the impact of restitution and community service as well as promising results on victim-offender mediation, victim impact panels, family group conferences, and related interventions.[119] A major distortion of this critique has been a tendency to portray all sanctions as negative and as detracting from the reintegrative process,[120] and a failure to distinguish theoretically and empirically between sanctions with a reparative focus and aim such as victim restitution and restorative community service, and sanctions with a solely punitive or deterrent intent.

In their list of programs that do *not* work, for example, Krisberg, Currie, and Onek[121] reinforce this tendency by including restitution and community service—along with "shock incarceration," "scared straight programs," and boot camps—in a category of interventions they conclude are ineffective, and possibly harmful. But sanctions that reinforce and affirm values about obligations to others and provide benefit to the community do not detract from rehabilitative goals, and it seems foolish at best not to consider the possibility that such sanctions could have independent rehabilitative impact. Are we to believe that meeting with one's victim, paying restitution, or completing community service is as demeaning, stigmatizing, and humiliating as being forced to clean toilets in a boot camp? Does community service in which youth work with adults to build a community shelter for abused women[122] provide the same experience as a chain gang?

Being required to face one's victim or face the community and work to repair the harm caused by one's crime may well be tougher and more painful for offenders than standard punishments focused on incarceration.[123] But, in lumping together such dramatically different sanctions as boot camps and restitution and discounting the contextual importance of the function of sanctions, critics ignore the intent of sanctions and reinforce by default the one-dimensional approach to rehabilitation. Most important, politically, they strengthen the hands of those policymakers promoting truly harmful retributive sanctions. In the absence of an alternative sanction model,[124] treatment is in any case most likely to be used as an add-on to destructive punishments whose impact is likely to counter any possible positive effects.

Advocates of restorative justice would not claim that reparative sanctions are rehabilitative panaceas. No one should expect dramatic reductions in recidivism as a result of exposure to restitution, community service, mediation, or any other programs in isolation, and too often many of the most promising restorative sanction programs have been poorly implemented.[125] Yet, despite the unfounded dismissal of the idea of sanctions as potentially rehabilitative, a number of restorative sanctions are gaining popularity precisely because they are assumed to be good for the offender, and increasingly this assumption is being supported by emerging theory and research. In addition to Schneider's empirical work on equity theory and processes, which appears to establish a link between completion of reparative sanctions and reduced recidivism among delinquent offenders,[126] there are recent promising findings and theory on the rehabilitative impact of community service.[127] When integrated into a comprehensive and holistic reintegrative strategy, such sanctions reinforce and, according to available studies, are likely to increase the rehabilitative impact of other interventions. When implemented in a way that also begins with an acknowledgment of harm to victims, actively involves community members in sanctions aimed at holding the offender accountable to the victim, and engages a support group for the offender (and the victim), such sanctions can also be a natural first step in a process to reintegrate offenders.[128]

Sanctions and Reintegrative Process

> When community people have input into who is accepted into a community sentencing process, they don't just pick the "cream puffs". . . they pick the guys who have been wreaking the most havoc on them for years. (B. Stuart, *Sentencing Circles: Making 'Real' Differences*, unpublished paper, Territorial Court of the Yukon, 1995)

At least as important as the actual sanction of restitution, victim service, or community service, however, is the process by which these sanctions are meted out to offenders. So vital is the nature of the decision-making process in restorative justice, in fact, that some proponents argue that process and outcome are not easily separated. Following the logic of aboriginal and indigenous settlement traditions, the argument suggests that simply "making connections" and hearing the voices of those with an interest in the crime in a respectful way is itself a positive outcome; in an effective process, solutions or outcomes are said to take care of themselves.[129]

An underlying assumption of restorative justice now being more frequently discussed is that sanction processes are more likely to enhance rehabilitation/ reintegration when they involve family, victims, and key members of the offender's community directly in the process.[130] In this regard, perhaps the most promising potential bridge between sanctions and rehabilitation in restorative justice practice has been the proliferation of new community decision-making models such as family group conferencing, circle sentencing, citizen boards, and various extensions of victim-offender mediation and victim-offender dialogue.[131] The excitement around such interventions is that in bringing citizens and victims together with offenders and the supporters of both offender and victim together in a family group conference or sentencing circle, much more than sanctioning or "shaming" may be accomplished. Among other things, conferences or circles contain some basic elements of a true offender support group.[132]

Yet, as is the case with restitution or victim-offender mediation programs, the impact of spending two hours in an FGC should not be expected to produce remarkable results and does not offer a complete model of rehabilitation.[133] There is nothing *easy* about the restorative justice process, and it will in fact require far more time up-front than formal court processes, as well as follow-up time . Offenders will not be quickly "cured," and, as Braithwaite and Mugford suggest, several family group conferences may be necessary before an offender "gets the message."[134] As an ex-felon who is now an active leader in a local community juvenile justice committee in northern Canada and mentor for young offenders participating in circle sentencing processes told Judge Barry Stuart, "I'm *still* a crook . . . I still want to sell and use drugs and fence stereo equipment. But if I do that, I lose this connection. It's this connection here [the community justice committee] that makes me *not* do it."

Moreover, if not carried out with a thorough grounding in restorative goals and values, FGCs and other processes may even exacerbate the reintegration problem.[135] There are empirical questions one may ask to determine if a specific sanction approach or process is likely to be helpful or harmful, and Braithwaite and Mugford's distinction between "conditions of successful reintegration ceremonies" that differentiate condemnation of the *act* from condemnation of the *actor*[136] and processes such as "shaming" that promote "status degradation," provide a useful benchmark in making this assessment.[137]

Practically, from a rehabilitative perspective, these community sanction models provide one possible gateway to engage community support for offender reintegration at a time when this is a very difficult political enterprise. Some have suggested, however, that what may be most important about these community sanction processes is their potential for increasing citizen participation in and support for reintegrative processes by providing a sense of ownership over a primary justice decision-making function.[138] As the quote from Judge Stuart at the beginning of this section suggests, citizen involvement may also widen the range of offenders viewed as acceptable for community sanctions to include serious and violent lawbreakers generally viewed as beyond eligibility for reintegrative processes. The "hook" to attract such community support is that citizens who had formerly been uninvolved and concerned about offenders only in the abstract, and then often as objectives of punishment, will be more willing to participate when given the opportunity for input into sanction decisions. Once involved in this way, restorative justice advocates assume, citizens will also be more likely to better understand the needs of the offenders (as well as those of victims) and to support a reintegrative agenda for offenders who fulfill their obligations through a restorative process of earned redemption.

Confronting Obstacles: A Discussion

Although the more obvious criticisms of restorative justice can be answered persuasively, numerous obstacles remain to widespread expansion of a restorative agenda in the United States. Both generic questions about restorative justice and specific questions about the prospects for offender reintegration based on development and expansion of processes of earned redemption need to be addressed.

Responding to Critics: Generic Concerns about Restorative Justice

Restorative justice advocates do not have all the answers for criminal justice reform or for changing the community response to crime. Although addressing the range of criticisms of this new paradigm is beyond the scope of this chapter, several of the most common questions about restorative justice can be at least provisionally answered.

1. *Limited Application.* Although some have dismissed restorative justice as relevant only to minor crimes, as a systemic intervention model restorative justice cannot be limited to one program, one type of offender or victim, or one part of the system. Restorative responses for cases diverted from the court or formal system (for example, community mediation and service to the community) and restorative efforts to prevent crime (such as, school-based mediation) are, however, likely to be very different from restorative responses to the most violent crimes (victim awareness education or community service within a secure facility). Currently, though their use is most common as part of diversion or as an option for probation, restor-

ative sanction and decision-making processes are being used at several points in juvenile and criminal justice systems in various parts of the world. Restorative sanctions may be ordered by judges or developed through community boards, mediation sessions, or other process at any point—including after institutional commitment.[139]

2. Lack of Concern with Due Process. Because a core principle of restorative justice is that the community should have input into how problems should be resolved and new responses to crime developed, restorative justice should be *flexible and adaptable to local communities* and prescriptive only with regard to these values and system goals. It is often this general emphasis on community involvement in nonadversarial decison making that has been the source of many questions about restorative justice. Such increased reliance on informal processes seems difficult to envision in a system in which formal rules and procedures are in part intended to protect offenders from the abuses of unrestricted retribution and may be especially troubling to those concerned about further slippage in current procedural safeguards.[140] No restorative justice advocates have argued that it is necessary or desirable to weaken constitutional safeguards for offenders,[141] and restorative justice processes are not undertaken in cases in which an offender has not admitted guilt or been found guilty. In most cases, the current court process is itself highly informal rather than truly adversarial;[142] however, it is based on negotiation and bargaining in the service of the retributive ends of the state (and the professional interests of attorneys) rather than the interests of fairness and due process.[143]

3. Victims, Communities, and Offenders as Obstacles. Numerous questions remain about the practicality and overall effectiveness of restorative approaches. Common concerns focus, for example, on assertions that "victims are angry and punitive and do not want to have anything to do with the offender"; "offenders have no empathy, are incompetent, and are incapable of restoring the loss or harm caused by their crimes"; "the community is apathetic and citizens do not wish to be involved"; or "juvenile justice workers are required to spend too much time in court or doing paperwork and have not been trained to work with the community." Interestingly, criminal justice professionals committed to achieving the restorative justice goals view these very rationales for opposing the approach as precisely the reasons a new mission is necessary.[144] That is, if victims are angry and offenders lack skills and empathy, a primary objective should be to develop interventions that facilitate *changes* in offender empathy and competency and attempt to meet the needs of victims and ask them for their input. If citizens seem apathetic, a primary objective should be to work toward reducing community apathy and non-involvement and strengthening neighborhoods by changing the nature of current practices and decision-making processes. Finally, if staff do not have time or skills to perform such tasks, it may be time to reexamine and consider changing priorities and incentives.

4. *Incompatibility with Other Criminal Justice Objectives.* It is unlikely that a restorative system would eliminate other traditional justice system goals. Rather, restorative justice would most likely seek to bring about changes in the priority of these goals.[145] For the most part, as Braithwaite and Mugford propose,[146] restorative justice values can exist side by side with most traditional goals of juvenile justice intervention such as rehabilitation and even deterrence and incapacitation. Proponents of restorative justice, for example, recognize the need for attempts to deter some offenders, as secondary responses when they willfully and repeatedly disregard restorative obligations, or to protect citizens by incapacitating a smaller group of predatory offenders who continually victimize others.[147] But restorative justice would give lowest priority to punishment for its own sake and would in practice challenge current "easy" solutions that simply reinforce retributive urges and devote additional resources to traditional punishment, treatment, and unimaginative approaches to enhancing public safety. From a restorative perspective, it is easy to get offenders to "take the punishment,"[148] but it is much more difficult—and more important—to get them to take responsibility. It is equally easy to get many offenders to submit passively to the requirements of treatment programs, but it is much more difficult—and more important—to get them to actively earn their way back into the community and involve themselves in meaningful, productive roles that can potentially change their image from liability to community asset. It is easy to routinely lock up offenders in the name of public safety. But it is more difficult and more important to promote genuine public safety by building community capacity to control and prevent crime.[149]

5. *The Need for More Research.* Although the experience of restorative justice initiatives thus far and the findings of restorative justice research do not support the claims of critics, the grain of truth in these assertions does in many ways reflect the view of some staff in today's criminal justice systems. Initially, potential problems can be seen as basic implementation challenges, which in turn suggest essential empirical questions. For example, a fundamental question that requires baseline data before court and other system decision makers decide to support community justice decision making is whether citizens really *want* these alternatives and are willing to be involved in neighborhood sanction processes. Alternatively, citizens may simply want more accessible or user-friendly courts and other criminal justice agencies. As Kathleen Daly suggests after examining restorative justice conferencing in Australia over a period of several months, cautious optimism is justified in assessing the potential benefits of restorative justice.[150] Restorative justice is in its infancy, but, in any case, the standard or benchmark for gauging success must be the reality of the current system rather than some ideal depiction of it.

Devolving Rehabilitation and Building Community: Offenders, Experts, Real People, and "Naturalistic" Reintegration

> The development of a [criminal justice] system that takes sole responsibility for authoritarian control, and of a department [police] that takes sole responsibility for removing people from civil society and feeding themselves into this system—such developments may be socially debilitating, even criminogenic. They perpetuate the illusion that the state, rather than civil society, is ultimately responsible for social order."[151]

Many baby boomers and older generations often recall a time when adults in their neighborhoods or small towns took responsibility for looking after neighborhood children other than their own. In effect, community members, with the encouragement and support of police, schools, and other institutions, often "took care of" problems that now end up in juvenile courts or diversion programs. One of the things neighborhood adults did, as Braithwaite[152] reminds us, is reinforce community standards, norms, and expectations. These adults set community tolerance limits, and through verbal or other sanctions (including telling their parents), often persuaded young people to refrain from whatever troublemaking or annoying behavior they were involved in. As adults were involved in expressing disapproval of behavior they viewed as wrong, they maintained a relatively strong system of informal social control. While it is possible to simply write off these actions as nostalgic memories of a different era—and some of these social control techniques were discriminatory and undemocratic—we can also examine cultural and structural forces that have fundamentally limited the capacity of neighborhoods to develop common tolerance limits.[153] Moreover, it is important to ask questions about the ways in which criminal justice intervention itself may have reinforced a process by which community adults and adult institutions appear to have become helpless and hapless in socializing young people.

Several developments in U.S. criminal justice have expanded the government's role in social control while undercutting the community's role. The movement away from informal, neighborhood policing that emphasized local responses to crime to centralized intake bureaus where juvenile justice professionals process young offenders through courts and treatment programs[154] is one example. Similarly, three decades of failure in the experience with juvenile diversion programs in the United States[155] can teach related lessons about the intrusiveness and expansiveness of early intervention programs and the social service bureaucracies that support them. The problem with diversion and the centralization and specialization of the response to crime was the failure to distinguish between interventions that strengthened youth commitments and youth-adult relationships and those that further stigmatized and excluded young people, isolated youth from conventional adults, and usurped the community's responsibility.

The problem, moreover, was not government itself, but a failure to define a suitable role for government. When the role of the justice system is not clearly defined in concert with the community's role, justice and service programs are likely to overextend their reach, and bureaucracies will often make matters worse by aggravating processes of marginalization. As McKnight observes:

> A preliminary hypotheses is that services that are heavily focused on deficiency tend to be pathways out of community and into the exclusion of serviced life. We need a rigorous examination of public investments so that we can distinguish between services that lead people *out of community and into dependency* and those that support people in community life. (Emphasis added)[156]

A relational approach to offender rehabilitation must at some point confront social service bureaucracies that focus primarily on deficiency and exclusion and that, in the attempt to provide help, actually minimize the prospects for bonding and relationship building. In place of this youth service and individual treatment model, a new intervention paradigm is needed that seeks to rediscover and, if necessary, reinvent ways for communities to begin to take back the responsibility for youth socialization and offender rehabilitation. Citizens who look closely at the causes of crime suspect that courts and justice systems have already reached beyond their competence in the effort to control crime, sanction offenders, or build safer communities.[157] Similarly, government cannot be solely responsible for rehabilitating offenders.

The good news is that most offenders "age out" of crime, or experience "maturational reform."[158] While this process doesn't happen magically, it typically has nothing to do with treatment programs. Rather, known institutional and social ecological factors—notably, a job, family ties (both to family of origin and family of choice), access to higher education, and community supports—are primarily responsible.[159] Moreover, the resiliency of young people in high-risk neighborhoods seems to be due to one relatively simple factor: the ongoing presence of one or more caring adults (not necessarily parents) who are able to provide them with ongoing support and access to roles that allow them to develop legitimate identities.[160] What is of most significance is the role of the relationships most young offenders eventually build with other law-abiding citizens in their own communities. Hence, effective strategies for long-term rehabilitation must maximize neighborhood ties and seek to enhance those nonprofessional adult relationships.

But naturalistic does not mean "naturally occurring." There is nothing accidental about reintegration, and a relational strategy based on restorative principles is not a libertarian approach. Moreover, there is nothing magical about "the community," and identifying and mobilizing citizens to allow for a greater community role in rehabilitation will require a very intentional strategy that redefines rather than seeks to eliminate the government role.[161] Hence, a naturalistic approach to rehabilitation would build on a general belief in the capacity of communities and nonprofessional adults, if encouraged and supported, to develop and assist young people in getting through problems such as delinquency and growing up. Relational rehabilitation would maximize use of informal support networks while minimizing use of formal social control and professional intervention services.

Such a strategy would redirect justice resources toward the difficult task of community building and would begin to redefine the role of the rehabilitation professional. In a naturalistic, relational rehabilitation approach such professionals would no longer view themselves or be viewed by their communities as "experts," providing service or treatment to change offender attitudes and behavior. Nor would their role be defined as "case manager," responsible for functions that limit the potential for astute professionals to enhance naturalistic reintegrative processes. Rather than monitoring offenders on community supervision, making referrals for service, and completing paperwork, justice professionals would focus on creative problem solving, community development, and relationship building, and the professional role in relational rehabilitation would thus be more one of catalyst for facilitating change in the role of offenders from liability to resource.[162]

Obstacles to Restorative Reintegration: The Challenge of Earned Redemption

Currently, in the United States we appear to lack two essential ingredients to make the restorative justice response to crime more than a marginal and ancillary feature of the current predominately retributive criminal justice response. To move forward with an agenda for offender reintegration based on earned redemption, it is necessary to consider how the restorative justice project, which necessarily consists of micro efforts to repair harm to victims and victimized communities, might interact with more macro efforts to build a supportive culture of redemption and to develop structural paths that support integration and reintegration. In the United States in particular, however, the prospect of a more systemic and societal application of earned redemption must confront both cultural and structural obstacles.

A Structure of Integration and Reintegration

One typical response to restorative justice arguments about offender reintegration is that when it comes to young people in much of the Western world, we lack even an approach to *integration*.[163] The increasing structural separation of young people from adults is indeed both a cause of crime and a formidable barrier to even a productive dialogue about offender reintegration.

Addressing this separation as an international problem of marginalization of young people will require a dramatic shift in work and educational policies and priorities. Such a shift requires a willingness to confront structural economic changes that have created an international crisis of youth marginalization.[164] This crisis is, of course, greatly exacerbated for minority young people, as illustrated graphically by rates of unemployment for sixteen- to nineteen-year-old African Americans that in recent years have run as high as three times those for whites (the white rate has averaged approximately 20 percent).

Having begun to address these issues, a comprehensive and meaningful reintegration policy aimed at young persons currently in (or near) the criminal and juvenile justice systems must therefore begin with an educational, employment, and youth development strategy. Such a strategy would be based on the premise that a functional economy cannot afford to "write off" huge segments of the youth population as liabilities, but must instead begin to view all young people as a resource.[165]

A second structural concern for advocates of a restorative approach to reintegration grows out of the fundamental premise of restorative justice that crime control and offender reintegration must begin and end in communities. This requires that advocates confront the fundamental challenge of "finding" and then engaging community. The magnitude of this structural challenge is illustrated clearly by criminologist Elliot Currie's sketch of an economy and social system that strains communities to the point at which they are unable to develop or sustain a sense of connectedness or bonding:

> If we wanted to sketch a hypothetical portrait of an especially violent society, it would surely contain these elements: it would separate large numbers of people, especially the young, from the kind of work that could include them securely in community life; it would encourage policies of economic development and income distribution that sharply increased inequalities between sectors of the population; it would rapidly shift vast amounts of capital from place to place without regard for the impact on local communities, causing massive movements of population away from family and neighborhood supports in search of livelihood; it would avoid providing new mechanisms of care and support for those uprooted, perhaps in the name of preserving incentives to work and paring government spending; it would promote a culture of intense interpersonal competition and spur its citizens to a level of material consumption many could not lawfully sustain.[166]

While the emphasis on the personal "communities of concern" around offender and victims as discussed above is a useful beginning in the effort to define community in terms useful for criminal justice intervention, this focus has little apparent relationship to a macro reintegration strategy based on earned redemption. One initial linkage proposed by Braithwaite and Parker is to begin to connect community sanctions and reintegration ceremonies to what they refer to as a "vibrant social movement politics."[167] The purpose of such a linkage is to address structural inequities directly implicated in race and class bias in the criminal justice process, while also checking the potential tyranny of both state and community. Infusing more macro, movement politics into such micro processes as FGC, victim-offender dialogue, or circle sentencing, on the one hand, runs the risk of altering the dynamic of these ceremonies in a way that may alienate some participants. On the other hand, broader community and social justice concerns that appear to be clearly grounded in movement politics have been a consistent feature of some of these efforts to devolve, and assume community control over, justice decision making. In fact, community control over justice processes has been a driving force among those Canadian and New Zealand aboriginals, although the devolution movement in these communities has been as much about local ownership as indigenous solidarity.[168] Similar initiatives could possibly build on anti-criminal justice system sentiments in African American and Hispanic communities in the United States in a way that encourages local community building to improve the response to crime.

A Culture of Redemption

Case One. In San Diego, the tragic shooting of the teenage son of a well-to-do San Diego businessman by a fourteen-year-old gang member after the man's son had refused to give him a pizza was to result in the transfer of the offender's case to adult court for disposition. Rather than seek waiver of his son's killer to adult court, the father, who blamed the state of California for allowing teenagers such easy access to guns, chose to reach out to the grandfather of the boy both for a resolution to this case and to develop a potential solution to the broader problem of youth violence. After a series of meetings that involved the extended families of the father of the victim and the offender, the father and grandfather formed a national coalition dedicated to remedying the two conditions the father blamed for his son's shooting: the ready availability of guns to teenagers and the need for training in peaceful alternatives to resolving conflict among young people.

Case Two. A St. Paul, Minnesota, man, whose home had been burglarized and his possessions (including several valuable antiques) badly damaged by a vandalism spree of two young neighborhood boys, recognized that his neighborhood lacked the sense of community he once felt. Feeling some personal responsibility for this breakdown in relationships as well as anxiety about his loss, the victim suggested to the prosecutor in the case that a meeting with the offenders be arranged in hope that he might involve them in an effort to do something in the neighborhood to restore a sense of community. After this suggestion was rebuffed by the prosecutor, who explained that the courts were "interested in consistency, not creativity," the man—with the support of victim-offender mediation case workers—arranged a block party in which the offenders were required to work with him to prepare a barbeque for neighborhood residents.

It is apparent that cultural expectations in those societies and communities that find an easy fit between restorative justice and criminal justice support and encourage offender confession and repentance for their wrongdoing. Once this occurs, it is also assumed that societal forgiveness and an effort to reintegrate the offender will be forthcoming.[169] Building support for earned redemption within a culture of blame and retribution based on what one observer labeled "constitutionalized revenge" presents enormous challenges. One of the greatest of these challenges is the mutually reinforcing character of a justice system focused on fixing blame and determining punishment by means of the most adversarial process in the world and the tendency of offenders to deny guilt—or admit to the lowest acceptable charge until a plea agreement can be negotiated.

On the one hand, the current attempt to "import" processes that use shame and remorse in ways that promote repentance, forgiveness, and resolution in such a culture runs a substantial risk of perverting these concepts. On the other hand, despite these cultural obstacles, the cases described above, however atypical they may appear in the American cultural context, are not unique. Moreover, the cultural significance of a few widely publicized cases that seem to stretch the concepts of forgiveness and repentance to the limit could enhance the strength of emerging grassroots support by providing a kind of "folklore" that illustrates a much wider range of possibilities in the community response to crime. In addition, consistent with Naroll's theory of "snowballs,"[170] as reintegrative sanction ceremonies are repeated and publicized often enough in what some see as a period in which policymakers are sensing that they have reached the limits of the punitive and treatment reactions, a community and cultural learning process may take place.[171] Such a process may allow these alternatives to slowly seep into the cultural repertoire of potential responses to crime and to the harm crime causes.

Proponents of restorative justice approaches are indeed engaged in micro attempts to "build community" from the ground up using the vehicle of sanctioning ceremonies. Though the prospects that such activity will bring about systemic change in criminal justice seem remote, other examples from community organizing suggest that it is often one signifying incident (such as a police shooting) that mobilizes neighborhoods to implement reforms. It might not stretch this analogy too far to argue that new awareness of the crime problem in a community, growing problems with neighborhood young people, concern about increased victimization, or a particularly disturbing case, could, in the context of an effective participatory community sanction model, provide a wake-up call to a few individuals who band together to initiate fundamental change in the response to crime.

Although the hope for cultural change in a direction supportive of earned redemption by means of even widely repeated demonstrations of successful restorative responses seems farfetched, Schweigert suggests that the emerging restorative justice agenda for "community moral development" has several characteristics in common with other successful social change movements.[172] This includes a blending of means and ends, or process and outcome (e.g., conflict resolution, informal social control mechanisms), which allows for multiple and ever widening impact as the means themselves result in outcomes unforeseen by the actors involved, yet consistent with the basic principles. Moreover, restorative justice reforms build on community assets and strengths,[173] follow the lead of "citizen politics" in their adaptability and focus on local communal traditions while using professionals as catalysts and facilitators, demand and encourage collaboration, and allow for "free space" or "space between places" in social relations where individuals and communities and the formal and informal intersect. The latter characteristic encourages victims, citizens, and offenders in conferences, mediations, and other processes to resolve conflict in a way that is potentially transformative for communities and that integrates affective ties and emotions based on communal norms with the universal norms of the legal system that provide rational, transcending standards. "Crime" as a violation of established law is linked in restorative justice to the more communal notion of crime as personal conflict and personal injury sanction ceremonies in which

> moral authority is demonstrated as government agencies and institutions act with respect toward all persons involved in the crime, effect a process that repairs the harm done by the crime, and ratify the authority and acts of those who resolve the crime. In short, impersonal rational moral authority is demonstrated by acts of reinstating offenders and restoring victims. The restorative process enables persons exercising communal moral authority to endorse the acts and hence the authority of agencies and institutions embodying universal norms. In this way, the moral authority of community traditions reinforces the authority of universal norms.[174]

Discussion moving from micro to macro process in this fashion while connecting the communal and universal will been seen by many as nothing less than utopian. Yet, as Belgian criminologist Lode Walgrave observes:

> Giving priority to reparation rather than retribution calls for a change in social ethics and a different ideology of society. That means a society governed with the aims of individual and collective emancipation, in which autonomy and solidarity are not seen as diametrically opposed, but viewed as mutually reinforcing principles. A society doing its utmost to avoid exclusion of its members, because it is a society which draws its strength not from fear but from the high social ethics by which it is governed. . . . Is this Utopia? Yes, but we need a utopia to motivate us and provide guidance for our actions in society. There is nothing more *practical* than a good utopia.[175]

Notes

1. Conservative philosophers have generally enshrined punishment as the cornerstone of moral authority and thus the priority for intervention in response to crime, and have little faith in the capacity of most offenders to change behavior except in response to the threat of coercive responses centered primarily on incarceration (E. van den Haag, *Punishing Criminals: Concerning a Very Old and Painful Question* [New York: Basic Books, 1975]). Liberal approaches have traditionally focused on rehabilitative approaches that seek to treat the assumed under-

lying causes of crime. Based on the idea that criminal justice intervention must be kept to a minimum, proponents of libertarian approaches emphasize procedural restrictions on the system because they are equally skeptical of the motives of those seeking to either punish *or* treat offenders (A. M. Platt, *The Child Savers: The Invention of Delinquency* (Chicago: University of Chicago Press, 1977) and are concerned that intervention, no matter what the intent, often makes matters worse. American Friends Service Committee (AFSC), *Struggle for Justice* (New York: Hill and Wang, 1971); M. Lemert, *Instead of Court: Diversion in Juvenile Justice* (Rockville, MD: National Institute of Mental Health, 1971); E. Schur, *Radical Nonintervention* (Berkeley: University of California Press, 1972).

2. B. Feld, "The Punitive Juvenile Court and the Quality of Procedural Justice: Distinctions Between Rhetoric and Reality," *Crime and Delinquency* 36 (1990); B. Feld, "The Criminal Court Alternative to Perpetuating Juvenile in Justice," in *The Juvenile Court: Dynamic, Dysfunctional, or Dead?* (Philadelphia: Center for the Study of Youth Policy, School of Social Work, University of Pennsylvania, 1993), 3-13; D. R. Gordon, *The Justice Juggernaut* (New Brunswick, NJ: Rutgers University, 1991); M. Tonry, *Malign Neglect, Race, Crime and Punishment in America* (New York: Oxford University Press, 1995).

3. H. Zehr, *Changing Lenses: A New Focus for Crime and Justice* (Scottsdale, PA: Herald Press, 1990); M. Umbreit, *Victim Meets Offender: The Impact of Restorative Justice and Mediation* (Monsey, NY: Criminal Justice Press, 1994).

4. F. T. Cullen and J. P. Wright, "The Future of Corrections," in *The Past, Present, and Future of American Criminal Justice*, ed. B. Maguire and P. Radosh (New York: General Hall, 1995).

5. The retributive/punitive paradigm that emerged in the juvenile justice system in the 1980s was in no way a pure "just deserts" approach. Rather, retributive justice, as implemented, combines the emphasis on the primacy of punishment philosophy and certain policy trappings (e.g., determinate sentencing guidelines) of just deserts with a general concern with deterrence, incapacitation, and more traditional punitive objectives.

6. F. T. Cullen and K. E. Gilbert, *Reaffirming Rehabilitation* (Cincinnati: Anderson, 1982); B. Krisberg, *The Juvenile Court: Reclaiming the Vision* (San Francisco: National Council of Crime and Delinquency, 1988); P. Gendreau and R. Ross, "Correctional Treatment: Some Recommendations for Successful Intervention," *Juvenile and Family Court Journal* 34 (1994): 31-40.

7. Tonry, *Malign Neglect*.

8. The libertarian concern with due process become strong in the 1960s and 1970s as the growth of law enforcement capabilities and the Supreme Court's response to this new state power created heightened awareness of threats to civil liberties. H. Packer, *The Limits of the Criminal Sanction* (Palo Alto, CA: Stanford University Press, 1968), 41, 296-316. Proponents of crime control ideologies, impatient with the due process concerns of libertarians, are interested in maximizing

intervention aimed at reducing risk of crime even at the expense of some encroachment on civil liberties, minimizing procedures and obstacles to efficiency in crime fighting, and maximizing use of incarceration. Unlike the more moralistic or "fundamentalist" position of conservatives (Sue Guarino-Ghezzi and Edward Loughran, *Balancing Juvenile Justice* [New Brunswick, NJ: Transaction Publishers, 1996]), however, proponents of crime control favor punishment as a means to the more ultimate ends of deterrence and/or incapacitation.

9. AFSC, *Struggle for Justice*; E. Schur, *Radical Nonintervention*; Feld, "The Criminal Court," 3-13.

10. Zehr, *Changing Lenses.*

11. Zehr, *Changing Lenses*; D. Van Ness et al., "Restorative Justice Practice," (Washington, DC: Justice Fellowship, 1989).

12. Zehr, *Changing Lenses*; Van Ness, "New Wine and Old Wineskins: Four Challenges of Restorative Justice," *Criminal Law Forum* 4 (1993): 251-76; G. Bazemore, "Three Paradigms for Juvenile Justice," in *The Practice of Restorative Justice*, ed. Joe Hudson and Burt Galaway (Monsey, NY: Criminal Justice Press, 1996).

13. R. Elias, *Victims Still: Political Manipulation of Crime Victims* (Newbury Park, CA: Sage, 1993); Bazemore, "Understanding the Response to Reforms Limiting Discretion: Judges' Views of Restrictions on Detention Intake," *Justice Quarterly* 11 (1994): 429-53.

14. Indeed, restorative justice is often equated with one program: victim-offender mediation. M. Umbreit, *Victim Meets Offender* (Monsey, NY: Criminal Justice Press, 1994); M. Wright, *Justice for Victims and Offenders* (Buckingham, England: Open University Press, 1991). There is good reason, however, for this emphasis on victims in restorative justice. Early research and theoretical discussion of practices such as restitution and even victim-offender mediation was, on the contrary, almost exclusively offender focused, giving primary emphasis to use of these sanctions to promote diversion or alternatives to incarceration. The term "restorative justice" is generally attributed to Albert Eglash, "Beyond Retribution: Creative Restitution," in *Restitution in Criminal Justice*, ed. J. Hudson and B. Galaway (Lexington, MA: Lexington Books, 1975). "Client" as used in this chapter refers to an individual or group that receives services from a governmental agency based on need and is targeted for intervention by the agency intended to change behavior or alter its current situation. A "coparticipant" is actively engaged in the government intervention process as a key decision maker.

15. G. Bazemore and M. Umbreit, "Rethinking the Sanctioning Function in Juvenile Court: Retributive or Restorative Responses to Youth Crime," *Crime and Delinquency* 41 (1995): 296-316; Zehr, *Changing Lenses.*

16. Although the term "earned redemption" has probably been used before in various contexts, I credit its use in the modern restorative justice movement to Dennis Maloney, Director, Deschutes County Department of Community Correc-

tions, Bend, Oregon.

17. K. Pranis, "Communities and the Justice System: Turning the Relationship Upside Down" (paper presented before the Office of Justice Programs, Forum on Community Justice, U.S. Department of Justice, Washington, DC, 1996).

18. Van Ness et al., "Restorative Justice Practice."

19. Bazemore, "Three Paradigms"; M. J. Dooley, *Reparative Probation Program* (Waterbury: Vermont Department of Corrections, 1995).

20. G. Bazemore, "What's New About the Balanced Approach?" *Juvenile and Family Court Journal* 48 (1997): 1-23.

21. Van Ness, "New Wine and Old Wineskins," 251-76; Zehr, *Changing Lenses.*

22. G. M. Weitekamp, "The History of Restorative Justice," in *Restoring Juvenile Justice: Changing the Context of Youth Crime Response*, ed. G. Bazemore and L. Walgrave (Monsey, NY: Criminal Justice Press, 1998)

23. Weitekamp, "History of Restorative Justice." See also, R. J. Michalowski, *Order, Law, and Crime* (New York: Random House, 1995); Van Ness et al., "Restorative Justice Practice."

24. Van Ness et al., "Restorative Justice Practice."

25. Weitekamp, "History of Restorative Justice."

26. Van Ness et al., "Restorative Justice Practice."

27. Zehr, *Changing Lenses.* Monarchs who succeeded William competed with the church's influence over secular matters and effectively replaced local systems of dispute resolution. In 1116, William's son, Henry I, issued the *Leges Henrici* securing royal jurisdiction over certain offenses against the king's peace, including arson, robbery, murder, false coinage, and crimes of violence.

28. S. Schafer, *Compensation and Restitution to Victims of Crime* (Montclaire, NJ: Smith Patterson, 1970).

29. J. Hudson et al., "Research of Family Group Conferencing in Child Welfare in New Zealand," in *Family Group Conferences: Perspectives on Policy and Practice*, ed. J. Hudson, B. Galaway, A. Morris, and G. Maxwell (Monsey, NY: Criminal Justice Press, 1996); A. Schneider, "Restitution and Recidivism Rates of Juvenile Offenders: Results from Four Experimental Studies," *Criminology* 24 (1986): 533-52; Umbreit, *Victim Meets Offender.*

30. Zehr, *Changing Lenses*; J. Hudson et al., "Research of Family," 1-16; Bazemore and Umbreit, "Rethinking the Sanctioning," 296-315.

31. E. Barajas Jr., "Moving Toward Community Justice," *Topics in Community Corrections* (Washington, DC: National Institute of Corrections, 1995); C. T. Griffiths and R. Hamilton, "Spiritual Renewal, Community Revitalization and Healing: Experience in Traditional Aboriginal Justice in Canada," *International Journal of Comparative and Applied Criminal Justice* 20 (1996); B. Stuart, "Circle Sentencing: Turning Swords into Ploughshares," in *Restorative Justice: International Perspectives*, ed. B. Galaway and J. Hudson (Monsey, NY: Kugler Publications, 1996): 193-206.

32. M. Young, "Restorative Community Justice: A Call to Action," (Washington, DC: National Organization for Victim Assistance, 1995); G. Bazemore and M. Schiff, "Community Justice/Restorative Justice: Prospects for a New Social Ecology for Community Corrections," *International Journal of Comparative and Applied Criminal Justice* 20 (1996): 311-35.

33. J. Robinson, "Research on Child Welfare in New Zealand," in *Family Group Conferences: Perspectives on Policy and Practice*, ed. J. Hudson, B. Galaway, A. Morris, and G. Maxwell (Monsey, NY: Criminal Justice Press, 1996): 49-64.

34. J. Belgrave, "Restorative Justice: A Discussion Paper" (Wellington: New Zealand Ministry of Justice, 1996); Dooley, *Reparative Probation Program*.

35. Bazemore, "What's New."

36. Young, "Restorative Communitive Justice."

37. M. Sparrow et al., *Beyond 911* (New York: Basic Books, 1990); M. Moore and R. Trojanowicz, "The Concept of Community," *Perspectives on Policy No. 6* (Washington, DC: United States Department of Justice, National Institute of Justice, 1988).

38. Griffiths and Hamilton, "Spiritual Renewal"; A. Melton, "Indigenous Justice Systems and Tribal Society," *Judicature* 70 (1995): 126-33.

39. M. K. Harris, "Moving into the New Millenium: Toward a Feminist Vision of Justice," in *Criminology as Peacemaking*, ed. H. Pepinsky and R. Quinney (Bloomington: Indiana University Press, 1990), 83-97; C. G. Bowman, "The Arrest Experiments: A Feminist Critique," in *Taking Sides: Clashing Views on Controversial Issues in Crime and Criminology*, ed. R. Monk (Guilford, CT: Dushkin Publishing Group, 1994), 186-91.

40. J. Braithwaite and P. Petit, *Not Just Deserts: A Republican Theory of Criminal Justice* (Oxford: Clarendon Press, 1992); Bazemore and Umbreit, "Rethinking the Sanctioning"; L. Walgrave, "The Restorative Proportionality of Community Service for Juveniles: Just a Technique or a Fully-Fledged Alternative?" *Howard Journal of Criminal Justice* 34 (1995): 228-49.

41. Philosophically and politically, a restorative approach is also consistent with insights from the new communitarianism (A. Etzioni, *The Spirit of Community* [New York: Crown Publishers, 1993]; D. B. Moore and T. O'Connell, "Family Conferencing in Wagga Wagga: A Communitarian Model of Justice," in *Family Group Conferencing and Juvenile Justice: The Way Forward or Misplaced Optimism?*, ed. C. Adler and J. Wundersitz [Canberra: Australia Institute of Criminology, 1994]) both in its demand for active involvement of citizens in community problem solving and skepticism about the ability of government to resolve problems (Van Ness et al., "Restorative Justice Practice"; B. Stuart, *Sentencing Circles: Making 'Real' Differences* (unpublished paper, Territorial Court of the Yukon, 1995). Restorative justice principles are also consistent with recent developments in both private sector and public management focused on reinventing organizational responses to "customers" (W. Deming, *Out of Crisis* [Cambridge, MA: MIT Center for Advanced Engineering, 1996]; L. Martin, *Total Quality Management in Organizations*

[Newbury Park, CA: Sage, 1993]), as well as with concepts from the environmental movement focused on sustainable growth.

42. Many of these new practices in fact address that portion of the reform agenda of restorative justice aimed at establishing a community-based alternative to the formal justice system and the need to transform justice decision-making processes to better accommodate the needs and interests of victims, offenders, and communities. Both are discussed in subsequent sections.

43. Zehr, *Changing Lenses*; J. Braithwaite and S. Mugford, "Conditions of Successful Reintegration Ceremonies: Dealing with Juvenile Offenders," *British Journal of Criminology* 34 (1994): 139-71.

44. H. Goldstein, "Improving Policing: A Problem-Oriented Approach," *Crime and Delinquency* 25 (1979): 236-58; H. Goldstein, "Toward Community-Oriented Policing: Potential, Basic Requirements and Threshold Questions," *Crime and Delinquency* 33 (1987): 6-30.

45. Zehr, *Changing Lenses*; Van Ness, "New Wine and Old Wineskins."

46. K. Pranis, "From Vision to Action," *Church and Society* 87 (1997): 32-42; Stuart, "Circle Sentencing."

47. Zehr, *Changing Lenses.*

48. Zehr, *Changing Lenses.*

49. Pranis, "From Vision to Action."

50. Stuart, *Sentencing Circles.*

51. Zehr, *Changing Lenses*; Bazemore and Umbreit, "Rethinking the Sanctions."

52. Zehr, *Changing Lenses*; H. Messmer and H. Otto, eds., *Restorative Justice on Trial: Pitfalls and Potentials of Victim Offender Mediation:International Research Perspectives* (Norwell, MA: Kluwer Academic Publishers, 1992).

53. S. Hillsman and J. Greene, "The Use of Fines as an Intermediate Sanction," in *Smart Sentencing*, ed. J. M. Byrne, A. Lurigio, and J. Petersilia (Newbury Park, CA: Sage, 1992), 123-41.

54. C. Shapiro, "Is Restitution Legislation the Chameleon of the Victims' Movement?" in *Criminal Justice, Restitution, and Reconciliation*, ed. B. Galaway and J. Hudson (Monsey, NY: Willow Tree Press, 1990), 73-80.

55. Elias, *Victims Still.*

56. M. Umbreit, "Holding Juvenile Offenders Accountable: A Restorative Justice Perspective," *Juvenile and Family Court Journal* 46 (1995): 31-41; Bazemore, "Understanding the Response."

57. Elaine Berzins, quoted in Stuart, "Circle Sentencing."

58. Wright, "Justice for Victims and Offenders"; Zehr, *Changing Lenses.*

59. Stuart, "Circle Sentencing."

60. Zehr, *Changing Lenses.*

61. Young, "Restorative Community Justice."

62. Indeed the experience with victim-offender mediation and some research on crime victims' attitudes suggest that victim mercy toward offenders may be less at

issue than the capacity of community groups and certainly public officials to for-give. Umbreit, *Victim Meets Offender*; K. Pranis and M. Umbreit, "Public Opinion, Research, Challenges, and Perceptions of Widespread Public Demand for Harsher Punishment," (Minneapolis: Citizen's Council, 1992).

63. Umbreit, *Victim Meets Offender*; Wright, "Justice for Victims and Offenders."

64. D. Karp, *Community Justice*, Research Seminar on Community, Crime, and Justice (Washington, DC: George Washington University/National Institute of Justice, 1997); Bazemore, "Three Paradigms."

65. R. J. Sampson and W. B. Groves, "Community Structure and Crime: Testing Social-Disorganization Theory," *American Journal of Sociology* 94 (1989): 774-802; Karp, *Community Justice*.

66. T. Hirschi, *Causes of Delinquency* (Berkeley: University of California Press, 1969).

67. S. Briar and I. Piliavin, "Delinquency, Situational Inducements, and Commitments to Conformity," *Social Problems* 13 (1965): 35-45; K. Polk and S. Kobrin, *Delinquency Prevention Through Youth Development* (Washington, DC: Office of Youth Development, 1972).

68. E. H. Sutherland and D. R. Cressy, *Criminology*, 10th ed. (Philadelphia: Lippincott, 1978).

69. Stuart, *Sentencing Circles*.

70. Braithwaite and Mugford, "Conditions of Successful Reintegration."

71. H. Garfinkel, "Conditions of Successful Degradation Ceremonies," *American Journal of Sociology* 61 (1956): 420-4; Stuart, *Sentencing Circles*; Wright, "Justice for Victims and Offenders."

72. H. Becker, *Studies in Sociology of Deviance* (New York: Free Press, 1960). At this interactional level, restorative justice is also consistent with a growing body of empirical research on the role of informal sanctions such as shame, embarrassment, and the role of significant others in promoting conformity to conventional norms (S. S. Tompkins, *Affect, Imagery, Consciousness* [New York: Springer Publication, 1992]; S. Retzinger and T. Scheff, "Strategy for Community Conferencing: Emotions and Social Bonds," in Galaway and Hudson, eds. Restorative Justice: International Perspectives [Monsey, NY: Kugler Publications, 1996]: 313-36).

73. Pranis, "From Vision to Action."

74. A. J Reiss and M. Tonry, eds., *Communities and Crime* (Chicago: University of Chicago Press, 1986).

75. Van Ness et al., "Restorative Justice Practice."

76. Van Ness et al., "Restorative Justice Practice"; Stuart, *Sentencing Circles*; Pranis, "From Vision to Action."

77. Stuart, "Circle Sentencing."

78. Van Ness et al., "Restorative Justice Practice."

79. N. Christie, *Limits to Pain* (Oxford: Martin Robertson, 1982); F. Schweigert,

Learning the Common Good: Principles of Community-Based Moral Education in Restorative Justice (St. Paul: University of Minnesota, 1997).

80. Stuart, "Circle Sentencing."

81. J. Braithwaite, *Crime, Shame, and Reintegration* (New York: Cambridge University Press, 1989).

82. Braithwaite and Mugford, "Conditions of Successful Reintegration."

83. G. Bazemore and S. Day, "The Return to Family Interventions in Youth Service: A Juvenile Justice Study in Policy Implementation," *Journal of Sociology and Social Welfare* 22 (1995): 25-50.

84. Reiss and Tonry, ed., *Communities and Crime.*

85. K. Pittman and W. Fleming, "A New Vision: Promoting Youth Development," Testimony to House Select Committee on Children, Youth and Families, Academy for Education and Development, Washington, DC, September 1991; J. H. Brown and J. E. Horowitz, "Why Adolescent Substance Abuse Prevention Programs Do Not Work," *Evaluation Review* 17 (1993): 5.

86. G. Melton and P. M. Pagliocca, "Treatment in the Juvenile Justice System: Directions for Policy and Practice," in *Responding to the Mental Health Needs of Youth in Juvenile Justice*, ed. J. J. Cocozza (Seattle: National Coalition for the Mentally Ill in the Criminal Justice System, 1992), 107-39.

87. R.W. Scott, *Organizations: Rational National, and Open Systems* (Englewood Cliffs, NJ: Prentice-Hall, 1987).

88. I.M. Schwartz, "Public Attitudes toward Juvenile Crime and Juvenile Justice: Implications for Public Policy," in *Juvenile Justice Policy*, ed. I. Schwartz (Lexington, MA: Lexington Books, 1992), 225-50.

89. Bazemore and Umbreit, "Rethinking Sanctioning."

90. Braithwaite and Mugford, "Conditions of Successful Reintegration," 5.

91. K. Polk, "Family Conferencing: Theoretical and Evaluative Questions," in *Family Group Conferencing and Juvenile Justice: The Way Forward or Misplaced Optimism?*, ed. C. Adler and J. Wundersitz (Canberra: Australian Institute of Criminology, 1994), 155-68; William Julius Wilson, *The Truly Disadvantaged* (Chicago: University of Chicago Press, 1987).

92. It is ironic that a discipline such as criminology so grounded in sociological theories about the complex and community-oriented causes of crime at times appears atheoretical and willing to beg the basic question of whether anyone should *expect* young offenders to be rehabilitated—habilitated and reintegrated—in settings that involve limited and relatively short-term individually focused treatment by experts detached from communities. This basic suspension of doubt is not apparently shared by average citizens (and juvenile justice professionals) when they remind us that young offender—even in the best treatment program—will go back to the same neighborhoods they came from. Although theories of crime have come primarily from sociology, it is clear that the treatment paradigm has been almost exclusively influenced by abnormal psychology and clinical social work.

93. Schneider, "Restitution and Recidivism"; Braithwaite and Mugford, "Conditions of Successful Reintegration."

94. Van Ness, "New Wine and Old Wineskins"; G. Bazemore and C. Terry, "Developing Delinquent Youth: A Reintegrative Model for Rehabilitation and a New Role for the Juvenile Justice System," 26 *Child Welfare* 5 (1997): 665-716.

95. This concept of "resonance" was first articulated by Troy Armstrong. See Armstrong et al., "The Balanced Approach in Juvenile Probation: Principles, Issues, and Application," *Perspectives* 1 (1990): 8-13.

96. Van Ness et al., "Restorative Justice Practice"; Stuart, "Circle Sentencing"; M. Brown and K. Polk, "Taking Fear of Crime Seriously: The Tasmanian Approach to Community Crime Prevention," *Crime and Delinquency* 42 (1996): 398-420.

97. Hirschi, *Causes of Delinquency.*

98. Bazemore and Terry, "Developing Delinquent Youth"; G. Bazemore, "After the Shaming, Whither Reintegration: Restorative Justice and Relational Rehabilitation," in *Restoring Juvenile Justice,* ed. G. Bazemore and L. Walgrave (Amsterdam: Kugler International Publications, 1998).

99. Christie, *Limits to Pain.*

100. T. Makkai and J. Braithwaite, "Reintegrative Shaming and Compliance with Regulatory Standards," *Criminology* 31 (1994): 361-85; Bazemore and Umbreit, "Rethinking the Sanctioning."

101. Wright, "Justice for Victims and Offenders."

102. E. Durkheim, *Moral Education: A Study in the Theory and Application of the Sociology of Education,* trans. E. K. Wilson and H. Schnuter (New York: Free Press, 1961); D. Garland, *Punishment and Modern Society: A Study in Social Theory* (Chicago: University of Chicago Press, 1990).

103. L. Zhang and S. F. Messner, "The Severity of Official Punishment for Delinquency and Change in Interpersonal Relations in Chinese Society," *Journal of Research in Crime and Delinquency* 31 (1994): 416-33.

104. Bazemore and Umbreit, "Rethinking the Sanctioning."

105. H. Packer, *The Limits of the Criminal Sanction* (Palo Alto, CA: Stanford University Press, 1968), 41, 296-316.

106. Braithwaite, *Crime, Shame, and Reintegration*; L.T. Wilkins, *Punishment, Crime, and Market Forces* (Brookfield, VT: Dartmouth Publishing Company, 1991); Garland, *Punishment and Modern Society.*

107. Durkheim, *Moral Education,* 181-2; cited in Braithwaite, *Crime, Shame, and Reintegration,* 178.

108. Griffiths and Hamilton, "Spiritual Renewal"; Wilkins, *Punishment.*

109. Durkheim, *Moral Education.*

110. Etzioni, *The Spirit of Community*; A. Schneider, *Deterrence and Juvenile Crime: Results from a National Policy Experiment* (New York: Springer-Verlag, 1990)

111. Braithwaite, *Crime, Shame, and Reintegration*; Garland, *Punishment and*

Modern Society; Wilkins, *Punishment*.

112. J. Butts and H. Snyder, *Restitution and Juvenile Recidivism* (Pittsburgh: National Center for Juvenile Justice, 1991); Schneider, "Restitution and Recidivism"; L. Walgrave and H. Geudens, "Community Service as a Sanction of Restorative Justice: A European Approach" (paper presented at the Council Meeting of the American Society of Criminology, Chicago, November 1996); M. Schiff, "The Impact of Restorative Interventions on Juvenile Offenders," in *Restoring Juvenile Justice: Changing the Context of the Youth Crime Response*, ed. G. Bazemore and L. Walgrave (Monsey, NY: Criminal Justice Press, 1998).

113. Schneider, *Deterrence and Juvenile Crime*; M. Umbreit and R. Coates, "Cross-Site Analysis of Victim-Offender Conflict: An Analysis of Programs in These Three States," *Juvenile and Family Court Journal* 43 (1993): 21-8.

114. Umbreit, *Victim Meets Offender*.

115. Schneider, *Deterrence and Juvenile Crime*.

116. S. Tomkins, *Affect/Imagery/Consciousness* (New York: Springer, 1992).

117. Stuart, *Sentencing Circles*; Griffiths and Hamilton, "Spiritual Renewal."

118. B. Krisberg et al., "What Works with Juvenile Offenders: A Review of Graduated Sanction Programs," *Criminal Justice* (1995): 20; Gendreau and Ross, "Correctional Treatment."

119. Schiff, "The Impact of Restorative Interventions."

120. Gendreau and Ross, "Correctional Treatment."

121. Krisberg et al., "What Works."

122. G. Bazemore and D. Maloney, "Rehabilitating Community Service: Toward Restorative Service in a Balanced Justice System," *Federal Probation* 58 (1994): 24-35.

123. M. Crouch, "Is Incarceration Really Worse? Analysis of Offenders' Preferences for Prison Over Probation," *Justice Quarterly* 10 (1993): 67-88.

124. Bazemore and Umbreit, "Rethinking the Sanctioning."

125. Bazemore and Maloney, "Rehabilitating Community Service"; Bazemore and Umbreit, "Rethinking the Sanctioning"; Polk, "Family Conferencing."

126. Schneider, *Deterrence and Juvenile Crime*.

127. Bazemore and Maloney, "Rehabilitating Community Service"; Walgrave and Geudens, "Community Service."

128. Braithwaite and Mugford, "Conditions of Successful Reintegration"; Stuart, *Sentencing Circles*.

129. Stuart, "Circle Sentencing."

130. Braithwaite and Mugford, "Conditions of Successful Reintegration"; Stuart, *Sentencing Circles*.

131. Bazemore, "The 'Community' in Community Justice"; M. Umbreit and S. Stacy, "Family Group Conferencing Comes to the U.S.: A Comparison with Victim-Offender Mediation," *Juvenile and Family Court Journal* 11 (1996): 29-39.

132. With the exception of victim offender mediation (VOM), few restorative

sanction processes have been rigorously evaluated to date. VOM studies show positive impact on offenders, clearly documented positive victim effects (M. Umbreit and R. Coates, "Cross-Site Analysis of Victim-Offender Conflict: An Analysis of Programs in These Three States," *Juvenile and Family Court Journal* 43 [1993]); and the various affect theories and related perspectives underlying the reintegrative shaming process in family group conferencing (Tomkins, *Affect, Imagery, Consciousness,* [1992]: 90; Scheff and Retzinger, "Strategy for Community Conferencing," 90; David B. Moore and Terry O'Connell, "Family Conferencing in Wagga Wagga: A Communitarian Model of Justice," in Alder and Wundersitz, ed., *Family Group Conferencing and Juvenile Justice*) are providing further impetus for expansion of sanction processes aimed at reintegration as well as at holding offenders accountable (Gabrielle Maxwell and Allison Morris, *Family Participation, Cultural Diversity and Victim Involvement in Youth Justice: A New Zealand Experiment,"* [Wellington, New Zealand: Institute of Criminology, 1992]; Hudson and Galaway, ed., *The Practice of Restorative Justice*).

133. C. Alder and J. Wundersitz, *Family Group Conferencing and Juvenile Justice: The Way Forward or Misplaced Optimism?* (Canberra: Australian Institute of Criminology, 1971); Bazemore, "After the Shaming."

134. Braithwaite and Mugford, "Conditions of Successful Reintegration."

135. Polk, "Family Conferencing"; Umbreit and Stacy, "Family Group Conferencing."

136. Braithwaite and Mugford, "Conditions of Successful Reintegration."

137. D. Kahan, "What Do Alternative Sanctions Mean?" *University of Chicago Law Review* 63 (1996): 591-653; Garfinkel, "Conditions of Successful Degredation."

138. Bazemore, "The 'Community' in Community Justice."

139. Belgrave, "Restorative Justice." Few advocates of restorative justice argue that a restorative approach is likely to, or should, completely replace existing justice systems (at least not in the near future) (see Christie, *Limits to Pain*). In fact, the most common debate is over the extent to which energies should be focused on developing a parallel, informal, or "community justice," system along the lines of the dual-track Japanese model (J. Haley, "Confession, Repentance, and Absolution," in *Mediation and Criminal Justice: Victims, Offenders, and Community,* ed. M. Wright and B. Galaway [London: Sage, 1989], 195-211), or on efforts to modify the current formal system by changing the role and function of professionals to support restorative practices and processes. The restorative vision is, however, one of an entire justice system and ancillary community networks, both with a variety of flexible options to meet the needs of the three clients at any point in the justice process.

140. Feld, "The Punitive Juvenile Court."

141. Messmer and Otto, eds., *Restorative Justice on Trial.*

142. J. Eisenstein and H. Jacob, *Felony Justice: An Organizational Analysis of Criminal Courts,* 2nd ed. (Boston: Little Brown, 1991); J. Hackler, *The Possible*

Overuse of Not Guilty Pleas in Juvenile Justice (Edmonton: Centre for Criminological Research, University of Alberta, 1991).

143. Even if restorative justice options were restricted to those who admit guilt through plea bargaining or other mechanisms, they would still be applicable for the vast majority of criminal and juvenile court cases. Moreover, in contrast to the "individualized" justice especially characteristic of juvenile courts and the traditional treatment model, restorative justice acknowledges and builds on group and community responsibility for crime (Van Ness, "New Wine and Old Wineskins"; F. W. M. McElrae, "A New Model of Justice," in *The Youth Court in New Zealand: A New Model of Justice*, ed. B. J. Brown (Wellington, New Zealand: Legal Research Foundation, 1993); J. Braithwaite and C. Parker, "Restorative Justice Is Republican Justice," in *Restoring Juvenile Justice*, ed. G. Bazemore and L. Walgrave (Amsterdam: Kugler International, 1998)) rather than simply directing blame—and thus sanctions or treatment—at individual offenders. In short, there is little debate that an adversarial system is needed, especially and primarily for decisions about guilt and innocence, but much agreement that this system could be improved if it received fewer cases and/or was modified to be more attentive to client needs.

144. Bazemore and Day, "The Return to Family."

145. Braithwaite and Mugford, "Conditions of Successful Reintegration"; P. Robinson, "Hybrid Principles for the Distribution of Criminal Sanctions," *Northwest University Law Review* 19 (1987): 34-6.

146. Braithwaite and Mugford, "Conditions of Successful Reintegration."

147. Braithwaite and Mugford, "Conditions of Successful Reintegration"; Young, "Restorative Community Justice."

148. Wright, "Justice for Victims and Offenders."

149. Barajas, "Moving Toward Community Justice."

150. K. Daly, "Shaming Conferences in Australia: A Reply to the Academic Skeptics" (paper presented at the American Society of Criminology, Chicago, November 1996).

151. D. B. Moore, "Illegal Action—Official Reaction," (Canberra: Australian Institute of Criminology, 1994): 9.

152. Braithwaite, *Crime, Shame, and Reintegration*.

153. Braithwaite, *Crime, Shame, and Reintegration*; Haley, "Confession"; R. J. Sampson and J. Wilson, "Toward a Theory of Race," in *Crime and Urban Inequality*, ed. J. Hagan and R. D. Peterson (Stanford, CA: Stanford University Press, 1995), 37-54.

154. Wilson, *The Truly Disadvantaged*.

155. J. T. Whitehead and S. P. Lab, *Juvenile Justice: An Introduction* (Cincinnati, OH: Anderson, 1996); M. Ezell, "Juvenile Arbitration: New Widening or Other Unintended Consequences," *Journal of Research in Crime and Delinquency* 26 (1992): 358-77.

156. J. McKnight, *The Careless Society: Community and Its Counterfeits* (New

York: Basic Books, 1995), 20.

157. Stuart, *Sentencing Circles.*

158. G. Bazemore, "Delinquent Reform and the Labeling Perspective," *Criminal Justice and Behavior* 12 (1985): 131-69; D. Elliott, "Serious Violent Offenders: Onset, Development Course, and Termination," (The American Society of Criminology 1993 Presidential Address) *Criminology* 32 (1994): 1-25.

159. Elliott, "Serious Violent Offenders."

160. M. Rutter, "Resilience in the Face of Adversity: Protective Factors and Resistance to Psychiatric Disorder," *British Journal of Psychiatry* 147 (1985): 598-611.

161. Karp, *Community Justice*; Bazemore, "The 'Community' in Community Justice."

162. This is not to suggest that treatment providers lack skill and commitment or that some treatments are not better than others, given the choices corrections administrators must make. Rather, the problem of avoiding "doing harm," like the obstacles to promoting positive youth development, is more systemic. Despite their unique professional focus, what the designating social service systems have in common is a deficit focus emphasizing the identification of needs and risks and the provision of services intended to correct presumed deficits and dysfunctions. Just as youth do not "grow up in programs," treatment and service programs are often irrelevant to the larger social ecology or context in which maturation occurs. S. Halperin et al., "Introduction," in *Contract with America's Youth: Toward a National Youth Development Agenda*, ed. S. Halperin et al. (Washington, DC: American Youth Policy Forum, 1995), 2-7.

163. K. Polk, "The New Marginal Youth," *Crime and Delinquency* 30 (1984): 462-80.

164. Polk, "New Marginal Youth"; Sampson and Wilson, "Toward a Theory."

165. Halperin et al., "Introduction," 2-7; Bazemore and Terry, "Developing Delinquent Youth"; A. Sum et al., "Confronting the Demographic Challenger: Future Labor Market Prospects of Out-of-School Young Adults," *A Generation of Challenge: Pathways to Success for Urban Youth, A Policy Study of the Levitan Youth Policy Network*, Monograph No. 97-03 (Baltimore: Johns Hopkins University, 1997): 13-45.

166. E. Currie, *Reckoning—Drugs, the Cities and the American Future* (New York: Hill & Wang, 1986), 12.

167. Braithwaite and Parker, "Restorative Justice."

168. Griffiths and Hamilton, "Spiritual Renewal."

169. Braithwaite, *Crime, Shame, and Reintegration*; Haley, "Confession."

170. R. Naroll, *The Moral Order: An Introduction to the Human Situation* (Beverly Hills, CA: Sage, 1983).

171. Stuart, *Sentencing Circles*; Braithwaite and Mugford, "Conditions of Successful Reintegration."

172. Schweigert, *Learning the Common Good.*

173. P. L. Benson, *Creating Healthy Communities for Children and Adolescents* (Minneapolis: Search Institute, 1996).

174. Schweigert, *Learning the Common Good*, 27.

175. L. Walgrave, "Beyond Retribution and Rehabilitation: Restoration as the Dominant Paradigm in Judicial Intervention Against Juvenile Crime" (paper presented at the International Congress on Criminology, Budapest, Hungary, July 1993), 9.

Chapter Three

Apology and Pardon: Learning from Japan*

John O. Haley

Mention to someone who has lived in Japan even briefly the role of apology and you are apt to evoke a smile, if not an effusion of tales of apologies given or received to expiate both slight and serious offenses. Even the most temporary expatriate quickly becomes familiar with the differences between the uses and effects of apology in Japan in contrast to the United States, Europe, and apparently even other parts of East Asia. Apology remains nevertheless one of the least explored social phenomena of Japan. It receives scant attention by all but a handful of the burgeoning number of persons who write on that society, including the Japanese themselves. For the most part the study of the cultural implications of apology has been relegated to dinner table or cocktail party anecdotes. Until recently, apology has been treated as an inconsequential, albeit interesting, quirk of Japanese social life. There has been no anatomy of apology.

Hiroshi Wagatsuma and Arthur Rosett, and more recently Takie Lebra[1] were among the first to give apology the undivided attention it deserves. In the work of these

---

* This chapter includes many of the ideas and arguments from previous publications by the author, particularly the following essays:

"Comment: The Implications of Apology," 20 *Law and Society Review*, 4 November (1986): 499.

"Victim-Offender Mediation: Japanese and American Comparisons," in H. Messmer and H. U. Otto, *Restorative Justice on Trial* (Amsterdam and Cambridge, MA: Kluwer Academic Publishers, 1992), 105.

scholars we are finally able to identify social phenomena that may be accurately described as cultural and perhaps even peculiar or unique to Japan. All three demonstrate what those who have spent any amount of time in both Japan and the United States have discovered by experience: apology is tendered in Japan in contexts that are far more likely to elicit an excuse or self-justification in the United States. To be sure, institutional or structural arrangements reinforce this contrast; for example, failure to apologize in Japan increases the likelihood of litigation and other forms of formal legal sanction. Nonetheless, in the use of apology in Japan or its neglect in the United States, we encounter broadly shared social behavior that is a mix of habit, expectations, and underlying values.

But what is of greatest importance to us here, beyond the interesting cultural observations about apology, is the important role apology appears to play in Japan's success at reducing crime rates since the Second World War. In this essay, I will attempt to show the significance of apology to this success through an examination of the nature of apology in both Japanese culture and Japan's criminal justice system. I shall then argue that we may learn many valuable lessons from Japan's approach to crime that can be applied in Western countries. But first, let me introduce the disparity between crime rates in Japan and the United States.

Crime in Japan and the United States

No contrast between Japan and the United States could be greater or should be more disturbing, at least for Americans, than Japan's postwar success and the United States' failure in efforts to reduce crime and its awesome social and material costs. Japan today has the lowest rates of crime of any industrial state. Japan's success is, however, not measured by its relatively low rates of crime. Rather, as illustrated by the statistics in Table 3.1, Japan's achievement is reflected in the gradual reduction of nearly all categories of crime except traffic-related offenses. Except for moderate increases in the early 1980s, Japan has experienced a steady decline in the number of Penal Code offenses other than "traffic professional negligence." More significant has been the steady decrease in the number of offenders (as identified by law enforcement authorities) throughout the postwar period, as indicated in Table 3.2, especially during the past two decades.

The statistics for the United States portray a far more dismal picture. As indicated in Table 3.3, crime rates per 100,000 persons tripled in the United States from 1960 to 1988. By the mid-1980s, the United States was experiencing over three times as many cases of larceny and five times as many homicides as Japan. The United States was not the exception, however. Except for homicides, crime rates in the United States were comparable to those in most West European states (see Table 3.4). The United Kingdom, for example, had nearly five times as many larcenies per capita as Japan. The United States and the Federal Republic of Germany had four times and France had three times as many larcenies as Japan. In every category of major crime, the number of offenders had decreased by extraordinary percentages: homicide by 40 percent, robbery by 60 percent, and rape by nearly 80 percent. In other words, during the past four and a half decades, Japan has somehow managed to ensure that fewer persons each year resort to non-traffic-related criminal behavior, while other industrial states have experienced steadily increasing crime rates and numbers of offenders.

Explanations of Japan's success have not been persuasive. Most observers do accurately attribute Japan's low crime rates to a variety of cultural, economic, and institutional factors.[2] Differences between Japan and the United States in terms of social cohesion, ethnic homogeneity, family stability, and respect for authority, coupled with steady improvement in living standards and high clearance rates for crime, surely contribute to the differences in crime rates between the two countries. However, such explanations may say more about the United States than Japan. Other industrial states share with Japan many if not all of these attributes. Although they may have lower crime rates than the United States, they too have experienced significant increases in crime during the postwar period. For example, the increase in crime rates between 1950 and 1980 in Sweden—which surely rivals Japan in terms of affluence, social stability, and cultural homogeneity—was greater than in the United States.[3] Indeed, Japan's principal feat is not its relative lack of crime but rather its reduction of criminal conduct and the number of persons who commit crimes.

Apology, Repentance, and Restoration

In the beginning of this chapter, I began to examine the nature of apology in Japan and its role in society. I would now like to continue this discussion in light of the observations concerning crime in Japan. Wagatsuma and Rosett observe that, for the Japanese, "the external act of apology becomes significant as an act of self-denigration and submission" in which "the relational elements" of Japanese culture are given expression as a "commitment to a positively harmonious relationship in the future in which the mutual obligations of the social hierarchy will be observed."[4] Apology also implies accountability. It expresses a willingness to put matters right and to make reparations for injury. These observations are quite consistent with the findings of Lee Hamilton and Joseph Sanders that as victims of wrongs Japanese generally tend to be less retributive than Americans and more willing to accept compensation to put an end to the matter.

> Across everyday life, accident, and crime vignettes, Japanese respondents are at least as willing as Americans to advocate that *something* should happen to perpetrators, but they had systematically different ideas about what that "something" should be. Judging an array of everyday life situations, the model sanction chosen by Japanese was some form of restitution; sanctions chosen by the Americans predominately served to isolate or punish the individual perpetrator.[5]

Table 3.1
Number of Reported Penal Code Offenses
and Offenders Cleared by the Police: 1946-1987

| Year | Number of Offenses Reported | | Number of Offenders | | Total Population | Ratio of Offenses Other Than Traffic Professional Negligence to the Population* |
	Total	Those Other Than Traffic Professional Negligence	Total	Those Other Than Traffic Professional Negligence		
1946	1,387,080	1,384,222	433,083	430,178	73,114	1,893
1947	1,386,020	1,382,210	477,061	442,819	78,101	1,770
1948	1,603,265	1,599,968	539,467	535,918	80,003	2,000
1949	1,603,048	1,597,891	566,943	561,512	81,773	1,954
1950	1,469,662	1,461,044	587,105	578,152	83,200	1,756
1951	1,399,184	1,387,289	596,258	573,909	84,541	1,641
1952	1,395,197	1,377,273	546,986	528,655	85,808	1,605
1953	1,344,482	1,317,141	520,057	492,214	86,981	1,514
1954	1,360,405	1,324,333	513,718	476,992	88,239	1,501
1955	1,478,202	1,435,652	534,060	490,683	89,276	1,608
1956	1,410,441	1,354,102	527,950	470,522	90,172	1,502
1957	1,426,029	1,354,429	544,557	471,600	90,928	1,490
1958	1,440,259	1,353,930	545,272	457,212	91,767	1,475
1959	1,483,258	1,382,792	557,073	454,898	92,641	1,493
1960	1,495,888	1,378,817	561,464	442,527	93,419	1,476
1961	1,530,464	1,400,915	581,314	451,586	94,287	1,486
1962	1,522,480	1,384,784	569,866	430,153	95,181	1,455
1963	1,557,803	1,377,476	606,649	425,473	96,156	1,433
1964	1,609,741	1,385,358	678,522	449,842	97,182	1,426
1965	1,602,430	1,343,625	706,827	440,563	98,275	1,367
1966	1,590,681	1,293,877	740,055	433,545	99,036	1,306
1967	1,603,471	1,219,840	802,578	402,738	100,196	1,217
1968	1,742,479	1,234,198	923,491	393,831	101,331	1,218
1969	1,848,740	1,253,950	999,981	377,826	102,536	1,223
1970	1,932,401	1,279,787	1,073,470	380,850	103,720	1,234
1971	1,875,383	1,244,168	1,026,299	361,972	105,145	1,183
1972	1,818,072	1,223,530	976,592	348,774	107,595	1,137
1973	1,728,726	1,190,534	931,346	357,725	109,104	1,091
1974	1,671,947	1,210,987	852,347	363,284	110,573	1,095
1975	1,673,727	1,234,279	830,128	364,069	111,940	1,103
1976	1,691,229	1,247,613	830,679	359,322	113,094	1,103
1977	1,704,995	1,268,391	822,218	363,043	114,165	1,111
1978	1,776,801	1,336,880	843,295	381,499	115,190	1,161
1979	1,738,407	1,289,360	840,285	368,078	116,155	1,110
1980	1,812,755	1,357,418	869,766	392,035	117,060	1,160
1981	1,925,796	1,463,188	904,609	418,128	117,884	1,241
1982	2,005,292	1,528,752	944,005	441,917	118,693	1,288
1983	2,039,181	1,540,689	963,497	438,658	119,483	1,289
1984	2,080,297	1,588,667	961,339	446,593	180,235	1,321
1985	2,121,410	1,607,663	970,226	432,107	121,026	1,328

Table 3.1 (continued)
Number of Reported Penal Code Offenses
and Offenders Cleared by the Police: 1946-1987

Year	Number of Offenses Reported		Number of Offenders			Ratio of Offenses Other Than Traffic Professional Negligence to the Population*
	Total	Those Other Than Traffic Professional Negligence	Total	Those Other Than Traffic Professional Negligence	Total Population	
1986	2,124,239	1,581,378	967,972	399,861	121,672	1,300
1987	2,132,592	1,577,929	983,891	404,722	122,264	1,291

Source: Ministry of Justice of Japan, Summary of White Paper on Crime (Tokyo, 1988-96).

* The ratio to the population is the number of reported offenses per 100,000 inhabitants.

Table 3.2
Number Offenders for Major Penal Code Crimes: 1963-1987

Year	Homicide	Robbery	Rape
1987	1,651	1,707	1,608
1986	1,692	1,842	1,577
1985	1,833	1,777	1,809
1984	1,788	2,031	1,907
1983	1,784	2,069	1,972
1982	1,768	2,072	2,420
1981	1,712	2,124	2,657
1980	1,760	2,064	2,667
1979	1,841	1,809	2,757
1978	1,843	1,748	2,876
1977	1,988	1,826	3,046
1976	2,113	2,045	3,394
1975	2,179	2,246	4,052
1974	1,870	2,111	4,485
1973	2,113	2,078	4,786
1972	2,188	2,398	5,464
1971	2,134	2,556	5,81
1970	2,146	2,845	6,430
1969	2,351	2,835	6,843
1968	2,297	2,974	7,725
1967	2,225	3,143	8,039
1966	2,278	3,799	8,210
1965	2,379	4,106	8,444
1964	2,501	4,019	8,384
1963	2,752	4,210	7,579

Source: Summary of White Paper on Crime (1988-1996)

Table 3.3: Estimated Number of Offenses Known to Police, United States: 1960-1988

	Population	Total Crime Index	Violent Crime	Property Crime	Murder and Nonnegligent Manslaughter	Forcible Rape	Robbery	Aggravated Assault	Burglary	Larceny Theft	Motor Vehicle Theft
1960	179,323,175	3,384,200	288,460	3,095,700	9,110	17,190	107,840	154,320	912,100	1,855,400	328,200
1961	182,992,000	3,488,000	289,390	3,198,600	8,740	17,220	106,670	156,760	949,600	1,913,000	336,000
1962	185,771,000	3,752,200	301,510	3,450,700	8,530	17,550	110,860	164,570	994,300	2,089,600	366,800
1963	188,483,000	3,109,500	316,970	3,792,500	8,640	17,650	116,470	174,210	1,386,400	2,297,800	408,300
1964	191,141,000	4,564,600	364,220	4,200,400	9,360	21,420	130,390	203,050	1,213,200	2,514,400	472,800
1965	195,526,000	4,739,400	387,390	4,352,000	9,960	23,410	138,690	215,330	1,282,500	2,572,600	496,900
1966	193,576,000	5,223,500	430,180	4,793,300	11,040	25,820	157,990	235,330	1,410,100	2,822,000	561,200
1967	197,457,000	5,903,400	499,930	5,403,300	12,240	27,620	202,910	257,160	1,632,100	3,111,600	659,800
1968	199,399,000	6,720,200	595,010	6,125,200	13,800	31,670	262,840	286,700	1,858,900	3,482,700	783,600
1969	201,385,000	7,410,900	661,870	6,749,000	14,760	37,170	298,850	311,090	1,981,900	3,888,600	878,500
1970	203,235,298	8,098,000	738,820	7,359,200	16,000	37,990	349,860	334,970	2,205,000	4,225,800	928,400
1971	206,212,000	8,588,200	816,500	7,771,700	17,780	42,260	387,700	368,760	2,399,300	4,424,200	948,200
1972	208,230,000	8,248,800	834,900	7,413,900	18,670	46,850	376,290	393,090	2,375,500	4,151,200	887,200
1973	209,851,000	8,718,100	875,910	7,842,200	19,640	51,400	384,220	420,650	2,565,500	4,347,900	928,800
1974	211,392,000	10,253,400	974,720	9,278,700	20,710	55,400	442,400	456,210	3,039,200	5,262,500	977,100
1975	213,124,000	11,256,600	1,026,280	10,230,300	20,510	56,090	464,970	484,710	3,252,100	5,977,700	1,000,500
1976	214,659,000	11,349,700	1,004,210	10,345,500	18,780	57,080	427,810	500,530	3,108,700	6,270,800	966,000
1977	216,332,000	10,984,500	1,029,580	9,955,000	19,120	63,500	412,610	534,350	3,071,500	5,905,700	977,700
1978	218,059,000	11,209,000	1,085,550	10,123,400	19,560	67,610	426,930	571,460	3,128,300	5,991,000	1,004,100
1979	220,099,000	12,249,500	1,208,030	11,041,500	21,460	76,390	480,700	629,480	3,327,700	6,601,000	1,112,800
1980	225,349,264	13,408,300	1,344,520	12,063,700	23,040	82,990	565,840	672,650	3,795,200	7,136,900	1,131,700
1981	229,146,000	13,423,800	1,361,820	12,061,900	22,520	82,500	592,910	663,900	3,779,000	7,194,400	1,087,800
1982	231,534,000	12,974,400	1,322,390	11,652,000	21,010	78,770	553,130	669,480	3,447,100	7,142,500	1,062,400
1983	233,981,000	12,108,600	1,258,090	10,850,500	19,310	78,920	506,570	653,290	3,129,900	6,712,800	1,007,900
1984	236,158,000	11,881,800	1,273,280	10,608,500	18,960	84,230	485,010	685,350	2,984,400	6,591,900	1,065,500
1985	238,740,000	12,430,000	1,327,440	11,102,600	18,980	87,340	497,870	723,250	3,073,300	6,926,400	1,102,900
1986	241,077,000	13,210,800	1,488,140	11,722,700	20,610	90,430	542,780	834,320	3,241,400	7,257,200	1,224,100
1987	243,400,000	13,508,700	1,484,000	12,024,700	20,100	91,110	517,700	855,090	3,236,200	7,499,900	1,288,700
1988	245,807,000	13,923,100	1,566,220	12,356,900	20,680	92,490	542,970	910,090	3,218,100	7,705,900	1,432,900

Table 3.4: Estimated Rate (per 100,000 Inhabitants) of Offenses Known to Police, United States: 1960-1988

	Population	Total Crime Index	Violent Crime	Property Crime	Murder and Nonnegligent Manslaughter	Forcible Rape	Robbery	Aggravated Assault	Burglary	Larceny Theft	Motor Vehicle Theft
1960	179,323,175	1,887.2	160.9	1,726.3	5.1	9.6	60.1	86.1	508.6	1,034.7	183.0
1961	182,992,000	1,960.1	158.1	1,747.9	4.8	9.4	58.3	85.7	518.9	1,045.4	183.6
1962	185,771,000	8,019.8	162.3	1,857.5	4.6	9.4	59.7	88.6	535.2	1,124.8	197.4
1963	188,483,000	2,180.3	168.2	2,012.1	4.6	9.4	61.8	92.4	576.4	1,219.1	216.6
1964	191,141,000	2,388.1	190.6	2,197.5	4.9	11.2	68.2	106.2	634.7	1,315.5	247.4
1965	195,526,000	2,449.0	200.2	2,248.8	5.1	12.1	71.7	111.3	662.7	1,329.3	256.8
1966	193,576,000	2,670.8	220.0	2,450.9	5.6	13.2	80.8	120.3	721.0	1,442.9	286.9
1967	197,457,000	2,989.7	253.2	2,716.5	6.2	14.0	102.8	130.2	826.6	1,575.8	334.1
1968	199,399,000	3,310.2	298.4	3,071.5	6.9	15.9	131.8	143.8	932.3	1,746.6	393.0
1969	201,385,000	3,680.0	328.7	3,351.3	7.3	18.5	148.4	154.5	984.1	1,930.9	436.2
1970	203,235,298	3,984.5	363.5	3,621.0	7.9	18.7	172.1	164.8	1,084.9	2,079.3	456.8
1971	206,212,000	4,164.7	396.0	3,768.8	8.6	20.5	188.0	178.8	1,163.5	2,145.5	459.8
1972	208,230,000	3,961.4	401.0	3,560.4	9.0	22.5	180.7	188.8	1,140.8	1,993.6	426.1
1973	209,851,000	4,154.4	417.4	3,737.0	9.4	24.5	183.1	200.5	1,222.5	2,071.9	442.6
1974	211,392,000	4,850.4	461.1	4,389.3	9.8	26.2	209.3	245.8	1,437.7	2,489.5	462.2
1975	213,124,000	5,281.7	481.5	4,800.2	9.6	26.3	218.2	227.4	1,525.9	2,804.8	469.4
1976	214,659,000	5,287.3	467.8	4,819.5	8.8	26.6	199.3	233.2	1,448.2	2,921.3	450.0
1977	216,332,000	5,077.6	475.9	4,601.7	8.8	29.4	190.7	240.0	1,419.8	2,729.9	451.9
1978	218,059,000	5,140.3	497.8	4,642.5	9.0	31.0	195.8	262.1	1,434.6	2,747.4	460.5
1979	220,099,000	5,565.5	548.9	5,016.6	9.7	34.7	218.4	286.0	1,511.9	2,999.1	505.6
1980	225,349,264	5,950.0	596.6	5,353.3	10.2	36.8	251.1	298.5	1,684.1	3,167.0	502.2
1981	229,146,000	5,858.2	554.3	5,263.9	9.8	36.0	258.7	289.7	1,649.5	3,139.7	474.7
1982	231,534,000	5,603.6	571.1	5,032.5	9.1	34.0	238.9	289.2	1,488.8	3,084.8	458.8
1983	233,981,000	5,174.0	537.7	4,637.4	8.3	33.7	216.5	279.2	1,337.7	2,868.9	430.8
1984	236,158,000	5,031.3	539.2	4,492.1	7.9	35.7	205.4	290.2	1,263.7	2,791.3	437.1
1985	238,740,000	5,206.5	556.0	4,650.5	7.9	36.6	208.5	302.9	1,287.3	2,901.2	462.0
1986	241,077,000	5,479.9	617.3	4,862.6	8.6	37.5	225.1	346.1	1,344.6	3,010.3	507.8
1987	243,400,000	5,550.0	609.7	4,940.3	8.3	37.4	212.7	351.3	1,329.6	3,081.8	529.4
1988	245,807,000	5,664.2	637.2	5,027.1	8.4	37.6	220.9	370.2	1,309.2	3,134.9	582.5

Civic Repentance

Table 3.5
Homicide and Larceny Rates, 1984-1986

Year/Item	Japan	United States	United Kingdom	Federal Republic of Germany	France
1984					
Homicide cases reported	1,823	18,690	1,613	2,760	2,712
Crime rate	1.5	7.9	3.2	4.5	4.9
Clearance rate	96.8	74.1	76.4	94.1	83.7
1985					
Homicide cases reported	1,847	18,980	1,819	2,796	2,497
Crime rate	1.5	7.9	3.7	4.6	4.5
Clearance rate	96.1	72.0	79.1	95.0	84.0
1986					
Homicide cases reported	1,744	20,613	2,160	2,728	2,413
Crime rate	1.4	8.6	4.3	4.5	4.4
Clearance rate	96.4	70.2	76.7	93.9	89.4
1984					
Larceny cases reported	1,365,705	10,608,473	2,655,858	2,583,635	2,196,587
Crime rate	1,136	4,492	5,349	4,223	4,006
Clearance rate	58.7	17.9	31.2	30.5	15.3
1985					
Larceny cases reported	1,381,237	11,102,590	2,705,430	2,628,933	2,217,344
Crime rate	1,141	4,651	5,436	4,309	4,027
Clearance rate	59.9	17.8	30.8	30.8	15.2
1986					
Larceny cases reported	1,375,096	11,722,700	2,893,996	2,720,277	2,041,268
Crime rate	1,130	4,863	5,797	4,456	3,693
Clearance rate	58.7	17.5	28.3	29.1	15.3

Source: Summary of White Paper on Crime (1988-1996)

Note: The statistics in reported homicide cases are based on the following criteria in the respective countries: Japan: murder, manslaughter, and robbery causing death (attempted cases are included); United States: murder and manslaughter (negligent manslaughter and attempted cases are not included); United Kingdom: murder, attempted murder, threat or conspiracy to murder, manslaughter, and infanticide (child destruction is not included); Federal Republic of Germany: murder (*Mord*), manslaughter (*Totschleg*), murder on demand (*Tötung auf Verlanger*), and infanticide (*Kindertötung*); France: murder (*assassinat*), manslaughter (*meurtre*), parenticide (*parricide*), infanticide (*infanticide*), and empoisonment (*empoisonnement*). Crime rate means the number of reported offenses per 100,000 population. Clearance rate means number of offenses cleared/number of cases reported x 100. The statistic on reported larceny cases is based on the following criteria in the respective countries: Japan: all kinds of theft; United States: larceny theft, motor vehicle theft, and burglary; United Kingdom: theft and burglary; Federal Republic of Germany: theft (*Diebstahl ohne erschwerende Umstände*) and weighted theft (*Diebstahl unter erschwerenden Umständen*); France: theft (*vol*).

To some commentators, apology is an exceptional feature of Japan's cultural landscape. In a recent paper, Takie Lebra[6] contrasts the use and meaning of apology in Japan with the conclusions reached in several recent studies, including the monograph by Nicholas Tavuchis.[7] While accepting the view that some characteristics of apology have universal, transcultural application, Lebra emphasizes the particularity of the Japanese context. She finds in the notion of "self" and the relationship between apology and empathy an element that appears to be peculiar at least in emphasis to the Japanese. Thus apology is used in Japan in contexts that often appear unusual and difficult to explain to anyone unfamiliar with Japan. In the Japanese context, Lebra notes, "empathy is a main ingredient of both apology and guilt."[8] Apology is an expression of personal sensitivity and sharing of injury and pain.

Lebra also observes that "empathetic apology" is usually not unilateral. She illustrates the point with the example of a father who apologized for his son's misbehavior, reported in a letter to the editor of the *Asahi Shinhun*.

> The boy was a troublemaker in school who intimidated his classmates and extorted money from them. His father, who was a former school principal, went to see the son's homeroom teacher in response to the latter's request. When he was told of his son's robbery, "he apologized with a deep bow, saying, 'I am very sorry.' Watching his father thus apologizing on his behalf, the offender was moved to tears. This was a turning point for him that changed his way of life completely." The message is that the father's surrogate apology aroused empathetic guilt in the culpable son, which turned out to be a breakthrough for the son much more effective than direct scolding and punishment.[9]

Apology is well integrated in Japan's justice system. Wagatsuma and Rosett point out that the cultural phenomenon of apology affects the Japanese legal system in two guises, for the role of *confession* in Japanese criminal law enforcement corresponds to the role of *apology* in other contexts.[10] There is little question that the use of apology relates closely to the frequency and type of litigation in Japan. Perhaps most importantly, the use of apology reduces the likelihood that a dispute will be taken to court. Japanese judges uniformly acknowledge that the failure of an injuring party to apologize and offer at least a nominal sum to express sympathy *(mimaikin)* is more likely to produce a lawsuit even in cases in which there is no dispute that the injuring party lacks any legal liability. Following the 1982 Japan Air Lines crash in Tokyo Bay,[11] for example, its president met with victims or their families to offer apologies and full compensation. No lawsuits were filed. The combination of apology and adequate compensation eliminated any incentive to sue.

Apology can also be an end in itself, and as such it serves as an important informal sanction. In suits brought against Japanese government agencies and business firms in pollution and drug-related injury cases, apology was as important an issue as damages for both the plaintiffs and the defendants.[12] In one series of cases,[13] for example, attorneys for the one foreign defendant note the astonishment of their client over the refusal of the president of at least one of the Japanese defendant firms to agree to the plaintiff's demand for an apology, which held up a settlement for months.[14]

As the preceding examples indicate, apology plays a large role in Japanese justice. Essential to this role is the formal discretionary authority of the police, prosecutors, and judges. Without the discretion to deal leniently with offenders on a particularistic basis, law enforcement authorities in Japan as in other industrial states would be bound by the rules of Japan's Penal Code and special criminal statutes that otherwise dictate a more generalized equality and a more punitive approach in responding to individual offenders. The three most critical institutional features of Japan's criminal justice system are thus the authority given to the police not to report minor offenses (*bizai shobun*) in cases where they deem it appropriate;[15] the authority of prosecutors to suspend prosecution where warranted by the nature and circumstance of the crime and the offender's attitude;[16] and the courts' broad authority to suspend execution of sentences.[17]

These features are clearly present at every stage of the Japanese criminal process. Those accused of an offense who confess and display remorse, who cooperate with the authorities and compensate or otherwise reach an accommodation with their victims, stand a reasonable chance of being released without further official action. For example, police statistics for 1978, as cited by George,[18] show that Japanese police cleared 599,309 (52.73 percent) of the 1,136,648 known cases of theft. Of the 231,403 offenders involved in these cases, only 15 percent (36,790) were arrested, and only 73 percent were reported to the prosecutor. In Tokyo, as George notes, "police do not transmit [to the procuracy] approximately 40 percent of referable cases because they involve minor property offenses, suspects have shown remorse, restoration has been made, or victims have expressed forgiveness."[19] The procuracy treats suspects reported by the police in similar fashion. In exercising the authority provided under article 258 of the Criminal Code, procurators suspend prosecution in roughly a third of all cases involving criminal code offenses. Again confession and repentance are primary considerations in granting such absolution. "Even an offender who had committed a rather serious crime might be relieved from prosecution," writes Procurator Kawada Katsuo, "if he was a first offender, if the injuries caused by the offense were compensated for, and if there was reasonable ground to believe that he would not commit another offense."[20] The pattern repeats in the trial process: Japanese courts have a conviction rate of 99.5 percent, yet routinely suspend jail sentences in two-thirds of all cases. The critical factor is the attitude of the accused: In over 80 percent of all cases there is confession.[21]

Japanese judges and procurators stress correction as a primary aim. They see their formal office as integral to a correctional process in which the identification, apprehension, and prosecution of offenders as well as the adjudication of guilt become secondary. Their formal roles as judge or prosecutor are thus subordinated to their concern for the rehabilitation of the accused and the correction, or at least the control, of proscribed behavior. Japanese judges, for example, justify suspending sentences based on the remorse shown (or not shown) by offenders with comments like "if a defendant doesn't show remorse he is more likely to commit another crime" or "if a person doesn't accept his own guilt, how can he be corrected?" Consequently, certain judges refuse to let even convicted defendants leave the courtroom until they confess and show remorse.

This ethos, which Daniel H. Foote aptly labels "benevolent paternalism" is an equally strong attribute of the Japanese prosecutorial and police establishments.[22] What Foote and others observe from the outside, David Johnson confirms from within the procuracy.[23] Over 10 percent of all prosecutors in Japan responded to his survey of their objectives. In order of priority (and percentage), their primary aims were to discover the truth (99.6 percent), to make "proper" charge decisions (97.9 percent), to invoke offender remorse (92.7 percent), to rehabilitate and reintegrate offenders (91.5 percent), to protect the public (91.1 percent), to treat like cases alike (90.7 percent), to respect the rights of suspects (83.9 percent), to reduce the crime rate (83.8 percent), and to give offenders the punishment they deserve (82.5 percent). Over two-thirds (67.6 percent) answered that repairing relations between offenders and victims was a goal, a slightly higher percentage than those who listed efficient disposition of cases (65.5 percent) and twice as many as those who considered maintaining the reputation of the procuracy (36.6 percent). Less than a quarter (21.9 percent) replied that maximizing punishment was a prosecutorial aim, and less than 10 percent responded that prosecuting and convicting as many cases as possible was an objective.[24] Johnson also inquired about the disparate factors prosecutors consider in suspending prosecution of convictable offenders. He found again by rank and percentage (in parentheses) that the seriousness of the offense, measured by the harm done, and the likelihood of reoffending were the two primary considerations (each 90.1 percent), followed by the repentance of the suspect (80.3 percent), the motive for the act (76.4 percent), whether the offender had compensated the victim (76 percent), the victim's views on the appropriateness of punishment (70.8 percent), and the offender's prior record (70.1 percent). The legally prescribed punishment ranked ninth (44.6 percent) and cooperation of the suspect with police and prosecutors ranked sixteenth (9.9 percent).[25] Johnson's evidence on the effectiveness of institutional controls to ensure that individual prosecutors internalize agency values and adhere to institutional standards is persuasive that these replies accurately apply to the procuracy as a whole.

As expressed by Minoru Shikita, the former director of the United Nations Asia and Far East Institute for the Prevention of Crime and Treatment of Offenders, "the relative effectiveness of the Japanese criminal justice system can be attributed to the fact that all of its subsystems recognize a unity of purpose and seek to achieve the dual aims of deterrence and rehabilitation under the guiding principle of reinforcement of moral responsibility."[26]

A very different set of attitudes is apparently held by judges and prosecutors in the United States. A federal district court judge in Seattle was perhaps representative of the prevailing American response when pointed out to me that his primary concern as a judge in criminal cases was to ensure fairness. "What concerns me most," he said, "is that the defendant—whether convicted or not—leaves my courtroom feeling that he or she has had a fair trial." Thus criminal justice authorities in the United States seem more likely than their counterparts in Japan to internalize their institutional roles and define their primary objectives in terms of their formal responsibilities:

for the police, to identify and apprehend the offender; for the prosecutors, to win convictions; for the judges, to ensure fair determinations of guilt; and for all, to ensure that justice is done with little if any consideration of the psychological or other needs and circumstances of the individual offender or victim, except as delineated by formally prescribed programs and procedures.

In Japan, it must be noted, the offender's attitude alone is insufficient to justify leniency. The family and community must also come forward and accept responsibility to ensure that steps will be taken to prevent future misconduct and to provide some means of control. Even this is not enough. The victim must pardon. Japanese law enforcement officials stress the importance of victim compensation and pardon as an essential element in the decision by the police whether to report the crime, by the prosecutor whether to prosecute, and the judge whether to suspend a prescribed sentence. I am told that in cases where prosecutors conclude that suspension of prosecution is otherwise justified but the victim refuses to express his or her willingness to forgive, extraordinary efforts may be made by officials to facilitate effective mediation to produce the requisite response by the victim.

Correction is a direct consequence of leniency toward offenders who demonstrate remorse and receive their victims' forgiveness. The most recent studies of recidivism in Japan confirm previous research[27] in showing that the more lenient the response by the authorities (see Table 3.5), the less likely the offender will commit another offense within three years. To be sure, these statistics can be read to indicate that Japanese law enforcement authorities have been extraordinarily prescient in assessing which offenders have the least risk of repeating criminal conduct. However, because by every account their judgment depends upon offender confession, demonstrable remorse, victim compensation, and pardon, these are themselves critical factors in determining risk. Therefore, the willingness of offenders to confess and demonstrate remorse and of the victim to pardon must either be a reliable indication of which offenders are less likely to repeat offending or are themselves determinative factors in the process of correcting deviant behavior. Both may be true.

Cultural Factors Alone?

Many, as noted, argue that Japan's record of crime reduction is simply a product of cultural factors, ranging from ethnic homogeneity to postwar prosperity. Such explanations are less persuasive when other societies with similar attributes but rising crime rates, such as Sweden, are compared, or considering the reality that most crimes, especially the most violent crimes, are committed even in Japan within subcultures and between persons who are not strangers.[28] In other words, profiles of crime do not support conventional cultural explanations. Whatever merit cultural factors—from social cohesion or ethnic and cultural homogeneity to family stability or high rates of literacy and educational achievement—may have in determining Japan's relative lack of crime, unless these variables are conceded to have become increasingly stronger and more pervasive during the past forty years, they alone do not explain the reduction of crime in postwar Japan.

Indeed, my greatest concern is that in accenting the role of apology in Japan and the United States as an example of an enduring cultural contrast, Wagatsuma and Rosett and others may unwittingly reinforce the view that there is nothing to learn from the Japanese experience. For many years I have badgered local law enforcement authorities as well as colleagues who teach criminal law and procedure and related areas in social science to examine the leitmotif of confession, repentance, and absolution in Japan and its implications for the United States and other countries. The invariable response is to brush off such pleas politely with observations on the uniqueness of Japanese social organization and references to Japan's social cohesion and homogeneity. Perceived differences in culture thus become fixed barriers to further inquiry. Nonetheless, there are parallels in the United States that at least hint that we have much to gain from a more careful scrutiny of the Japanese experience. Let me describe two of these parallels.

Parallels

First, there is evidence that the impact of apology in preventing litigation is similar in the United States and Japan. The Japanese experience echoes in the comments made by trial lawyers experienced in medical malpractice suits that a physician's failure to express sympathy and concern for the patient or the family promptly after an adverse operation or treatment significantly increases the likelihood of litigation. As an experienced Alabama lawyer once told me, "I have never seen a malpractice case where the doctor said he was sorry or made an effort to show concern for the feelings of the patient and the family." Sending a bill after an operation has gone badly is even more likely to provoke a lawsuit, as many insurers and hospital risk managers in the United States have learned. According to Dr. Loren C. Winterscheid, former associate dean and medical director of the University of Washington School of Medicine in Seattle, the desire to avoid such legal actions underlies the procedures followed for the University Hospital.[29] In cases in which the physician or other medical attendant is clearly responsible for the unsatisfactory outcome of treatment or even in which there is some question or doubt as to responsibility, the hospital's risk managers intercede. They meet with the patient or the family, apologize, and attempt to compensate or ameliorate the expenses by not billing at all or at least discounting the costs. "Risk managers are persuaded," says Dr. Winterscheid, "that early intervention is very important—going to the patient, apologizing, explaining what happened and why, and compensating for the costs."[30] Yet there appear to be no studies to show whether or why such measures are effective. Our American *tatemae* (myth) depicts an adversarial, individualistic culture in which apology has little significance. Yet we, like the Japanese, seem to have an underlying *honne* (reality) in which apology is a critically important behavioral determinant.

A second example is victim-offender mediation. In Japan, mediation between victims and offenders is generally used in cases where direct negotiation between the wrongdoer and the injured party is difficult or considered inappropriate. In such instances, third-party intervention or assistance is a normal—but informal— societal response. Resorting to mediating go-betweens has been historically a common pattern of conflict negotiation in Japan.[31] Japanese parents and teachers are thus likely to respond to conflicts between children more as mediators than as judges or adjudicators.[32] Mediation is also preferred to adjudication as a means of ensuring party control over the outcome by the parties to a dispute or conflict. Again, Japanese take for granted the utility of mediators in facilitating negotiation between victims and offenders for compensation and pardon as well as their availability. There are no victim-offender mediation programs in Japan. No mediator training agencies exist. There are no statistics or studies. Mediation is a normal aspect of daily life. Those in a position of authority or influence have been expected to act as go-betweens or intermediaries in the settlement of disputes. Negotiating the restitution for victims of crime may be a more serious and perhaps more onerous task; nonetheless, it is one many persons are expected to undertake on behalf of those with close family, community, or friendship ties. The restorative model and all of its essential elements have thus fit quite naturally within the Japanese cultural and institutional matrix.

In contrast, few aspects of everyday Japanese experience are as unusual or alien to American patterns of behavior as victim-offender mediation. Not only is the idea of direct negotiation between victims and offenders, with or without the help of third-party mediation, exceptional; but, despite the growth of formal mediation in resolving civil disputes, even in less serious interpersonal conflicts, the role of mediator has had scant customary or cultural support. Unlike Japanese, Americans are seldom expected in daily social life to seek the assistance of a mediator, much less perform the functions of one. Adjudication, not mediation, remains the dominant paradigm for dispute resolution involving third-party intervention in the United States and perhaps most other societies in the West. The norm is to rely on third parties to decide or judge disputes, to control the outcomes, and to impose solutions. Judging is the role that comes most naturally to us as parents, neighbors, and citizens. In this respect the statement by William L.F. Felstiner and Lynne A. Williams in their limited study of a community-based mediation project in California remains quite telling. Mediation fails, they conclude, if the parties' "attitude toward all dispute resolution is dominated by a court model."[33] The participants will thereby "discount mediators as impotent judges and will feel that the authoritative stance of mediation debases legitimate expectations."[34] The idea of the mediator as "judge," impotent or otherwise, is as inappropriate a description of the role of the mediator as the assumption that normative rules not determined or accepted by the parties themselves could be applied. Felstiner and Williams themselves appear to be equally bound by the cultural framework they describe. Never mentioned is the empowerment of the participants, especially the victim, intrinsic to mediation as a process. Victim-offender mediation thus appears to be less countercultural in terms of the relationship between victim and offender than with respect to the role of the mediator and the idea of the participants' maintaining control over the outcome.

Despite the cultural reasons that would seem to preclude victim-offender mediation as an effective approach to criminal justice in the West, a program begun in the mid-1970s by a small group of Mennonites and other concerned Christians in Elkhart, Indiana, indicates that victim-offender mediation does indeed work in vastly different cultural settings. The program was formed as an alternative process for dealing with criminal offenders by providing an opportunity for mediated negotiation, restitution, and reconciliation.[35] Volunteer victim-offender mediation programs have been established in communities throughout North America during the past two decades. The number of such programs in the United States grew from at least thirty-two in 1985 to sixty-seven in 1989[36] in over forty cities or counties in two dozen states. Seattle is home to one of the earliest programs (although, tellingly, to avoid misunderstanding and criticism from victims' groups, the Seattle program dropped "Reconciliation" from its title, changing its name from Victim Offender Reconciliation Program to the more neutral and culturally acceptable Mediation Services for Victims and Offenders).

Victim Offender Reconciliation Program (VORP) provides mediation training and a service intended to foster reconciliation between the offender and the victim as well as between the offender and the community. The benefit to victims in terms of healing the injury and enabling forgiveness with compensation is, however, a primary premise of all VORP efforts. Some programs work only with adult offenders. Others limit their efforts to juvenile offenders. Many do both. The severity of the crime is not necessarily restrictive. Some programs handle cases that have previously diverted from adjudication. Others provide mediation only after a determination of guilt. Referrals are usually made by cooperating judges and probation officers. Ideally, defense attorneys and prosecutors also refer cases.

Victim Satisfaction and Offender Correction

The evidence of victim satisfaction as a result of face-to-face confrontation with the offender and mediation of a restitutionary response is overwhelming. From the first experiments with victim-offender mediation by the American Arbitration Association in the late 1960s to the various mediation programs throughout the United States (as noted above for the VORP program), Canada, and Europe, victims have expressed much greater satisfaction with the criminal justice system and have received more in compensation than through any alternative approach.[37]

All studies on VORP-sponsored mediation confirm the benefits to victims. A 1985 study by Robert B. Coates and John Gehm was one of the earliest and most ambitious attempts to evaluate victim responses.[38] Theirs, however, was a very limited assessment, with only thirty-seven victim respondents from one of three Indiana communities. No attempt was made to evaluate the extent of any change in the participating victims' attitudes toward various approaches to the treatment of offenders, or their level of anxiety, fear, or other psychological states. Nor did Coates and Gehm undertake to compare the attitudes of victims who had participated in a VORP-sponsored mediation with those who did not because of either unwillingness by the offender or the victim's refusal.

In 1986, I attempted to compile what data was available on the outcome of cases mediated under VORP auspices in the United States, Canada, and the United Kingdom. Questionnaires were sent to all known VORP and similar victim-offender mediation programs (approximately sixty-five) with a request for whatever statistics were available on victim satisfaction in addition to comparable local court or other law enforcement agency data, as well as any available information on relative rates of recidivism (as defined by the respondent) and the rates of offender completion of restitution agreements. We received responses from sixteen programs in the United States, nine in Canada, and eleven in the United Kingdom. No program, however, could provide data based on a rigorously controlled study of outcomes. Because of financial limitations and lack of staff and expertise, no respondent had strictly monitored the results of its efforts over time, except in keeping track of offender compliance with mediated restitution contracts. Moreover, no attempt was made to gauge in detail or depth victim responses to mediation, such as whether victims who are able to confront offenders and demand accountability become less fearful and more willing to substitute a restorative approach for a retributive one.

All VORP respondents indicated a high level of "victim satisfaction." Most are based on informal surveys and, in only a few instances, written evaluations of mediation. Seattle VORP (United States) reported that 57 percent of all participating victims indicated a high degree of satisfaction, 14 percent were simply "satisfied," and 29 percent were neutral; 91 percent stated that the process was helpful. The Langley, British Columbia (Canada) program reported that 92 percent of its victims expressed satisfaction. The only other response on this question from the Leeds (United Kingdom) Reparation Project indicated that 78.6 percent of the victim participants were highly satisfied and 14.3 percent moderately satisfied. These responses confirmed Coates and Gehm's finding that 59 percent of victims participating in mediation with offenders are satisfied and 97 percent would participate again.[39]

In the early 1990s, University of Minnesota professor Mark S. Umbreit supervised the most thorough and persuasive research on victim-offender mediation.[40] His two-and-a-half year study of victim-offender mediation programs in California, Minnesota, New Mexico, and Texas fully confirmed what previous research had revealed about the high level of victim satisfaction, the high rate of offender compliance with compensatory settlements, and the increased sense of fairness felt by both victims and offenders with respect to the process. A subsequent study of four Canadian programs resulted in nearly identical findings.[41]

Convincing assessment of the corrective effect of victim-offender mediation has been more elusive. Empirical research on recidivism is constrained by several difficulties. One is inconsistency in definition—whether, for example, arrest rather than conviction counts and what time frame is used. In the case of reported VORP data, the problems are compounded by doubts as to reliability. Finally, in nearly all cases, face-to-face mediation with the victim is a brief and less significant experience for the offender. It is hardly likely to counter the effects of an otherwise adversarial and punitive system. Nevertheless, at least as an impressionist measure, the 1986 VORP responses (Table 4) do suggest that victim-offender mediation has a significant effect in correcting deviant behavior. No program had collected comparable data for offenders who had not participated in mediation. Although emphasizing that the results are not statistically significant, both Umbreit[42] and Tony Marshall,[43] summarizing a British Home Office study, note similar findings. The findings by a more recent study of the Leeds (United Kingdom) Mediation Service indicate a more significant reduction of recidivism.[44] Apology and pardon through mediation—however brief the experience—has at least some corrective effect on offenders.

All studies report a high rate of offender compliance with their restitution agreements. In both my 1986 survey and Umbreit's studies, the rates ranged from 64 percent to 100 percent. Most hovered at the 80th percentile.[45] As in the case of recidivism, however, most respondents did not have data on the rate of compliance with court-ordered restitution for comparable cases. And what data was available could not be verified.

The empirical support for the contention that victim-offender mediation is beneficial in facilitating victim satisfaction, offender correction, and the community involvement in general is persuasive. Hundreds of thousands of cases have been mediated. All available evidence indicates that they have produced the benefits claimed. There is no evidence that any of the programs have failed to live up to these expectations. In other words, in nearly every instance where victim-offender mediation has been tried, by all accounts it has been more successful than the formal criminal justice system in meeting the needs of victims and enabling a change in the behavior of offenders.

Yet, despite the growth of VORP and other programs for victim-offender mediation, these efforts remain marginal. They tend to be located in smaller, predominantly rural or suburban communities. Only about a dozen major metropolitan or major urban centers are served.[46] As volunteer organizations, they are dependent on private community support. Most are closely tied to churches and religious groups. With a few notable exceptions, they are funded mostly by donations with little if any public funding.

Although VORP and other victim-offender mediation efforts appeal to deeply held values of at least significant segments of the American public, the retributive demands of American culture seem stronger. For some, the potential of reconciliation is in itself sufficient justification for the resort to mediation. For others, the ideal of a nonpunitive, forgiving approach has equally influential appeal. Community values therefore sustain their growth. Yet, the general public and law enforcement authorities remain unconvinced. For a restorative approach to expand, these are the first hurdles that must be overcome.

Role of Law Enforcement Authorities

The public and, most important, law enforcement officials need to be persuaded that victim-offender mediation does contribute to offender correction and victim satisfaction without significant risks to the community. The concerns and objections of law enforcement officials must be addressed effectively. Without the support of judges, prosecutors, and police, victim-offender mediation and other elements of the restorative model cannot expand. The Japanese model is premised on official control. Although victims are empowered in the process, law enforcement officials do not relinquish their authority to make the ultimate decisions with respect to treatment of offenders. The restorative approach has become the predominant pattern in Japan because police, prosecutors, and judges recognize its success in correcting offenders and satisfying victim and public needs. Until the law enforcement community as a whole in the United States is convinced of the benefits of a similar approach, VORP and similar attempts to introduce features of restorative justice seem likely to succeed only where, as in Japan, law enforcement authorities themselves take a leading role, often beginning with an individual judge, prosecutor, or sheriff willing to allow experiment.

A significant example of the success of a restorative program managed by law enforcement authorities is the Seattle Drug Court—a diversion program for defendants in substance abuse cases who are willing to acknowledge the need for correction and their personal accountability. The Seattle program commenced in July 1994 as a result of the combined efforts by the King County prosecutor, Norm Maleng, and a King County Superior Court judge, Ricardo Martinez. By August 1996, over 2,000 addicts had participated and 500 had completed the program successfully. In order to enter, the participants, limited to defendants charged with possession of controlled substances without prior convictions for sex or violent offenses or any pending felonies, had to agree to enter a three-phase drug treatment program involving a comprehensive, court-approved treatment plan developed in the initial orientation and assessment phase as well as a post treatment monitoring program. Defendants entering the program were required to waive their rights to a speedy trial and a jury trial. If they successfully completed the program as contracted, the charges would be dismissed. If not, there would be a trial without jury based on agreed facts contained in the police report.[47] The first full evaluation of the project, published in July 1995,[48] gave the first five months of the program high marks for success in dealing with drug offenders. Between August and December 1994, 262 defendants were determined to be eligible and were referred to the program. Of these, 43 percent (113) decided not to participate. Of the 41 percent (106) who chose to enter the program, 80 percent (85) remained active. Only 14 percent (15) failed, in most cases because of a new offense or failure to participate in treatment as required. Five percent (5) withdrew voluntarily, apparently because of the rigorous requirements of treatment.

Take the case of Mike Carpenter. As he graduated from the Seattle program, receiving his diploma and formal notice of dismissal of the drug possession charges, he turned to the courtroom where his mother and fiancee were sitting, holding back tears. "My name is Mike," he said. I am an alcoholic and an addict. I'm not gonna stand here and tell you that it was easy. It takes a lot of work. My moment of clarity came when I was on the deck of my boat, smoking crack, and looking at a knife and a bucket. I was gonna cut my wrists and bleed into the bucket so that I didn't mess up the boat."[49]

The Seattle experiment is not unique. Similar programs have been initiated in Chicago; New York City; Philadelphia; Miami; Portland, Oregon; Oakland; and St. Paul. Nearly all have had positive outcomes in terms of lower rates of incarceration and recidivism.[50] Among the features found to be critical for success was the strong support of all concerned law enforcement authorities—judges, prosecutors, and the police, as well as the leadership of an active judge able to motivate and encourage defendants to complete the treatment program. Not noted or assessed, however, was a presumably equally significant factor, the extent to which the defendant could turn to a supportive family or friends, in other words, some sort of community.

The Seattle Drug Court, like too many others, has been an isolated example. It demonstrates the potential, however, for coordinated efforts among various programs with the support and participation of law enforcement officials based on the principles of apology and pardon. Noteworthy among such coordinated efforts is the Australian "family conferencing" program,[51] which was influenced by both the New Zealand example[52] and John Braithwaite's theory of social control,[53] a model explicitly based on Japan. As in the case of Japan, the Australian program is managed by criminal justice authorities—the police. It also expands more familiar North American victim-offender mediation efforts by including the widest feasible circle of those hurt by the offense, potentially anyone affected negatively as well as the extended family and friends of the offender. The process proceeds in a manner that is otherwise nearly the same as victim-offender mediation, with a trained police officer as facilitator. Each participant relates how he or she was affected. The offender is thus confronted with the fullest possible accounting of the consequences of the act but is also given the opportunity to explain and to express remorse. The family becomes an important source of disapproval as well as restoration. The offender is not left as an outcast, but is enabled by the experience to begin to earn his or her way back into the community by accepting responsibility, including corrective future action, and making acceptable amends.

Other countries are trying similar measures, such as Canada with its growing practice of "circle sentencing"[54] and New Zealand with "family group conferences" for all juvenile offenders. Each program demonstrates that nearly all of the most effective efforts to correct offenders reflect elements of the Japanese approach as a model of "restorative justice," with integration of these elements into a coherent system of criminal justice.

As these efforts suggest, outside of Japan a growing—but largely unsynthesized—literature affirms the importance of acknowledgment of guilt and restitution of victims to the psychological rehabilitation of offender, and attitudes of victims toward the offender within the formal criminal justice system. Early studies by Elaine Walster, Ellen Berscheid, and G. William Walster remain especially noteworthy for evaluating the Japanese approach.[55] They and others[56] found that offenders attempt to relieve distress experienced after committing a crime involving harm to others by justification, derogating the victim, and denying responsibility or restitution. Although decades of research on recidivism have yielded few conclusive findings,[57] studies that deal with even discrete facets of a restorative approach to criminal justice note similar results.[58] Limited intervention—for example, a few hours of victim-offender mediation—cannot be expected to have a significant effect on the offender. Such caveats noted, considerable empirical data supports the notion that in lieu of incentives for denial, encouraging offender remorse and acceptance of the need for correction—often including medical treatment—and victim reparation, along with the prospect of being able to rejoin and participate as an accepted member of the community, does tend to reduce recidivism.

Public Attitudes

An added benefit of the Japanese approach is that, as noted, an emphasis on victim reparation and restoration reduces societal demands for revenge and retribution and thus political pressures to limit the discretion of law enforcement authorities even to experiment with restorative alternatives to our prevailing retributive approach. As direct apology and reparation reduces victim anger and fear and victims become more satisfied with the criminal justice system, they tend to support approaches that facilitate efforts by law enforcement authorities to provide effective means for offender correction. In other words, societal demand for retributive punishment is reduced and the authorities are then able to tailor their responses in ways that are most likely to lead to a change in the offender behavior. The now abundant empirical evidence on victim-offender mediation in the United States and Canada indicates that victims who through mediation have been able to confront the offenders directly are not only more satisfied with the criminal process itself but also, if negotiated restitution is attempted, become less inclined to view whatever penalty is imposed as inadequate.

Victim satisfaction would also explain why the Japanese are more tolerant of leniency and are more willing to accept whatever punishment the law prescribes. As Hamilton and Sanders note, the Japanese surveyed were considerably more likely to prefer a response to criminal behavior that tends to restore relationships in comparison to the Americans who favored sanctions that tend to isolate and outcast offenders.[59] It appears therefore that the Japanese approach contributes a dynamic process of positive reinforcement in which correction is more likely both to succeed and to be a more socially acceptable and politically feasible objective.

There is hope. However gradually, the lesson of apology is being learned. Whether embedded in the society, as in the case of Japan and other communitarian cultures, or institutionally constructed, as in the case of New Zealand and an increasing number of experimental programs in the United States, Australia, and Canada, efforts to institute restorative approaches in criminal justice are demonstrating the efficacy of apology and pardon in very different cultural and institutional contexts. This is not to say that the Japanese or any other criminal justice system can or should be fully replicated in the United States. What we have to learn about apology from Japan is simpler and more basic—that restorative approaches are successful in correcting offenders, empowering and healing victims, and restoring community. The Japanese experience thus provides insights for other industrial societies seeking to establish a more humane and just system of criminal justice, one free from the human and economic costs of overcrowded prisons, increasing crime, and victim alienation. The lesson learned is that restorative justice works.

Notes

1. H. Wagatsuma and A. Rosett, "The Implications of Apology: Law and Culture in Japan and the United States," *Law & Society Review* 20 (1986): 461-98; T. Lebra, "Apology and Self: The Japanese Case" (paper presented for panel on "Righting Wrongs: Compensation, Apology, and Retribution in Contemporary Pacific Societies," ASAO Meeting, Kona, HI, February 1995).

2. Y. Suzuki, "Crime," in *Kodansha Encyclopedia of Japan* 2 (Tokyo: Kodansha, 1983), 46.

3. S. Stack, "Social Structure and Swedish Crime Rates: A Time-Series Analysis, 1950-1979," *Criminology* 20 (1982): 509.

4. Wagatsuma and Rosett, "Implications of Apology," 478.

5. V. L. Hamilton and J. Sanders, *Everyday Justice* (New Haven: Yale University Press, 1992), 323-4.

6. Lebra, "Apology and Self."

7. N. Tavuchis, *Mea Culpa: A Sociology of Apology and Reconciliation* (Stanford, CA: Stanford University Press, 1991).

8. Lebra, "Apology and Self," 20.

9. Lebra, "Apology and Self," 22-3.

10. Wagatsuma and Rosett, "Implications of Apology."

11. This incident has been widely reported in the United States. See, for example, "For Japanese Lawsuits Are the Last Resort," *Dallas Morning News,* 15 August 1985, 15A.

12. J. Gresser et al., *Environmental Law in Japan* (Cambridge, MA: MIT Press, 1981), 36; J. Haley, "Sheathing the Sword of Justice in Japan: An Essay on Law Without Sanctions," *Journal of Japanese Studies* 8 (1982): 275; F. Upham, "Litigation and Moral Consciousness in Japan: An Interpretive Analysis of Four Japan Pollution Suits," *Law & Society Review* 10 (1976): 597.

13. The SMON (subacute-myelo-optico-neuropathy) litigation involved nearly two dozen separate private damage actions against several of Japan's leading pharmaceutical firms by victims of injuries attributed to use of the drug Clioquinol. The cases, as well as the terms of settlement and a summary of the Hiroshima District Court decision, are described in English in *Law in Japan: An Annual* 11 (1978), 99-117.

14. Haley, "Sheathing the Sword," 275.

15. Code of Criminal Procedure, art. 246.

16. Code of Criminal Procedure, art. 248.

17. Code of Criminal Procedure, art. 25.

18. B. J. George, "Discretionary Authority of Public Prosecutors in Japan," *Law in Japan: An Annual* 17 (1984): 52.

19. George, "Discretionary Authority," 51; M. Shikita, "Integrated Approach to Effective Administration of Criminal and Juvenile Justice," in *Criminal Justice in Asia: The Quest for an Integrated Approach,* ed. B. J. George, Jr. (Tokyo: UNAFEI, 1982), 37.

20. K. Kawada, "Suspension of Prosecution" (paper prepared for the United Nations Asia and Far East Institute for the Prevention of Crime and Treatment of Offenders, Tokyo, 1978), 1.

21. Haley, "Sheathing the Sword," 271.

22. D. H. Foote, "The Benevolent Paternalism of Japanese Criminal Justice," *California Law Review* 80 (1992): 317-90.

23. D. Johnson, "The Japanese Way of Justice: Prosecuting Crime in Japan," (Ph.D. diss. in Jurisprudence and Social Policy, University of California, Berkeley, 1996).

24. Johnson, "The Japanese Way", 265.

25. Johnson, "The Japanese Way", 295.

26. Haley, "Sheathing the Sword," 236.

27. S. Dando, "System of Discretionary Prosecution in Japan," *American Jour-*

nal of Comparative Law 18 (1970): 518-31; George, "Discretionary Authority," 383, n. 163.

28. *White Paper on Crime* (Tokyo: Ministry of Justice of Japan, 1992), 63.

29. L. Winterscheid, telephone conversation with author, January 1986.

30. Winterscheid, telephone converation.

31. D. F. Henderson, *Conciliation and Japanese Law* (Seattle: University of Washington Press, 1965).

32. L. Peak, "Learning to Go to School in Japan: Problems Adjusting to Pre-school Life" (paper presented to the Japanese Studies Seminar, University of Washington, Seattle, 1988).

33. W. Felstiner and L. Williams, "Mediation as an Alternative to Criminal Prosecution: Ideology and Limitations," *Alternative Rechtsformen und Alternativen zum Recht: Jahrbuch fur rechtssoziologie und Rechtstheorie [Alternative Law, Modes of Law, and Alternatives to Law: Yearbook for the Sociology of Law and Legal Theory]* 6 (1980): 195-214.

34. Felstiner and Williams, "Mediation as an Alternative," 213.

35. M. Umbreit, *Crime and Reconciliation: Creative Options for Victims and Offenders* (Nashville, TN: Abington, 1985), 99.

36. PACT Institute of Justice, *Victim-Offender Reconciliation and Mediation Program Directory* (Valparaiso, IN: Pact Institute of Justice, 1989), 2.

37. J. Haley, "Victim Offender Mediation: Lessons from the Japanese Experience," *Mediation Quarterly* 12 (1995): 233-48.

38. R. B. Coates and J. Gehm, "An Empirical Assessment," in *Mediation and Criminal Justice*, ed. M. Wright and B. Galaway (London: Sage, 1989).

39. Coates and Gehm, "An Empirical Assessment," 9.

40. M. Umbreit, *Victim Meets Offender: The Impact of Restorative Justice and Mediation* (Monsey, NY: Criminal Justice Press, 1994).

41. M. Umbreit, "Restorative Justice Through Mediation: The Impact of Programs in Four Canadian Provinces," *Restorative Justice: International Perspectives*, ed. B. Galaway and J. Hudson (Monsey, NY: Criminal Justice Press, 1996), 373-85.

42. Umbreit, *Victim Meets Offender*; Umbreit, "The Development and Impact of Victim-Offender Mediation in the United States," *Mediation Quarterly* 12 (1995): 263-76.

43. T. Marshall, "Restorative Justice on Trial in Britain," *Mediation Quarterly* 12 (1995): 217-31.

44. J. Wynne, "Leeds Mediation and Reparation Service: Ten Years' Experience with Victim-Offender Mediation," in *Restorative Justice: International Perspectives* (Monsey, NY: Criminal Justice Press, 1996), 445-61.

45. J. Haley, "Victim-Offender Mediation: Japanese and American Comparisons," in *Restorative Justice on Trial*, ed. H. Messmer and H. U. Otto (Amsterdam and Cambridge, MA: Kluwer Academic Publishers, 1992), 105-130; M. Umbreit,

"Restorative Justice Through Mediation," 373-485.

46. PACT Institute, *Program Directory*.

47. Executive Summary, King County Superior Court Demonstration Drug Diversion Court Project, Seattle (1994). Available from the Honorable Judge Ricardo S. Martinez, King County Superior Court, 516 Third Ave., Seattle, WA 98104.

48. *Evaluation of the King County Drug Diversion Court* (Seattle: Urban Policy Research, 1995).

49. "Choosing Hugs, Not Drugs," *Seattle Times*, 2 August 1996, B3.

50. *King County Drug Diversion Court*, 2.

51. J. Braithwaite and S. Mugford, "Conditions of Successful Reintegration Ceremonies: Dealing with Juvenile Offenders," *British Journal of Criminology* 34 (1994): 139-71.

52. M. Brown, "Empowering the Victim in the New Zealand Youth Justice Process" (address to the Eighth International Symposium on Victimology, Adelaide, Australia, August 1994); F. McElrea, "The New Zealand Youth Court: A Model for Use with Adults," in *Restorative Justice: International Perspectives*, ed. B. Galaway and J. Hudson (Monsey, NY: Criminal Justice Press, 1996), 69-83.

53. J. Braithwaite, *Crime, Shame, and Reintegration* (Cambridge, UK: Cambridge University Press, 1989).

54. C. Griffiths and R. Hamilton, "Sanctioning and Healing: Restorative Justice in Canadian Aboriginal Communities," in *Restorative Justice: International Perspectives*, eds. B. Galaway and J. Hudson (Monsey, NY: Criminal Justice Press, 1996), 175-91; B. Stuart, "Sentencing Circles: Purpose and Impact," *National* 3 (1994): 13; Stuart, "Circle Sentencing: Turning Swords into Ploughshares," in *Restorative Justice: International Perspectives*, ed. B. Galaway and J. Hudson (Monsey, NY: Criminal Justice Press, 1996), 193-206; C. LaPrairie, "Altering Course: New Directions in Criminal Justice" (unpublished paper, 1994).

55. S. Macauley and E. Walster, "Legal Structure and Restoring Equity," *Journal of Social Issues* 27 (1971): 17-95; E. Walster and E. Berscheid, "When Does a Harm-doer Compensate a Victim?" *Journal of Personality and Social Psychology* 6 (1967): 35-41; E. Walster et al., "New Directions in Equity Research," *Journal of Personality and Social Psychology* 25 (1973): 151-76; E. Walster et al., "The Exploited: Justice or Justification?" in *Altruism and Helping Behavior*, ed. J Macauley and C. Berkowitz (New York: Academic Press, 1970), 179-294.

56. G. Sykes and D. Matza, "Techniques of Neutralization: A Theory of Delinquency," *American Sociological Review* 22 (1957): 664-70.

57. M. Maltz, *Recidivism* (New York: Academic Press, 1984).

58. B. L. Baxter et al., *The Effectiveness of Deferred Prosecution in Reducing DWI Recidivism: An Update* (Seattle: University of Washington, Alcohol and Drug Abuse Institute, 1993), 93-101; P. van Voorhis, "Restitution Outcome and Probationers' Assessments of Restitution: The Effects of Moral Development," *Criminal Justice and Behavior* 12 (1985): 259-86.

59. Hamilton and Sanders, *Everyday Justice*, 40.

PART TWO

Chapter Four

Repentance, Psychotherapy, and Healing: Through a Jewish Lens

Estelle Frankel

"Great is repentance for it brings healing to the world."
(Talmud Yoma 86b)

In the lives of observant Jews, rituals of repentance serve a healing function that has parallels with that of psychotherapy in our contemporary lives. Like psychotherapy, repentance enables people to come to terms with themselves by healing the pain and mistakes of the past. By transcending linear time, both psychotherapy and repentance deconstruct the past and free the individual from its determinism. Though psychotherapy and repentance generally address different domains of life—that of the psyche as compared to the ethical and spiritual—their common aim is to enable healing.

In both theory and practice, psychotherapy and repentance can inform and enrich each other. As a psychotherapist who has spent many years immersed in the study of Jewish thought, I have attempted to apply my knowledge of Judaism to my work as a psychotherapist. When I listen to my clients reveal their inner states as they progress through the different stages of healing, the words of ancient Jewish texts often echo between the lines of their life narratives. In particular, Jewish mystical teachings on repentance, or *teshuvah,* as it is called in Hebrew, have illuminated my work as a psychotherapist, offering a meaningful framework for understanding the various stages of the healing journey.

Before I go any further into the comparison of teshuvah and psychotherapy, it seems important to point out two significant differences. First, Judaism is based on a set of ethical and spiritual ideals that provide an objective yardstick against which observant Jews have traditionally measured themselves. Teshuvah involves a return to these ideals and a conscious turning from a "self"-centered existence to a "God"-centered one. In contrast, psychotherapy helps the individual to get in touch with the truth within oneself. This process of psychotherapeutic self-realization usually enables the individual to achieve a greater reliance on subjective, inner truth and personally defined values.

The second area of difference involves the fact that individual teshuvah is just one aspect of Judaism's broader, messianic vision of *tikkun olam*—the repairing and redeeming of the world. In this sense, teshuvah differs dramatically from the narrower aims of psychotherapy by addressing communal healing rather than primarily addressing the healing of individuals and families. Teshuvah goes to the heart of Jewish theology, wherein lies the promise of redemption for a suffering world and the injunction that every individual work to bring that about.

In Judaism, therefore, individual repentance represents just one part of the larger goal of collective repentance, which is seen as the catalyst for world redemption. As individual teshuvah culminates in a transformation of the individual, collective teshuvah offers the promise of messianic redemption—the possibility that the imperfect and broken world we live in will someday be transformed. The work of the truly pious Jew does not stop with the achievement of personal redemption, but extends to the collective effort of bringing about world redemption.

Rabbi Abraham Isaac Kook, early-twentieth-century mystic, kabbalist, and philosopher, as well as the first chief rabbi of pre-state Israel, wrote extensively on both the universal-collective as well as the individual dimension of teshuvah. Rabbi Kook's mystical sensibilities enabled him to see these two dimensions as parts of a continuum:

> The individual and the collective soul, the world soul, the soul of all realms of being cries out like a fierce lioness in anguish for total perfection, for an ideal form of existence . . . through the fact that penitence is operative in all worlds, all things are returned and reattached to the realm of divine perfection. . . . General penitence, which involves raising the world to perfection, and particularized penitence, which pertains to the personal life of each individual . . . all constitute one essence . . . an inseparable whole.[1]

Rabbi Kook's vision of teshuvah as the inherent force within creation—the force that guides all things toward perfection—provides an important foundation to our discussion. It also places the individual's journey of repentance and healing within a much larger context of meaning, because the Jewish mystical tradition from which Rabbi Kook drew his philosophy emphasizes that the righteous acts of repentance of each individual have cosmic consequences.[2] In fact, every single *mitzva*, or good deed, has the power to tip the balance of good and evil in the world. Rabbi Kook's vision of teshuvah is therefore an essentially optimistic view of the world. Despite the evil and destructive forces that exist, the world is essentially evolving toward a greater perfection. This optimistic belief empowers individuals to feel that their actions matter, and in doing so, contributes to its own self-fulfillment.

Repentance as Return or Restoration

Before turning to a discussion of communal rites of repentance and their place in Judaism's larger collective vision, let us explore the meaning and benefits of individual repentance and the therapeutic healing journey. Although teshuvah is classically translated as "repentance," its Hebrew root *la'shuv* actually means "to return," implying that repentance involves a return to a point of origin. Teshuvah as "return" suggests that our original state of being is to be spiritually and morally aligned with the divine will. Jewish mysticism postulates that at the core of every person is a soul that is pure and holy, a spark of the divine.

The Jewish notion of a "supraconscious" soul as the center of the self is fundamentally a different way of viewing psychic structure from that postulated by psychoanalytic theorists. When the longing to be aligned with the God-self is included among the drives and needs of the individual, a different psychic structure constellates—one in which spiritual wholeness may be as motivating a force as emotional needs and drives.[3] When a person sins or drifts off course from her essential alignment with the spiritual, this divine spark, which always remains pure, will call her back, beckoning her to return to her true essence.

But to err is part of the human condition. As one rabbi said, the only perfect world would have been no world. For the world to exist and survive its own tendency toward imperfection, teshuvah was a necessary principle, hence the talmudic notion that teshuvah existed prior to creation. A number of rabbinic sources make reference to this idea. For example, it is said in Genesis Raba (Chapter 1:5): "Great is repentance in that it preceded creation."

Another way to understand this saying is based on the notion that with creation, duality begins. In this sense, teshuvah is the means to return to that state of primal unity that existed prior to creation, and this is a gift of God's grace to humankind. In this sense, too, teshuvah can be understood as a perpetual process for the religious person. So long as one exists in the flesh as a separate, unique being, teshuvah offers the means by which one can return to one's essential unity with God.[4]

In fact, without the possibility of teshuvah, creation could not have sustained itself, because this principle of teshuvah as a self-correcting mechanism, in the sense of *la'shuv*, or "return," is built into creation and can be observed at the cellular level. Cell biologists have found that DNA coding errors occur quite commonly during cell replication as a natural consequence of existing in an imperfect environment. Cells deal with these DNA deviations by releasing repair molecules that have the ability to recognize and repair damaged or mutated cells. When the repair molecules fail to operate, disease can result, as we find in cancer cells. Thus, error, as well as the mechanism to recognize imperfections and to self-repair, is basic to the fabric of the universe.

In psychotherapy, healing is also frequently described as a process of return or restoration. Though usually framed in "secular" terms, psychotherapy offers a means to restore psychic wholeness. Just as teshuvah involves a return to one's true spiritual and ethical nature, psychotherapy aims to restore a sense of psychic wholeness that was once there but somehow was lost. Just as "sin" is seen by religion as somehow separating us from God, from one another, and from our true selves, similarly, in the psychological realm, unresolved conflict or trauma can leave us feeling internally divided, emotionally isolated, and cut off from our full potential.

While religion speaks of a return to the God-self, psychotherapists speak of a restoration of or return to the client's true or real Self. Ego and self psychologists speak of a real self using the lowercase *s*. Jung, on the other hand, referred to the Self with a capital *S*, to imply that there is a Self that transcends the personal, individual ego. Unlike the ego, the larger Self has access to the spiritual and archetypal realms. Jung's notion of healing and individuation as a movement toward the larger Self is very much akin to the Jewish notion of teshuvah as a return to a God-centered existence.

These terms reflect the differing ethos of religious versus psychological thinking, yet as we examine these two worldviews in greater depth, we find striking parallels that suggest their commonality. Psychology (in particular, psychoanalysis) may have attempted to replace religion in people's lives, yet many of its practices may unconsciously derive, albeit in secularized form, from the ancient Jewish formula for teshuvah.[5] But, as we examine the classic components of repentance in Jewish thought, their psychotherapeutic counterparts become evident.

The Stages of Individual Repentance and Their Psychotherapeutic Parallels

Maimonides, the medieval philosopher and codifier of Jewish law, systematically outlined the process of teshuvah for individuals in his monumental work the *Mishneh Torah*.[6] As one studies his formulation of the stages of teshuvah, the parallels to the psychotherapeutic journey become evident. Teshuvah, like analytic forms of therapy, always begins with awareness. In order to change, people have to recognize what it is they have done wrong. In Hebrew, this step is referred to as *hakarat ha'chet*, which literally means awareness of how one has "missed the mark."

It may sound simple, but honest awareness is not so easily achieved. People employ numerous psychological mechanisms of defense—including denial, repression, and projection—to protect themselves from the pain of facing the truth. In psychotherapy, much attention is paid to the analysis of these defenses as obstacles to understanding and change. Because a person cannot achieve awareness unless the enactment of defenses is fully understood, the analysis and working through of defenses, which is known as resistance analysis, is the crucial first step in the process of psychotherapy.

In the Jewish tradition, the second step of teshuvah is actualized through the act of *vidui,* or confession. Verbal acknowledgment of one's mistakes epitomizes the teshuvah process; without confession, teshuvah is not possible. In other words, awareness of one's mistakes in one's mind or heart is an important first step, but, in and of itself, it is not sufficient. Teshuvah demands a verbal articulation of one's inner process. This act of verbalization potentiates the process of teshuvah and is its defining characteristic.

Rabbi Joseph B. Soloveitchik, one of Judaism's most articulate contemporary teachers on the subject of teshuvah, speaks of the emotional potency of confession: "Confession compels man—in a state of terrible torment—to admit facts as they really are, to give clear expression to the truth. This indeed, is a sacrifice, a breaking of the will, a tortuous negation of human nature. Both remorse and shame are involved in this process."[7]

Soloveitchik emphasizes the need to overcome pride and defensive shame in order to look oneself straight in the eye and confess. He likens the humbling effects of confession to the symbolic sacrificial offering: "Just as the sacrifice is burnt upon the altar so do we burn down, by our act of confession, our well-barricaded complacency, our overblown pride, our artificial existence."[8]

In therapy, it is the telling or confessing of the client's personal pain, secret conflicts, regrets, and longings that enables her to face the truth, no matter how painful that may be. The client may not even know what she is going to say until the words are uttered, and it is frequently in the act of telling or confessing that she may begin to achieve insight and clarity. Through the telling, the client's life becomes a coherent story, and her true self is revealed. To achieve this truthfulness, however, the client must often overcome feelings of shame and humiliation.

The feeling and expression of regret or remorse is the second essential step of teshuvah, according to Maimonides, and it too is deemed an integral part of confession. The expression of regret and remorse for one's mistakes is what enables the penitent to learn the deepest lessons from the past.

In psychotherapy, painful feelings of regret often emerge just as the client is beginning to change and experience emotional growth. He or she may express deep regret over certain life choices that turned out to be unwise or even tragic, or weep in regret over the years spent living with crippling inhibitions. As the client develops the capacity to feel greater empathy for others, past actions and behavior patterns that previously were not viewed as wrong are suddenly perceived as hurtful or immoral. Ironically, as the client begins to heal in therapy, her newfound ability to feel more open and loving can bring up painful feelings of regret or grief for a lifetime spent shut down.

The process of healing and reconnecting with one's true self inevitably brings up painful feelings of loss. Avoidance of this pain is usually what holds someone back from healing. The courage to grieve and mourn the losses of the past is what ultimately frees the individual to move on and change.[9] In grieving, the patient relinquishes the defensive fantasy that the past can be somehow undone. By facing and accepting the fact that the past is over—however painful that may be—the client can reclaim her true self. Though regret and mourning mark an important stage in the healing process, this stage must be followed by work on self-forgiveness and acceptance for healing to be complete.

Maimonides' third step of teshuvah involves the resolve never to repeat the mistakes of the past. This step requires projecting oneself into the future and imagining doing it differently. One's resolve is tested when presented with a situation parallel to the one in which one previously had erred. When a person resists repeating his or her past mistakes in such a situation, then and only then is repentance considered complete. In fact, it is viewed as a grace from God when fate presents a parallel situation, because only then can one be sure that her repentance is complete. In Maimonides' words: "What is complete repentance? That in which the former transgressor is afforded an opportunity of repeating his sin but stays his hand and refrains from doing so because he has repented, and not out of fear or due to incapacity."

Just as life seems to provide us with endless opportunities to repeat old patterns, one could say that life is continually providing us with opportunities to finally get it right. In psychotherapy we help our clients become aware of their "compulsion to repeat." Therapists often reframe this as the client's unconscious attempt at mastery of the past. Clients can also develop awareness of these repetitious patterns in the context of the therapy relationship through transference analysis, the working through in the here and now of emotions whose origins are in the past. Clients thereby begin to replace the destructive old patterns with new understandings and behaviors.[10]

As with teshuvah, however, therapy is not complete until the client is free to respond in a conscious and healthy fashion, rather than blindly obeying his or her unconscious preprogramming. Perhaps one could say that therapy enables the client to exercise her "free choice" rather than be a prisoner of the past. Interestingly, Maimonides introduces a discussion of "free will" in the middle of his treatise on teshuvah, suggesting that repentance is possible only when people take responsibility for their choices.

Lastly, Maimonides adds personal apology, asking for forgiveness, public confession, and restitution as additional requisites of teshuvah over sins involving harm to other persons. Though complete restitution is not always possible, one must do whatever is possible to make amends toward all those wronged by one's actions.

I am not sure how many psychotherapists are equipped to offer their clients guidance on how to go about offering restitution. Clinical training doesn't necessarily prepare us to respond to such moral dilemmas. The popular twelve-step addiction recovery programs have adopted restitution as well as many other aspects of teshuvah into their programs, and restitution is seen as crucial to the recovery process of addicts. Psychotherapists might consider the potential therapeutic value that acts of restitution offer the client—not just in terms of relieving guilt, but in building a sense of moral responsibility for one's actions. In working with former addicts, criminals, and perpetrators of abuse, a discussion of restitution should be considered an essential part of the healing process.

Psychotherapists have been criticized for their general reluctance to take such moral stands with clients.[11] As William Doherty and Robert Bellah have pointed out, many psychotherapists are stuck in the "expressive individualism" of psychoanalysis and the human potential movement. The field of psychotherapy hasn't fully adjusted to the fact that many more of the clients who seek therapy today do not have the "moral capital" that clients of earlier generations had. The term "moral capital," coined by public policy scholar James Q. Wilson, is used to describe the strong grounding in moral, social, and ethical values that Freud and other pioneering intellectuals took for granted when creating psychoanalysis as a technique aimed at liberating the individual from excessive guilt and repression. According to Wilson, this moral capital is largely depleted now, and therapists can no longer see themselves primarily as agents of liberation.

Though contemporary psychoanalytic theorists speak of the need to augment clients' missing ego functions—even the need to provide the missing voice of conscience at times—these theories have not changed the popular image of the psychotherapist as having his or her hands tied when it comes to moral issues in therapy. Generally, these therapeutic strategies are aimed at work with clients who clearly have inadequate psychic structure, or severe personality disorders. One psychotherapist who has pioneered the work of confronting moral issues with this type of client is Dr. Otto Kernberg. He has worked extensively with severely narcissistic patients and asocial personalities and has written about the importance of confronting dishonesty in the patient (or client) and helping the patient develop a sense of moral integrity.[12]

But when it comes to challenging the moral choices of higher-functioning clients—that is, clients who are simply operating in line with the self-centered ethic of American individualism—psychotherapists are extremely reluctant to directly engage their clients in moral discourse. Yet, even as therapists avoid direct confrontation of moral issues, there is no escaping the fact that they bring their own set of morals and values to the relationship.

The fact that the therapist can never be entirely objective or neutral with the client has been acknowledged by intersubjectivity theory. According to this ap-

proach, the therapist and the client's psychology are viewed as inevitably inter-
twined, and the healing process involves a collaboration of the therapeutic pair.
The therapist, who is a participant as well as an observer of the process, is encouraged to make use of his or her inevitable subjective emotional responses as a
therapeutic tool with the client. This is done by making use of selective self-disclo-
sure, which may at times include being forthright in response to the client's moral or
ethical dilemmas.

The role of the therapist as "moral guide" is a whole discussion in itself, but its
relevance to the larger issue here is for the contemporary therapist to begin to
consider how the values inherent in an ancient spiritual tradition, such as Judaism,
might be applied to psychotherapeutic practice. In the Jewish tradition, healing
always includes the moral dimension; the notion of a healer's being "morally neutral" is incongruous with a Jewish approach. Judaism clearly sees righteous living
as an important component of a person's mental health, which suggests that the
process of clarifying the client's as well as the therapist's moral or ethical values
can be an asset in treatment.

As a therapist rooted in a feminist, non orthodox Jewish tradition, I am clear that
I bring a certain set of values and morals to my work. I am not so naive as to think
that I can entirely separate out my personal ideals from my work. I try not to
inappropriately impose my personal beliefs or choices on my clients; however, I
am aware that the questions I ask and guidance I offer are frequently guided by my
personal values, as well as by therapeutic technique. Whether or not I engage my
clients in direct moral discourse, my values and morals clearly inform my work, and
at times I find it can be a powerful therapeutic tool to selectively use Jewish legends
and teachings to convey moral lessons.

The Elevation of Sin in the Mystical Tradition

In the final chapter of the laws of repentance, Maimonides expands his discussion to include repentance over negative character traits such as anger, hatred, envy,
scoffing, greed, vanity, and food addictions, in addition to single acts of wrongdoing. He quotes a famous saying from the Talmud (Berachot 34b) that states, "Where
repentant sinners stand, the thoroughly righteous cannot stand." This saying
awards the repentant sinner a special status, an elevation above that of the righteous person who never sinned.

Maimonides also discusses a qualitatively different kind of repentance—one
that Soloveitchik calls "repentance of redemption." Whereas Maimonides has previously spoken of the repentance of expiation and acquittal—the ways in which
one can erase the negative effects of past wrongdoing—in his final chapter,
Maimonides alludes to the mystical dimension of teshuvah, in which a complete
transformation of character and rebirth is possible. At this level of teshuvah, one's
sins are not just erased but are transformed into merits. Repentance of redemption

involves a kind of spiritual alchemy—transforming sin into merit, sinner into saint, vice into virtue. Negative character traits that previously held the individual back are refashioned into virtues—propelling the repentant to levels of holiness she would never have achieved had she not sinned and been compelled to repent.

How does this alchemy occur? Soloveitchik speaks poignantly of the inner pain and struggle that "Repentant Man" faces in his lonely process of repentance. Like loss of a loved one, sin leaves us lonely and longing to regain God's loving presence. Just as we often don't know how much we need and love someone until we lose him or her, in the spiritual domain, the love for God is not always sufficiently appreciated until we sin and feel the resultant loss of connection. Through repentance, a deep longing to regain God's love and closeness is unleashed. The longing can be so strong that the repentant sinner is propelled by a force of holiness that far surpasses that of the righteous person who has never experienced spiritual estrangement. Soleveitchik describes this unique capacity to "elevate sin" that Repentant Man achieves as a result of this longing: "a man who has sinned and has repented may be able—if he proves worthy—to utilize the dynamism of the forces of evil which had enveloped him before and elevate them, and to make them operate on behalf of the forces of good." It is through the experience of sin that Repentant Man may discover within himself a reservoir of new energy that can now be directed toward the spiritual and the good.

Reb Tzaddok Ha'cohen of Lublin, Poland, a late-nineteenth-century Jewish scholar, also wrote on the transformational power of teshuvah. In his voluminous writings on Chassidic thought, he integrated many talmudic, kabbalistic, and psychological insights on repentance. In one of his great works, *Tzidkat Ha'tzaddik,* Reb Tzaddok says: "By the very quality in which one is lacking or wounded, by that very quality one finds one's unique gift or strength."[13] In other words, our most special gifts and strengths often derive from our very weaknesses and vulnerabilities. To base his idea in traditional sources, Reb Tzaddok quotes a well-known legend about Adam and Eve: "'And they (Adam and Eve) sewed (garments) from the leaves of the fig tree.' Through that which was their downfall they were redeemed." Adam and Eve clothed themselves with the leaves of the very tree that led to their temptation, sin, and subsequent exile from paradise. This legend suggests that sometimes our most calamitous mistakes lead us to our calling and to our most redeeming qualities.

Reb Tzaddok finds a parallel notion in the talmudic saying that Messiah was born on Tisha B'Av, the day on which the Temple in Jerusalem was destroyed. The redeemer and the possibility of redemption are born out of the very ashes of destruction. This powerful metaphor often inspires me when I treat individuals whose lives, as they have known them, have been destroyed by tragic circumstances—death, divorce, natural disaster, war. By finding the redemptive seeds of hope and renewal that lay hidden in the ashes of the past, these clients are helped to face their despair and loss.

I am not suggesting that therapists use these ideas as moral imperatives with clients. Rather, let us keep these teachings in mind as a potentially more expansive perspective than the one a person may be experiencing at the time of a personal tragedy. Then, over time, therapists might refer to these ideas to find ways to help clients discover the redemptive possibilities.

In another text, Reb Tzaddok offers concrete examples of the transformation of negative character traits into virtues. He begins by acknowledging that "every person has a unique passion or desire, and that very thing which evokes the greatest amount of attachment or desire is also a vessel for receiving God's blessing, if one returns to God with all of one's heart." One example is about the transformation of greed, in which Reb Tzaddok interprets the story of Moses' grandson, Yonatan. In the Book of Judges, Yonatan is described as an opportunist who sold out to idolatry for monetary gain. Yet, later, in the Book of Chronicles, Yonatan is renamed Shavuel, which literally means "a returnee to God," and he is said to be King Solomon's appointee over the treasures of the Holy Temple in Jerusalem. According to Reb Tzaddok, King Solomon recognized the potential that lay dormant in Yonatan's lust for money and helped him channel this passion to a sacred cause:

> He (Shavuel) restored this particular passion to its source by recognizing that all wealth is God's. . . . Also, a blessing fell upon the treasures through Shavuel, because God had made him a creature whose passion was money. Therefore he possessed tremendous power in this realm. And once he repented with his entire heart, God's blessing for abundance was channeled through him.

This teaching story provides a wonderful example of how teshuvah transforms a personal deficit into a gift. Passions and drives are not seen as essentially bad, but simply in need of redirection; the same intensity of passion that was directed toward selfish temptations of the flesh can be channeled into an equally deep passion for truth or service.

Applying Mystical Concepts of Repentance in Psychotherapy

For the psychotherapist, it is important to recognize a client's latent talents and gifts that may initially manifest as part of the presenting symptomatology. Thus, we can view the client's neurosis or presenting problem as potentially containing clues, if not the key, to healing. Indeed, the client's symptoms may be his or her best attempt at healing. Instead of solely aiming to eliminate painful symptoms, we can look for the wisdom hidden in the symptoms, that is, for the opportunity for healing offered by the crisis. The following cases illustrate this application.[14]

Gene, a thirty-five-year-old architect, revealed in therapy that he was having an affair with a woman he worked with. He didn't understand how he had gotten into this "mess," as he called it, since he was actually happily married and loved his wife and kids. What emerged in therapy was that Gene had been an artist before studying architecture. He had hoped that he would always continue doing art, but had decided that it would be easier to make a living with a career in architecture. Feeling overwhelmed by the demands of his job, Gene had given up on his artwork. The passion he sought through an affair was really a desperate attempt to fill the void created by his abandonment of his artwork. In therapy, Gene found that he is a person for whom passion is a life requirement, and fulfilling this need through affairs would very likely be disastrous. By understanding and accepting his need for passion, Gene was motivated to recommit himself to finding a way to balance the demands of his career with his love for art.

As Gene's psychotherapist, one might have been inclined to view his affair through only a classic psychoanalytic lens—to see his behavior as an unconscious attempt to undermine his successful marriage out of an identification with his father, who had failed in love. But this interpretation would not have provided the wonderful opportunity to help Gene reconnect with his passion and then redirect it in a constructive way.

Sarah was a forty-year-old teacher who suffered from episodes of debilitating depression. Though not in a crisis when she started therapy, Sarah wanted to explore the origins of her mood swings. She also felt very isolated and found it difficult to sustain deep and lasting friendships. Sarah's emotional development had been arrested by the untimely death of her mother when she was a child. Since then, she had basically been a loner. She did, however, find great solace in her study of various spiritual traditions. As an adult she had found a meaningful role for herself as an esteemed teacher in her spiritual community.

Sarah had been in previous therapies for her recurrent depressions. In the course of these therapies she learned that the painful abandonment she experienced when her mother died had impaired her ability to trust in others. It was easier for her to form an attachment to a spiritual being, or God, than to people who could hurt her as her mother had hurt her by dying. Previous therapists Sarah had worked with had viewed her spirituality as basically defensive, as some expression of a search for the lost love object of childhood (her mother). Despite the psychoanalytic accuracy of these interpretations, Sarah was unable to use them to make the needed changes in her life.

In our work together, I stressed that forming deep and meaningful bonds with friends would require that she understand and more fully reconcile with her grief over the loss of her mother. In addition to providing her with therapeutic rituals for the expression of her childhood grief, I also validated her spiritual sensitivity as a gift that had been activated by that very same trauma. By seeing her emotional pain not just as a handicap, but also as the source of her greatest gift, Sarah was able to resolve her depression and deepen her sense of self.

Maxine, a fifty-three-year-old client with a history of chronic depression, started therapy following the death of her husband. Her depression had become so severe that she could not function at work. Being unable to work reinforced her view of herself as worthless and added to her relentless list of self-recriminations. Through-out her life she had avoided facing deep feelings of worthlessness and nonentitlement to a life of her own. She would "justify her existence," to use her words, by overachieving and always taking care of others.

Using Reb Tzaddok's philosophy, I suggested that we view her depressive symp-toms, including the fatigue and dysfunction, also as an opportunity for healing. I suggested that the symptoms of her depression were challenging her to learn about "unconditional" self-love, the missing ingredient in her upbringing. The depres-sion, though painful, could be seen as freeing her from having to satisfy her criti-cal and demanding inner voices, since she was clearly unable to meet their de-mands at this time. Interpreting her depression as an opportunity to potentially heal an old wound helped reduce Maxine's self-recriminations, and thus we achieved a first step toward lessening her chronic self-hate.

Evan, a thirty-nine-year-old professional, came into therapy to deal with a substance abuse problem that had nearly destroyed his picture-perfect life. A child prodigy and Ivy League university graduate, Evan had achieved a measure of success in his field by the age of thirty that few achieve in a lifetime. Happily married and soon to be a father, Evan seemed to be leading a charmed existence; however, a series of disappointments, including an unexpected layoff from his job, sent him into a depression. Initially, Evan avoided dealing with his depression through the use of drugs. It wasn't until his wife threatened to leave him over the drug use that he sought out therapy. At this point Evan was suicidally depressed. Keeping Reb Tzaddok's "messiah metaphor" in mind, I began planting seeds of hope by helping Evan see that this crisis was not only inevitable, but also a neces-sary rite of passage into a more mature stage of life. Evan had never learned to deal directly with pain and disappointment. His turning to drugs was a reflection of this inability, and the drug use further disabled him emotionally. By viewing his current experience of "failure" as the very medicine needed for his healing, we were able to begin the work of deconstructing the narcissistic defenses that glued him together. The new Evan would never be as "picture perfect" as the old Evan, but he would become more whole and strong as he faced and accepted his own imperfection as well as life's disappointments.

****

Another way in which I draw on Reb Tzaddok's teaching is with clients who are excessively self-critical and who tend to dwell on their unfortunate fate or neurotic tendencies. I might ask if there is anything good or special about them that also derives from this very fate or characteristic they seem to hate. This type of question often pleasantly surprises clients and enables them to be more self-forgiving. When people are able to connect their painful memories or experiences with some redeeming outcome, they frequently experience a crucial psychological shift. What seemed to be arbitrary bad luck in their lives suddenly takes on new meaning and purpose.

This teleologic approach to healing offers the hope of finding a deeper meaning and purpose in the pain and mistakes of the past. Since the suffering that people feel is very much tied to the story they tell themselves, finding meaning in pain can diminish their sense of suffering.

As I mentioned at the opening of this essay, both teshuvah and psychotherapy achieve their aims through a transcendence of linear time. Through teshuvah, the penitent person brings the awareness and closeness to God that she has achieved back to the time of the sin, enlightening the sin itself by bringing God's loving presence to that dark time. In other words, the past is enlightened by the future consciousness and good deeds that result from the penitent's repentance.

In the Jewish mystical tradition, teshuvah involves accessing the Y-H-V-H (commonly translated as *Yahweh*) name of God that stands outside of time. The Hebrew letters Yod-Heh-Vav-Heh comprise a composite of three Hebrew words: *hayah* (was), *hoveh* (is); and *yihiyeh* (will be). YHVH, also known as *shem havayah* (holy name of Being), encompasses all of time. Past, present, and future join as one in this name. The name YHVH is also traditionally associated with God's transcendent and compassionate qualities, in contrast to *Elohim*, associated with divine judgment, limit-setting, and strict adherence to the laws of nature. It is in evoking the compassionate and time-transcendent quality of YHVH that the workings of linear time are rectified and transformational teshuvah is a possibility. Rabbi Joseph Soloveitchik has spoken of this phenomenon of teshuvah existing within qualitative time rather than quantitative time:

> Man lives in the shadow of the past, future and present simultaneously . . . the future determines the direction and indicates the way. . . . There exists a phenomenon whose beginning is sin and iniquity and whose end is *mitzvot* and good deeds, and vice versa. The future transforms the trends and tendencies of the past.[15]

Psychotherapy also employs a variety of "time-travel" techniques that facilitate the healing of childhood pain and trauma. It is generally accepted that the unconscious mind is not bound by time. Events and emotions from the past, even the distant past, can be experienced with an immediacy as though they were happening now. The work of transference analysis provides an opportunity to experience time as expanded or contracted. By using methods such as free association, guided visualization, or hypnosis, the client can be guided back in time to a particular trauma or painful memory. Through the compassionate reaching out from the adult, healthy ego-self to the memories of hurt from the past, healing begins to occur. The pain of the past is touched and transformed by the love and compassion of the present.

At such moments in therapy, clients often experience a transforming shift. Instead of trying to forget and not feel the pain of the past, it is a moment of deep connection to all of who one is, was, and is becoming. When a person can look back and see how everything she has endured, including all the pain, suffering, and mistakes, has led her to become who she is today—when she can embrace it all with a sense of forgiveness for herself and others—healing occurs. At such moments, the painful memories of the past are recontextualized by the higher state of consciousness reached in the present. When a person open-heartedly embraces all that she has been through, a bittersweet experience of "at-one-ment" occurs, a moment in which one feels whole or at one with the many parts of oneself.

Messiah as Archetypal Image of
Wounded Healer/Repentant Sinner

The heroes of a culture usually provide an accurate reflection of its most esteemed values, not only reflecting a culture's values, but also creating and recreating the culture by providing role models to emulate. In Jewish history it was frequently the repentant sinner or wounded healer—not the righteous saint—who was chosen as the hero or ideal leader. The very first high priest mentioned in the Bible was the repentant sinner Aaron. Though he had participated in the "primal" sin of fashioning the golden calf, he was, as the high priest, later endowed with the power to bring atonement to the people for all their sins.

Another major figure from Jewish history who embodied the archetype of the repentant sinner/wounded healer was King David. His profile provides a potent metaphor and teaching story for those seeking to redeem a painful past. David was the grandson of Ruth the Moabite, a convert and outsider whose legitimacy was questioned by some leaders of her generation. As Ruth's grandson, David was a descendant of Moav, the despised offspring of Lot's incestuous relations with his eldest daughter (Genesis 19). On his father's side, David descended from Peretz, one of the twins born of Tamar's incest with her father-in-law, Judah (Genesis 38). As if these stories were not enough to sully David's reputation, yet another rabbinic legend suggests that David was conceived when his father attempted to have sex with his maidservant and only unwittingly slept with his wife. Numerous other scriptural and rabbinic stories of illicit sexual relationships also surround David's birth.[16]

As king, David's reputation was further sullied when he committed two grave sins. Despite all this, he was not only forgiven by God, he was also awarded the messianic title. What is particularly striking about this is that it stands in contrast to the story of his predecessor, King Saul, who was dethroned for a failure to obey

God's command in the war against Amalek. Biblical commentators all ask why Saul was punished so severely for a single mistake, whereas King David, who committed two cardinal sins—adultery and murder—was forgiven. The answer given is that King Saul, instead of acknowledging his mistake, made excuses for it, whereas King David immediately confessed his sins when confronted by the prophet's reprimand, and he then proceeded to spend the rest of his days engaged in sincere repentance.

As the one chosen to be the messianic prototype, King David provides a model in which the redeemer need not be perfect, but he must be able to face his failings with honesty and humility. It is the integration of power with vulnerability and saintliness along with sinfulness that characterizes the Jewish messiah. To heal the wounded world and raise up all that is fallen, Messiah must himself be connected to all the evil that is crying out for redemption. Only a wounded healer/repentant sinner can be the messianic redeemer.

In classic rabbinic hyperbole, the Talmud includes the existence of "family skeletons" as an advantage for leaders because of its humbling effect: "One should not appoint any one as leader of a community, unless he carriers a basket of reptiles[17] on his back, so that if he becomes arrogant, one could tell him: Turn around and look behind you." (Talmud Yoma 22b)

It is interesting to note that David was a direct descendant of Judah, who, like David, was a repentant sinner and was also awarded the task of leadership.[18] When confronted with his sin of unwittingly impregnating his own daughter-in-law, Tamar,[19] Judah immediately admitted his folly. In fact, one of the meanings of the Hebrew root of the name Judah is "to admit" (*le'hodot*). Judah and David both represent leaders who fell prey to temptations, yet succeeded in redeeming their folly.

Their example stands in striking contrast to contemporary American culture, especially in the political arena, where politicians prey on any opportunity to expose their opponents' flaws. Unfortunately, contemporary political discourse holds no appreciation for a leader's potential and right to repent—no second chances exist for today's politicians. This atmosphere makes it practically impossible for leaders to openly admit their mistakes and express their remorse. Yet the ability to admit one's mistakes and to suffer the private as well as the public humiliation that it may entail is crucial to the process of teshuvah.

In choosing the repentant sinner as the prototype for its redeemer, Jewish theology embraced real life rather than perfection as its ideal. In a similar vein, the Bible opens with the garden of Eden story as if to say human history begins with a mistake and will inevitably include many other mistakes. Human existence necessitates that fixing and healing will be needed. Just as the world could not exist without teshuvah, no individual can live without forgiveness.

In my clinical work, I am frequently struck by how little awareness or understanding people have of how forgiveness and atonement can be part of the healing process. When people have no frame of reference for forgiving themselves or others who have wronged them, they carry around an enormous amount of guilt and resentment from the past. With such clients, I often use the stages of repentance laid out by Maimonides to teach a process they can learn that facilitates their achievement of forgiveness.

Overcoming shame is another theme that frequently emerges in psychotherapy. For some clients, the very need for therapy is a source of shame. For others, exposing their pain and vulnerability and allowing themselves to "receive" from the therapist may be experienced as humiliating. Clients often enact complex defenses against feelings and memories to ward off painful feelings of shame. Psychotherapy is not likely to be effective unless experiences of shame are uncovered and worked through.

With certain clients I have attempted to reduce their feelings of shame by drawing on the theme of the wounded healer. By reflecting that it is a sign of ultimate strength to be able to admit and reveal one's weaknesses, I help them to view the experience of shame as an opportunity to develop the positive quality of humility. Transforming shame into humility is particularly effective with the narcissistic client whose grandiose self must be deconstructed in order for his or her true feelings to emerge. By developing the quality of humility, such patients find a face-saving way to give up self-inflation.

In working with survivors of sexual or child abuse, I see the work of healing and self-forgiveness often aided when the perpetrator undergoes a process of repentance. Unfortunately, this is not always a possibility. But when the perpetrator is a parent, close relative, or friend, the adult victim may need to confront the perpetrator about the abuse to hasten his or her own healing. Such confrontations may also be necessary in order to reestablish an honest relationship.

As one client of mine put it: "I need my father to acknowledge and stop denying that what went on was abuse—not just 'discipline.' Until he faces the truth I can't have a close or honest relationship with him." When I asked this client what stopped him from confronting his father in the past, he replied: "When I tried to approach the subject in the past, my father felt so bad that I started feeling guilty and I couldn't bear to destroy him." I suggested that he try again by presenting it to his father in the context of the possibility of repentance and forgiveness. Perhaps his father would be more able to bear his painful feelings of guilt if he knew that ultimately it would lead to a healing between him and his son, whom he did love. When confronted in this fashion, the father was finally able to admit his mistakes and express deep feelings of regret over the past. Hearing his father's sincere regret helped my client overcome his own shame and denial over the abuse, and ultimately enabled him to rebuild a more honest relationship with his father.

On a number of occasions I have been able to arrange family therapy sessions for individual clients of mine who were victimized by another family member. These sessions have been beneficial not only to my clients but to the perpetrators as well. When those who have been abusive have the opportunity to express remorse and ask for forgiveness, they can be freed up from carrying a lifelong burden of guilt and alienation from a loved one.

Communal Rites of Repentance and Their Function in Healing

Many ancient societies observed periodic communal rites of repentance. These rites were seen as essential for the harmonious functioning of the community. The shaman or high priest functioned in much the way that psychotherapists do today, only the focus included the well-being of the community as well as that of its individual members. Psychotherapy in part fills the void that was created by the breakdown in these religious practices.

For observant Jews, the High Holy Days, beginning with Rosh Hashana (the Jewish New Year) and ending ten days later on Yom Kippur (the Day of Atonement), provide a structure for individual and communal repentance and healing. The Ten Days of Repentance (*asseret y'mai* teshuvah), as this period is known, provides a highly articulated system for self-reflection and for letting go of guilt. It is also a time in which Jews go out of their way to ask one another for forgiveness for the ways in which they have wronged each other in the past year, so that interpersonal conflict and grudges are not carried into the new year.

A Rosh Hashana ritual known as *tashlich* (literally, "casting off") provides an opportunity to "cast off" whatever needs to be discarded from the past. Jews observe this rite by symbolically throwing their "residue" from the past year into a body of moving water. Such rituals, when observed with conscious intention, can serve a therapeutic purpose. Drawing on the symbolism of the *tashlich* ritual, I have occasionally devised therapeutic rituals for clients who have been unable to let go of something from the past that they recognize is no longer useful. Symbolic ritual enactment of psychic contents can empower clients to make the needed changes that they have been unable to make through insight alone. Research on the psychology of ritual has shown that the psyche responds particularly well to ritual because it speaks in the language of the unconscious—the language of symbol and metaphor.[20]

The structure of the Ten Days of Repentance follows the stages of repentance laid down by Maimonides. Just as repentance begins with serious soul-searching and self-assessment, this period of time begins with Rosh Hashana, which is known as the Day of Judgment. This is a time when Jews figure out how their lives have steered off course so that they can reset their inner moral and spiritual compass. During the ensuing days that fall between Rosh Hashana and Yom Kippur, Jews continue to soul-search and attempt to mend whatever needs healing with friends, family, and community. The Ten Days of Repentance culminate on Yom Kippur, the Day of Atonement, when judgment gives way to forgiveness, when *din* (God's letter-of-the-law, judging quality) is replaced by *rachamim* (God's compassionate, womblike quality). These holidays are structured so that judgment precedes for-giveness; however, judgment must ultimately yield to forgiveness. By creating this yearly cycle for repentance, these holidays provide people with a way to release their resentments and limit their neurotic guilt.

The Integrative Function of Rites of Atonement

In ancient times, observance of the high holidays included a series of mystical rites performed by the high priest in the Jerusalem Temple. The symbolism of these rites, particularly the Yom Kippur rites of atonement, offers insight into the integra-tive healing power of teshuvah. When examined through a psychological lens, these ancient rites contain profound insights that can be applied to both contem-porary individual psychotherapy and communal healing.

The first rite, known as the scapegoat offering, involved drawing lots over two identical goats. One was chosen to be sacrificed in the Jerusalem Temple, while the other was sent off alive to *Azazel* (the wilderness) after the priest had confessed and transferred all the sins of the people onto it (Leviticus 16). According to Nachmanides, a medieval mystic and biblical commentator, the Yom Kippur scape-goat (*seir la'azazel*) was actually an offering to the "other side," seen symbolically as a gift or bribe to Satan (*shochad la'satan*).[21] The symbol of the scapegoat sug-gests that, on the holiest day of the year, one must extract a blessing even from one's nemesis. In a sense, the *seir la'azazel* is a rite of divine unification. God and Satan must make amends on Yom Kippur, so that nothing that exists is outside of the divine realm of the "One." This hints at the spiritual challenge of Yom Kippur, which is to heal and transform all the sins of the past through repentance, by bringing it all back to a God who is nondualistic or "One."

In psychological terms, the unification of God and Satan can be seen as sym-bolizing the reintegration of that which was previously split off from conscious-ness or relegated, in the Jungian sense, to the "shadow," to those parts of the self that are unacceptable to one's conscious image of oneself. We might also view the rapprochement between God and Satan as a metaphor for the psychological capac-ity for integration of good and bad. Instead of banishing one's bad self to the netherworld or *azazel*, as the scapegoat ritual seems to imply, Nachmanides' inter-pretation of the rite suggests the opposite—it is an attempt to make peace with Satan, God's banished evil side. By viewing the deity as one who has made peace with his dark or destructive side, the devout, in their imitation of God, follow a healthier psychological role model than that of a deity viewed as all good.

In psychotherapy, the capacity for integration of good and bad feelings about oneself and others is considered an important developmental goal. This capacity for integration is essential for a three-dimensional emotional maturity, for sustain-ing positive self-esteem, and for the ability to establish long-term intimate relation-ships. Many clients in therapy struggle with an inability to sustain their good feelings about themselves or others when they also experience negative feelings. Without the capacity for integration, such clients frequently isolate themselves from others in order to maintain their fragile one-sided view of themselves, or they find that their emotional lives are a virtual roller-coaster ride, alternating between love and hate.

The second ancient rite unique to Yom Kippur is the *ketoret,* or incense offering, and it also hints at the theme of integration. On this one day a year, the high priest would enter a space in the Jerusalem Temple known as the Holy of Holies and offer the *ketoret,* which consisted of eleven spices, one of which was called the *chelbenah,* or galbanum. Though the *chelbenah* smelled bad by itself, it was an essential ingredient of the sweet-smelling incense offering, and without it the offering was not complete. The inclusion of the *chelbenah* in the *ketoret* has been interpreted as a symbol of the need for inclusiveness and collectivity when trying to achieve atonement. In commemoration of this rite, Jews begin the Yom Kippur prayers by formally welcoming and including the sinners among them to join in the communal healing rites. Just as unity among all Jews, from sinners to saints, is a requisite for achieving atonement, so too, in the intrapsychic realm, we each have a *chelbenah*—a quality that by itself can be quite a nuisance. When we deny or reject this part, it remains split off, as part of our shadow and potentially an adversarial force. But once fully integrated, the *chelbenah* is often the key that unlocks the door to finding our wholeness. Rabbi Kook spoke eloquently of this reintegration of evil:

> fragmentation, and then every particular being stands by itself, and evil is evil in and of itself, and it is evil and destructive. When he repents out of love there at once shines on him the light from the world of unity, where everything is integrated into one whole, and in the context of the whole there is no evil at all. The evil is joined with the good to invest it with more attractiveness, and to enhance its significance.[22]

These ancient rites model how both individual integration and communal unity are essential aspects of atonement and healing. The vital message of Yom Kippur is that no part of the self, nor any individual from the collective community, may be cut off or separated from the whole. The special healing power of Yom Kippur can only be accessed when the people join as a collective to repent. In the collective, something greater constellates than the simple sum of individuals. When the people join together, they atone for one another—what one individual may lack, another makes up for, and vice versa. One person's weakness may evoke another person's strength. In both the material realm as well as the spiritual domain, the poor and needy provide those who are better off with opportunities to manifest their generosity.

This sense of communal responsibility and interconnectedness is reflected in the Yom Kippur confessional prayer, which is chanted in the plural. On Yom Kippur, Jews cease to view themselves as isolated individuals. Each individual takes a measure of responsibility for the sins of the collective. Part of the healing power of this holiday is based on the reconnection of individuals to the community at large.

On Yom Kippur, therefore, Jews revisit the covenant that the Israelites established with God at Mount Sinai that was based on the notion of *arevut,* or communal interdependence.[23] Every man or woman who stood at Sinai took it upon him or herself to be *arevim* (responsible and interconnected) with one another. The spiritual metaphor embedded in the Sinai experience is that we come into covenant with the Divine "One" only when we perceive how humanity is "One." The Sinai experience is about collective enlightenment, not just individual enlightenment.

Yom Kippur commemorates the Sinai experience by providing an annual rite of reentry into covenantal community. As part of the larger whole, each individual's path of repentance is made less lonely and less shameful. In the context of communal repentance, it is easier for each individual to face and admit his or her shortcomings. The communal dimension greatly reduces the shame involved in admitting one's mistakes. Also, it is easier to change old patterns when one's family members, friends, and community are simultaneously engaged in a process of repentance. This communal model for healing offered by the High Holy Days ensures that the individual's growth will be supported not just by his or her immediate family, but by the entire community as well.

When the larger social systems in which we live are open to change, we are less likely to be drawn back into old destructive patterns. The tendency to be drawn back into pathological dynamics has been recognized by systems-based theorists as a serious drawback of individual psychotherapy. In systems-based therapies, therefore, the individual is viewed as a part of a family system and social milieu, and the psychology of the individual cannot be understood outside this largest context.

If communities of all types could find ways to translate these processes of repentance into practices that emotionally and spiritually engage their members, enormous healing potential might be tapped. For example, though we might not agree with Louis Farakkhan's aims or message, we can see that he recognized this potential in designing the Million Man March as a day of "atonement." Farrakhan struck a deep chord for many African American men because he acknowledged the human need for rituals of healing and atonement as well as the need to feel a sense of belonging to community. People find it difficult to move on and change when the pain and mistakes of the past hold them hostage. Rites of atonement enable people to move beyond the past that has held them hostage; people are thus able to mourn the past, forgive themselves and others, and create a better future.

With a deeper understanding of the therapeutic and healing potential of Jewish rites of repentance, psychotherapists and community leaders can create viable new rituals of healing and repentance for individuals and for groups. Though we may have lost access to the actual practice of these ancient rituals, we can still tap into their wisdom and use their powerful symbolism to guide us on the healing journey.

As we begin to see the limitations of the "age of individualism," we see the relevance of ancient religious wisdom that is rooted in a communal perspective and directed toward creating communities of meaning. Individual psychotherapy may play an important role in healing, but it cannot replace the importance of community in people's lives. By emphasizing that atonement and healing are achieved in the context of one's connection to community, Jewish rites of repentance offer a model of healing that transcends the narrow scope of psychotherapy. And by viewing healing as a community affair, these rites validate the importance of people's social networks in their emotional and spiritual well-being.

While psychotherapy may help the individual heal from the damaging effects of living in a world in which oppression has left its mark, *tikkun olam*—the repairing of the world, of which individual teshuvah is just a part—aims at ending that oppression at all levels of society, beginning with the individual and culminating in each and every institution of society. Ultimately, it is the communal effort at repentance that brings the promise of redemption—the possibility that the imperfect and broken world we live in will someday be transformed.

Notes

1. For a more extensive discussion of collective repentance, see Abraham Isaac Kook, *The Lights of Penitence*, trans. by Ben Zion Bokser (New York: Paulist Press, 1978).

2. One such reference is in the Talmud: "Great is repentance, for on account of an individual who repents, the sins of all the world are forgiven" (Talmud Yoma 86b).

3. For a fuller discussion of this notion, see Rabbi Adin Steinzaltz, "Chassidism and Psychoanalysis," in *The Strife of the Spirit*, ed. Arthur Kurtzweil (NJ: Jason Aronson, 1988), 182-91.

4. Steinzaltz, "Chassidism and Psychoanalysis," 98-109.

5. For an in-depth study of the ways in which Freud may have unconsciously drawn on a variety of concepts from the Jewish mystical tradition in his early psychoanalytic formulations, see David Bakan, *Sigmund Freud and the Jewish Mystical Tradition* (Princeton, NJ: Van Nostrand, 1958).

6. Moses Maimonides, "The Laws of Repentance," in *The Book of Knowledge* from the *Mishneh Torah* (Jerusalem: Mossad ha'Rav Kook Publishers, 1976).

7. Pinchas H. Peli, *Soloveitchik on Repentance: The Thought and Oral Discourses of Rabbi Joseph B. Soloveitchik* (New York: Paulist Press, 1984), 95.

8. Peli, *Soloveitchik on Repentance*, 95.

9. For an in-depth discussion of the role of mourning in psychotherapy, see Peter Shabad, "Repetition and Incomplete Mourning: The Intergenerational Trans-

mission of Traumatic Themes," *Psychoanalytic Psychology*, 10,1 (1993), 61-75.

10. In psychoanalytically oriented psychotherapies, the client's feelings toward the therapist are viewed as the means to access feelings that originate in the client's past. Working with these "transferred" feelings in the here-and-now encounter between the therapist and patient provides an opportunity to heal unresolved dynamics from the client's past.

11. For a discussion of the role of morality in psychotherapy, see William Doherty "Bridging Psychotherapy and Moral Responsibility," *The Responsive Community* 5, 1 (Winter 1994/95) and Robert Bellah et al, *Habits of the Heart: Individualism and Commitment in American Life* (Berkeley: University of California Press, 1985).

12. See Otto Kernberg, *Severe Personality Disorders: Psychotherapeutic Strategies* (New Haven and London: Yale University Press, 1984).

13. All quotes from *Tzidkat Ha'tzaddik* are based on my as yet unpublished translations from the original Hebrew text: Reb Tzaddok Ha'cohen of Lublin, *Tzidkat Ha'tzaddik* (Jerusalem: "A" Publishers, 1968).

14. To protect the privacy of my patients and to maintain professional confidentiality, I have changed their names and identifying personal characteristics.

15. See Rabbi Joseph Soloveitchik, *The Halakhic Mind: An Essay on Jewish Tradition and Modern Thought* (New York: Seth Press, 1986).

16. Because of these stories, some leaders of his generation considered David to be a *mamzer*—the illegitimate son of Jesse.

17. The Hebrew word for reptiles used here, *sheratzim*, implies untouchability. In ancient times, one who had physical contact with *sheratzim* required subsequent purification.

18. In Genesis 49:10, Jacob blesses Judah with the symbolic staff of eternal leadership.

19. Genesis 38:26.

20. For a discussion of the therapeutic use of ritual, see Estelle Frankel, "Creative Ritual: Adapting Rites of Passage to Psychotherapy for Times of Major Life Transition," (master's thesis, California State University, 1982).

21. See Nachmanides' commentary in Leviticus 16.

22. Kook, *The Lights of Penitence*, chapter 12, 5.

23. The expression, "Every Israelite is responsible for (connected with) every other Israelite" is found in numerous sources, including: Talmud Shavuot 39; Talmud Sota 37; Talmud Rosh Hashana 29.

Chapter Five

Racial Reconciliation: Can Religion Work Where Politics Has Failed?

Patrick Glynn

The first signs of a thaw in our long decade of discontent about race in America came in June 1997 with President Clinton's announcement of a new White House initiative on racial reconciliation. With the bitter memories of the Rodney King incident, the 1992 Los Angeles riots, and the O. J. Simpson verdict finally beginning to fade, the president evidently gauged the nation ready to revisit the subject of race in a calmer vein. The new initiative was modest by any measure. The president offered a few edifying words on the need for racial harmony, called for a year-long national "conversation on race," and pledged to establish an advisory board to study and encourage the grassroots efforts on racial reconciliation that are already under way. It is emblematic of the diminished role of the federal government in setting the national agenda that Mr. Clinton would not, or could not, contemplate doing more.

But in truth, the real action on race relations in the 1990s has been unfolding at the grassroots level. The most important development has been the emergence of a major racial reconciliation movement among white and black Evangelical Christians. From rather modest beginnings in the early 1990s, the movement is rapidly growing into a national force. Several Evangelical organizations, including the Southern Baptist Convention and the National Association of Evangelicals, have launched fresh initiatives on race during the decade. But the backbone of the new reconciliation effort is the Promise Keepers organization—American Evangelism's new fast-expanding, all-male crusade—which has made racial reconciliation a major theme of its revival. Founded in 1990 by former University of Colorado football coach Bill McCartney and targeted at Protestant men, the movement has by now drawn well over two million to its revival rallies—typically held in major sports stadiums around the country.[1] The organization staged its own "million-man march" on Washington in October 1997, with racial reconciliation as a prominent theme.

Religiously based and largely confined to the Protestant community, the Evangelical racial reconciliation effort has so far played to a somewhat limited constituency. But its influence on national life is growing. Moreover, in both its theory and practice, the movement is pointing the way toward some fundamentally new, and potentially promising, approaches to the challenge of achieving racial harmony. In particular, the religiously oriented tactics of the Evangelicals often show a capacity for transcending many of the problems that have typically sabotaged our national political conversation on race in recent years.

The Capacity for Collective Apology

Few controversies could have better exemplified the awkwardness of our current national dialogue on race—or the need for a fresh reconciliation discussion—than the brief but heated quarrel over Congressman Tony Hall's proposal for a national "apology" to black Americans for slavery. The controversy exploded when the president, following his June speech, indicated he might support the idea. Hall's well-meaning suggestion managed to draw angry criticism from both white and black commentators and add steadily to the national sense of racial irritation before falling by the political wayside two months after it was introduced.

What was wrong with the idea of an apology? Even many who lashed out at the proposal acknowledged that slavery was a terrible evil with disastrous consequences persisting to our own day. The question was, Who should apologize to whom? The original perpetrators and victims, it was pointed out, were long dead. Moreover, the majority of America's contemporary white population could hardly be reckoned as descendants of slaveholders. As columnist Richard Cohen wrote,

> Why should I, as some in Congress propose, apologize for slavery? After all, during that era my ancestors were all in Europe, living with very few civil rights themselves. The ones who remained all perished in the Holocaust, and the ones who emigrated to America all arrived poor and went to work in sweatshops.[2]

A number of African American commentators, including Jesse Jackson, took the position that the apology was essentially a "meaningless gesture," at least in the absence of more serious efforts at restitution to blacks for the harmful effects suffered as a result of slavery and discrimination.[3] Yet opinion polls registered a troubling—though by now familiar—racial split on the issue: while roughly two-thirds of white respondents opposed the apology, two-thirds of blacks said they favored it.

It is precisely such nettlesome issues—collective and historical guilt, restitution—and the often confused emotions accompanying them that complicate reconciliation efforts, whether one is talking about whites and blacks in the United States, Catholics and Protestants in Northern Ireland, or Serbs, Croats, and Muslims in the former

Yugoslavia. How does one cope with major injustices of lasting impact whose perpetrators are long gone? At what point does one declare an amnesty on old grievances? Which is the more important focus for reconciliation efforts—historical grievances or present wrongs?

Typically, in such situations, each group has fallen into the habit of viewing the other as collectively responsible for the wrongdoing of its members. But, reasonably enough, no individual is willing to assume responsibility for the sins of his or her entire ethnic group or race, dating back to who-knows-when. All this tends to pose almost insuperable problems for politicians seeking to encourage calm discussion and rational resolution of such disputes—whether in an international or a domestic setting.

Yet many problems that seem insurmountable in a political context diminish greatly when one shifts to a religious, or perhaps we should say a spiritual, venue. Evangelical religious leaders have had much better luck with the apology approach than have the politicians. In 1995, the Southern Baptist Convention was widely praised for its resolution apologizing for past support of slavery and racism.[4] The Southern Baptists were not alone. In the same year, the president of the National Association of Evangelicals publicly confessed and repented of past racism by white Evangelicals in an emotional meeting between white and African American Evangelicals that culminated with a laying on of hands by black ministers and a breaking-of-bread ceremony.[5] A few months earlier, white and black Pentecostals engaged in mutual reconciliation at a meeting that evoked powerful emotions and climaxed in a foot-washing ritual.[6] In February 1996, the Promise Keepers organization sponsored a major gathering in Atlanta's Georgia Dome of more than 39,000 male pastors of diverse racial, ethnic, and denominational backgrounds, under the theme "Breaking Down the Walls." At the end of the rally, wrote *Christianity Today*, "Pentecostals and Baptists prayed together; Anglos and men of color embraced. Suspicions had given way to respect, even love, for fellow believers with different beliefs."[7]

No one would claim that such gestures or ritual moments constitute an instant cure for the problem of racial tension, even within the Evangelical community itself. (Evangelical activists themselves continually stress the need to translate such momentary sentiments into concrete, day-to-day action.) Nonetheless, there has been a greater willingness among observers, including many African Americans, to accept such acts of repentance as sincere—and a greater capacity of such religious gestures to evoke genuine emotion and a sense of hope and change. This may be in part because apologies on the part of church organizations involve a damaging admission of guilt: For a church to own up to serious sin is a humbling gesture indeed. (This may be one reason Pope John Paul II has generally earned high marks with commentators for his numerous recent apologies, whether for past Church support of slavery and racism, for the injustices done to Galileo, or—most recently—for the sixteenth-century massacre of Protestants by Catholics in France. There was a time when it was thought that being the pope meant never having to say you're sorry.)

But there is also a general recognition that the religious or spiritual motivation is by nature fundamentally different from, and usually purer than, the political one. "It is one thing for the Southern Baptists to repent for their racism, as they did in 1995; repentance is part of their religion. Congress will inevitably find it quite awkward," wrote Deborah Sontag in the *New York Times*.[8]

All this raises a further question. While reconciliation—and domestic peace between factions—seems a political necessity, is political action alone sufficient to achieve it? Political leaders who have engaged in the politics of reconciliation—from Nelson Mandela to Mikhail Gorbachev—often made implicit appeals to religious values. The Evangelical movement makes this appeal explicit. In effect, the Evangelical activists accept as their working premise that "only a miracle" will bring true reconciliation between the races, and they then proceed to try to bring this miracle about—an unusual approach that may help explain their comparative success to date.

Religious Versus Secular Approaches

The activities of the reconcilers take various forms. The public apologies have constituted only a small part of the movement's efforts, albeit the most widely publicized one. At the core of the movement is a small group of grassroots activists who have actually been involved in building and sustaining experimental interracial congregations in inner-city areas—in some cases going back as far as the 1970s.

The 1992 Los Angeles riots provoked soul-searching about race relations in the nation in general and in the Evangelical community in particular. Partly in response to heightened concern about the lack of racial harmony in the country, each of two black-white interracial ministry teams—Spencer Perkins and Chris Rice from Jackson, Mississippi, and Raleigh Washington and Glen Kehrein from Chicago—published books describing their experiences.[9] Tragically, Perkins died in 1998 at the age of forty-three. Very similar in theme, the books exhorted fellow Evangelicals to pursue better relations with believers of different races and outlined theories and techniques to guide the reconciliation process. The books received wide notice in the Evangelical press, and articles on race-related issues multiplied in *Christianity Today* and other Evangelical publications.[10] It was probably this newly race-sensitized climate—marked by a certain measure of guilt among Evangelicals for having neglected the race issue—that prompted the public apologies from the Southern Baptists, Evangelicals, and Pentecostals in the mid-1990s.

At around the same time, McCartney's Promise Keepers movement was picking up steam. A veteran of one of the nation's most integrated venues—the locker room—McCartney was already committed to the racial reconciliation idea. He had already included a promise to overcome racial and denominational differences in the "seven promises" that members of Promise Keepers make. He actively embraced the themes of the new Evangelical reconciliation literature of the early 1990s, folding ever more reconciliation-related content into the Promise Keepers' increasingly well-attended rallies.[11] Eventually, he hired Washington—a black former Army colonel turned Evangelical minister and reconciliation activist—as Vice President for Reconciliation, and invested considerable sums in building a staff to work on disseminating the reconciliation message through local church communities.

Three features distinguish the Evangelicals' approach to racial reconciliation from secular-based approaches such as conflict-resolution theory or multiculturalism: (1) an explicitly religious or spiritual motivation; (2) a sense of sin; and (3) a belief in the efficacy of ritual and in the reality of divine intervention in human relationships and human affairs. All three factors give the Evangelicals certain advantages vis-à-vis more conventional secular approaches.

Religious Motivation

Evangelicals understand the biblical prescription for human relationships as going well beyond such secular criteria as reasonableness, fairness, or even justice. Gospel values, they repeatedly emphasize, are different from—and more demanding than—those of the secular world. *"Civil rights* is a political concept," explained Perkins and Rice; "the *brotherhood* spoken of by biblical and contemporary prophets is a much higher calling."[12] Evangelical reconciliation activists speak frequently of having a special mission or "calling" to pursue racial healing, which they argue is shared to different degrees by all Christians.

This means that reconciliation activists can insist on a higher standard of conduct than the political realm normally demands of us. The criterion is no longer simply "justice," but rather "love your neighbor as yourself" and "bless those who persecute you." Equally important, in the context of the religious setting, the emphasis is no longer on the justice one gets, but rather on the mercy one gives. The reconciliation activists emphasize the obligation of the Christian to leave his or her "comfort zone," in the words of Washington and Kehrein, and go out of the way to encounter and be kind to the person of a different skin color.[13]

The reconciliation activists argue that such a shift in perspective from the political to the spiritual is essential if aggrieved races and other groups are to achieve a "more perfect union." Political dialogue, premised on mere justice or rights and responsibilities, is insufficient, they argue, as experience has shown. Indeed, they explicitly contrast their premises with those of the secular-based politics and social engineering of the Great Society era.

It is precisely the failure of the secularly oriented Great Society, a number of them argue, that points to the need for a new, explicitly religious or faith-based approach to racial divisions. "The humanistic optimism of 1965 is totally discredited," writes white Evangelical reconciler John Dawson. "The politician, educator, and scientists have failed," leaving the task to the Church.[14] "Someone forgot to tell us along the way that you can't legislate people's attitudes," claimed Perkins and Rice.[15] "Changing laws will not change hearts. The civil rights movement has run its course, and we've gotten just about all you can expect to get from a political movement." And according to Washington and Kehrein, "The L.A. riots are a reminder of how integration efforts have not brought an end to the prejudice in people's hearts. Neither Congress nor the president can apply a remedy to cure our country's ills. . . . We . . . say that Christ is the answer."[16]

Evangelicals say that in the absence of the spiritual imperative, it is simply impossible to find the motivation necessary to endure the difficulties of the reconciliation process. Wrote Perkins, an African American and son of perhaps the most famous black Evangelical, John Perkins: "To be honest, if I were a white non-Christian, I don't know if I'd have any motivation to care. But I am a Christian, and claiming that distinction carries responsibilities."[17] By the same token, like many Evangelicals, Perkins saw the reconciliation effort as a means to vindicate Christianity in the eyes of secular society. Christianity can demonstrate its validity by succeeding where secular techniques have failed.

> Together we are changing the way we do Christianity, making it visibly distinguishable from the world by our ability to embrace brothers and sisters from diverse racial and ethnic backgrounds. As our world becomes more multicultural, this unique trait will become even more crucial to our witness, providing credibility for a gospel competing among the many voices in the new global village.[18]

Sense of Sin

Secular thinkers have long looked askance at the powerful sense of sin that pervades the Calvinist worldview of the Evangelical Christian. But whatever its possible drawbacks, the Evangelical's strong sense of human sinfulness—matched with a belief in the possibility of divine forgiveness—tends to facilitate the reconciliation dialogue.

In a certain sense, it is precisely the problem of sin that tends to limit the effectiveness of the major alternatives to religious-based reconciliation techniques—conflict-resolution theory and the multiculturalist paradigm. In its emphasis on the need to find common ground, conflict-resolution theory tends to insist that parties to a dispute overlook grievances and avoid the issue of blame. That is perhaps one reason why conflict-resolution techniques often break down if wounds are deeply felt and the conflict is highly emotional in nature. Multiculturalism, on the other hand, is far more attuned to the historical and emotional dimensions of conflict; it is also focused on the issue of blame. But it tends to perpetuate the cycle of grievance by transforming oppressor into victim and vice versa. It also assesses blame on a collective basis, which is itself a form of injustice.

Yet if one is in the habit of admitting that one is a sinner and acknowledging the general sinfulness of the human race, it is in a sense easier to confess one's sins and admit wrongdoing publicly. There is always shame in wrongdoing, but less so if one is part of a community that acknowledges that wrongdoing is not an exceptional phenomenon in human life and that confessing wrongdoing is the necessary prelude to receiving divine forgiveness.

The acknowledgment of common guilt even makes possible what Evangelical reconciler John Dawson calls "identificational repentance." It is possible and also not inappropriate, Dawson argues, to express regret for the wrongs that have been perpetrated by the collectivities to which one belongs—one's nation, one's city, one's race, one's tribe. Citing a number of biblical precedents for such gestures, Dawson writes:

> Repentance, reconciliation, and healing could take place if Christians from the black and white community joined together in identification with the sins and griefs of our forbears. . . . The new resident of the city might think, "That's not my problem. I just moved here last year." However, when God puts you in a city you become part of the Church there and you inherit its legacy, good and bad. The unfinished business of the Church is now your responsibility, too.[19]

Behind all this lies a simple psychological truth: imputing blame normally aggravates conflict, while accepting blame tends to defuse it. By putting the onus on the believer to acknowledge and confess his or her own sin, the Evangelical reconcilers create a psychological setting more conducive to mutual support than mutual recrimination.

Ritual and Divine Action

Yet the whole process depends in the final analysis on the belief in God's ability to provide healing and forgiveness where it would be impossible to arrive at such a resolution through human means alone. Whether or not one shares the theological beliefs of the Evangelicals who engage in reconciliation efforts and ceremonies, one can easily see how the mere belief in the possibility of divine forgiveness—and in divine aid at arriving at reconciliation—could provide a strong psychological impetus for positive group interaction, as well as a sanction for the release of powerful emotions. Faith provides a sense of safety that permits people to express and release strong emotions constructively, and in a way that they may not be inclined to do in ordinary social settings, even or especially political ones.

Transforming Individuals

Of course in many ways the toughest question—and certainly the one that most nags at the reconciliation activists themselves—concerns how speeches, prayers, and ritual acts of forgiveness aimed at racial reconciliation translate into change in people's day-to-day lives. Promise Keepers is investing considerable effort in spurring ongoing reconciliation activities at the local church level. Moreover, Promise Keepers materials encourage members to go out of their way to engage with those of different races and ethnic groups for purposes of advancing reconciliation. There are already a number of reports of successful local efforts under way—organizations in which men of different races have come together for purposes of promoting reconciliation in their communities. But only time will tell how extensive or how lasting the effects of this movement will be.

Politics strives to transform people by altering the structure of society; religion strives to change society by transforming individuals. In this respect, the racial reconciliation movement of the 1990s differs importantly from the racial equality movements of the past. In those earlier movements the main goal of religious activists—Evangelical William Wilberforce, who led England's antislavery movement; the Quakers of American Abolitionism; or Dr. Martin Luther King, Jr.—was to spur politicians to action. But in postmodern societies, where the greatest challenges we face are increasingly less purely political in nature than behavioral and attitudinal, or even moral and spiritual—social change can be expected to come increasingly from grassroots community and religious activists like the Evangelical reconcilers, who strive to change the nature of society one community, and one soul, at a time.

Notes

1. Information on the Promise Keepers organization is available at *www.promisekeepers.org*.

2. Richard Cohen, "The Trouble with Apologizing for Slavery," *Washington Post*, 19 June 1997, A21.

3. Quoted in Paul Leavitt and Robert Silvers, "Poll: Congress Shouldn't Make Apology for Slavery," *USA Today*, 2 July 1997, 5A.

4. Joe Maxwell, "Black Southern Baptists: The SBC's Valiant Efforts to Overcome Its Racist Past," *Christianity Today*, 15 May 1995, 26-31.

5. "First Stride in a Long Walk," *Christianity Today*, 12 December 1994, 58.

6. "Pentecostals Renounce Racism," *Christianity Today*, 12 December 1994, 58.

7. "Clergy Conference Stirs Historic Show of Unity," *Christianity Today*, 8 April 1996, 88.

8. Deborah Sontag, "Too Busy Apologizing to Be Sorry," *New York Times*, 29 June 1997, Section 4, 3.

9. Spencer Perkins and Chris Rice, *More Than Equals: Racial Healing for the Sake of the Gospel*, (Downer's Grove, IL: InterVarsity Press, 1993); Raleigh Washington and Glen Kehrein, *Breaking Down Walls: A Model for Reconciliation in an Age of Racial Strife*, (Chicago: Moody Press, 1993).

10. See, for example, Andres Tapia, "The Myth of Racial Progress," *Christianity*

Today, 4 October 1993; "'Deeper Than a Handshake,'" *Christianity Today*, 12 December 1994; "Racial Reconciliation Tops NAE's Agenda," *Christianity Today*, 3 April 1995.

11. "McCartney Preaches Reconciliation," *Christianity Today*, 16 June 1995; Edward Gilbreath, "Manhood's Great Awakening," *Christianity Today*, 6 February 1995.

12. Perkins and Rice, *More Than Equals*, 25.

13. Washington and Kehrein, *Breaking Down Walls*.

14. John Dawson, *Healing America's Wounds* (Ventura, CA: Regal Books, 1994), 23.

15. Perkins and Rice, *More Than Equals*, 25.

16. Washington and Kehrein, *Breaking Down Walls*, 23, 12-3.

17. Perkins and Rice, *More Than Equals*, 93.

18. Spencer Perkins, "A Small Digression: Fly Away Home," Race and Reconciliation On-Line, originally available at *www.netdoor.com/com/rronline*.

19. Dawson, *Healing America's Wounds*, 211.

Chapter Six

Repentance in Political Life: Case Studies of American Public Figures

David E. Carney

Some years ago, Amitai Etzioni noted that some public figures violate laws or social mores and do not express remorse, do not offer to mend their ways—in short, do not repent.[1] Etzioni further explained that the public figures often added insult to injury by further offending the laws and mores they violated in the first place, instead of attempting the make society whole. Although there is no agreement in the minimal literature about whether public figures should be held to higher standards than the rest of society because they lead, are role models, and voluntarily chose public life, they certainly are not exempt from the laws and mores that govern all of us, a point not all of them seem quite to have fully accepted.

At issue are not merely laws but also governing moral values, the social mores by which we live. Senator Bob Packwood was not charged with criminal acts arising from allegations of making numerous unwanted sexual advances, yet he ultimately resigned from the Senate because of his sexual indiscretions. Similarly, political strategist Lee Atwater's attack advertisements helped his candidates win elections, yet he felt the need to apologize to his targets when he was diagnosed with an inoperable malignant brain tumor.

This chapter sets out to study in some detail nine public figures to assess Etzioni's observations and to provide the reader with insights into the motives and reactions of public figures who are forced to address their transgressions. The discussion purposely focuses on the descriptive, leaving the analytical and normative to the reader. Three sets of public figures and their reactions to allegations of wrongdoing are discussed. Considered first are two members of the Nixon administration: Charles Colson and G. Gordon Liddy, who transgressed because of their roles in various "dirty tricks." Two sets of men are considered from the Reagan years: Oliver North and Robert McFarlane from the Iran-contra affair; and Michael Deaver and Lyn Nofziger, who had legal problems arising out of alleged violations of lobbying regulations. The final section examines three political figures with a variety of problems: Lee Atwater, Bob Packwood, and Washington, D.C., mayor Marion Barry.

Two methodical observations must be made before proceeding. First, the set chosen is illustrative rather than a sample of some precisely defined universe of public figures out of which those studied are selected by some statistical method. They all are from the last generation and they seem to include a goodly subset of those who got into trouble. Certainly one could have chosen a different list, one that, for instance, would include Senator Gary Hart, Senator Edward Kennedy, and Senator Wilbur Mills. In this sense, it is best to consider those studied as illustrative rather than definitive. Note, though, that a cursory examination suggests that those excluded from this preliminary study conducted themselves no differently from those included.

Second, the "case studies" that follow are very uneven in their scope for the simple reason that the actions of some of those studied were much more extensive and elaborate, whereas the missteps of the others were much less involved. For the same reason, much more information is available on some than on the others. No purpose is served by forcing all the case studies into the same procrustean bed to generate artificial uniformity.

Nixon Administration Officials: One Found Religious Repentance; One, None at All

Charles Colson and G. Gordon Liddy were aides to President Richard Nixon and emerged from the scandals of the period with criminal records. Both were trained lawyers and had reputations as men who would stop at almost nothing in support of Nixon. Yet they have followed very different paths in the intervening years. Colson found Christianity even before his criminal proceedings had run to conclusion. While in prison, Colson began an active ministry. Liddy has been proudly defiant since Watergate and has parlayed his image into a career as a talk-radio host.

Charles Colson

Charles Colson possessed a fierce loyalty to Nixon; he once told the news media that he would walk over his own grandmother to get Nixon reelected. Known as Nixon's "hatchetman" and for being "incapable of humanitarian concerns," Colson was Nixon's special counsel in early 1973, when the president began his second term.[2] Described as an "evil genius," Colson possessed an overbearing persona so feared in Washington that his mere presence set people on edge and generated an almost palpable tension. He was exposed to—and participated in—a considerable number of what he himself has called White House "dirty tricks."[3]

In February 1973, Colson resigned to return to his law practice. It was then that *Newsweek* raised the first suspicions about Colson's involvement in criminal affairs: the magazine reported an accusation that Colson had instigated the Watergate break-in at the Democratic National Committee headquarters eight months earlier. Another report soon followed: In April, the *Washington Post* headline read: "Aides Say Colson Approved Buggings."[4] Although neither of these charges proved to be true—Colson likely was aware of the Watergate plans, yet he was not implicated in the burglary— the reports troubled Colson. The media seemed on the verge of cracking the Watergate mission. Colson chose to plead to obstruction of justice charges to avoid further implication in the Watergate affair.

Colson's plea centered around his role in the smear job targeting Daniel Ellsberg, the former Defense Department analyst who released to the *New York Times* what has become know as the *Pentagon Papers*—the Pentagon's extensive, classified history of American involvement in Vietnam prepared during the Johnson administration.[5]

Determined to prevent future leaks of government secrets, a group known as the "Plumbers" had been put to work by the Nixon White House. Colson had "persuaded the Plumbers to adopt a plan to destroy Ellsberg's 'public image and credibility.'"[6] Colson and his aides sought to share with journalists what they considered incrimi- nating information about Ellsberg, such as evidence that he was linked to left-wing causes, in the hopes that Ellsberg would be discredited, helping to prepare the ground for the conviction of Ellsberg for the leak.

Under Colson's supervision, the office of Ellsberg's psychiatrist, Dr. Lewis J. Fielding, was burglarized in search of documents that could be used to portray Ellsberg as mentally unstable.

Because Ellsberg was on trial at the time for disseminating the *Pentagon Papers*, Colson was charged with obstruction of justice for attempting to discredit Ellsberg and negatively influence the outcome of his trial. Colson pleaded guilty to these charges and as a result was sentenced in 1974 to a seven-month prison term.

Yet just before his plea, a profound transformation took place in the man. Colson underwent a spiritual conversion, which he attributes to the gestures of a Christian friend who read to him a passage from C. S. Lewis's "Mere Christianity" on the topic of pride.[7] Colson replaced his devotion to Nixon with a devotion to Christ.

Colson's new faith proved to be the inception of his repentance. Upon entering Maxwell Prison, he was befriended and ministered to by a country preacher.[8] His time in the penal system was consumed by a deepening embrace of Christianity. "I real- ized that I had been in prison for a purpose," he stated in a 1990 interview, "and believed it was God's call in my life that I devote myself to encouraging a movement of Christian people to go into prisons."[9] He came to believe that, although incarcera- tion might keep criminals out of society temporarily, the system failed to "change a heart" and cultivate strong moral values in offenders.[10]

Colson emerged from confinement in 1975, determined to make a difference in the prison system. This conviction led him to found the Prison Fellowship Ministries. Prison's fellowship's objective is to reform convicts' characters by converting them to Christianity. Under his tutelage, the small organization has grown to include 310 full-time staff members and 40,000 volunteers.[11] Twenty years, over six hundred prisons, and more than thirty countries later, Colson received the Templeton Prize for Progress in Religion.[12] The one-million-dollar award that comes with the prize was awarded to him personally, but he chose to donate it to the Prison Fellowship.[13]

Although Colson himself indicates that he reflects on his own past "with repentance," his statements about how much blame he actually deserves contain a measure of ambiguity.[14] Appearing for his sentencing, Colson exhibited an odd mix of repentance for general misdeeds and nonrepentance for the specific wrongdoings to which he had pleaded guilty. He started off by explaining to Judge Gerhardt Gesell:

> I entered my plea to this offense because I believed it right as a matter of law and right as a matter of conscience.
> Even though I believed myself innocent of the two matters for which I had been indicted, I knew that to spend possibly the next several years as a defendant would accomplish nothing. If I were acquitted, some would feel I had "beaten the rap." If I had been found guilty, others who know me would believe the verdict unjust. But most important, that period in my life would have been spent in self-centered activity with no ultimate value to myself or to society.[15]

Colson told Judge Gesell, "I pray that this plea will help fulfill a larger purpose. I pray it will serve the ultimate ends of justice—both personal justice in that I am accepting responsibility for my crime and social justice in that this plea may have some impact in deterring others with any individual's right to a fair trial."[16] Although Colson argued he had not committed the crimes in question, he explained later in his statement:

> As time went on it weighed heavily on me that while I might not have been guilty of the specific offenses for which I was going to be indicted, I could not regard the sum of my conduct in the White House as guiltless. . . . It came home to me when Your Honor reminded my counsel and others that this is a government of laws and not of men. I should never have needed such a reminder.[17]

Colson told Gesell that remaining a defendant would prevent him from cooperating with the special prosecutor and the House Judiciary Committee. Colson explained:

> The work of these two bodies, the successful and just resolution of the matters under investigation by them, it seemed to be, was far more important than the possibility of my eventual public vindication. I shall be cooperating with the prosecutor, but that is not to say that the prosecutor has bargained for my testimony, that there was any quid pro quo; there was not. I reached my own conclusion that I have a duty to tell everything I know that is relevant to these

important issues, and a major reason for my plea was to free me to do so.[18]

Colson continued, justifying his misdeed while at the White House. He explained that he worked hard and served Nixon in a way that he thought was loyal; however, "[c]ontrary to my view at the time, one who serves in public office is not doing anyone a favor. He or she is privileged to hold that office in public trust. One's loyalty should go beyond the man he serves to the institutions and people that have reposed that trust in him."[19] He said that "self-pride" was an important factor because

> I lost my perspective to a point where I instinctively reacted to any criticism or interference with what I was doing or to what the President was doing as unfair and something to be retaliated against. . . .
> I now realize how easy it is for even strong and well-disciplined men to lose their perspective under pressure. In my case, . . . I only took time to refer to [constitutional law] when it was a necessary source document for preparing arguments over such matters as the nomination of Supreme Court Justices. I never once even remotely thought that my conduct might trespass upon the Constitution or anyone's rights under it.
> I had one rule—to get done that which the President wanted done. And while I thought I was serving him well and faithfully, I now recognize that I was not—at least not in the sense that I never really questioned whether what he wanted done was right or proper. He had a right to expect more from me. I had an obligation to do more for him.[20]

Colson's remorse is not always readily apparent. In response to a later question of whether he felt guilt for his misdeeds, Colson answered, "I still have a hard time about that. On the one hand, it is difficult for me as a Christian not to repent, and not to repent publicly. On the other hand, was what I did really so bad? It was no worse than what goes on in every administration. We just got caught."[21] He also told a journalist, "Winston Churchill said, 'The truth is so precious that it has to be guarded by a squadron of lies.' Often in politics there are cases where that is correct. . . . There are plans which have to be secret if they are to work."[22]

Colson further argued that as a Christian he "could have helped Nixon in some very, very fundamental ways in which [he] did not."[23] He said his advice would have been to tell the truth about Watergate. Colson said of his role during Watergate, "I used to argue with Nixon. I used to take him on. Some of the tapes that have never been published show me really telling him off about Watergate. 'Tell the truth. Get rid of it.' And he didn't like it. He got angry at me."[24] In retrospect, Colson thought that if he had been more firm in his belief in Christ then he would have been more forceful in opposing Nixon rather than struggling over aspiring to do whatever Nixon wanted.

In the final analysis, though Colson appears ambivalent, he has shown considerable remorse. His cooperation with Watergate prosecutors and above all his devotion to his ministry show some commitment to restitution and a strong desire to restructure his life. In effect, Colson comes rather close to a model penitent, recognizing human imperfections. In effect, he stands out compared to the other public figures under study, most sharply when compared with fellow Nixon aide G. Gordon Liddy.

G. Gordon Liddy

G. Gordon Liddy learned to fight in the army, to formulate arguments in law school, and to work the nuts and bolts of Washington in the Justice Department and as Special Assistant to the Secretary of the Treasury for Organized Crime. All these skills were put to the test in 1972 when Liddy was assigned to the Committee to Re-Elect the President (CRP). Nixon created this body to have full control over his own reelection campaign, taking it out of the hands of the Republican National Committee.

Although CRP was involved mainly in campaigning for Nixon, it also engaged in espionage efforts against the Democratic Party, anti-Vietnam War protesters, and others among Nixon's adversaries. When appointed to CRP, Liddy was placed in full control of conducting "dirty tricks" as head of the "covert operations unit."[25] Liddy warmed to the task, planning a number of espionage initiatives he entitled "Operation Gemstone." The clandestine actions Liddy planned for the operation included:

> CRYSTAL, an electronic surveillance to be directed at the Democratic convention from a houseboat; SAPPHIRE, a spying caper relying on prostitutes working out of a lush houseboat bedroom wired for sound; and TURQUOISE, a disruption scheme relying on what Liddy called "a commando team of Cubans" to sabotage all of the [Democratic] convention hall's air-conditioning units.[26]

Other plans included kidnapping leaders of expected demonstrations outside the Republican National Convention and photographing documents contained in the Democratic National Committee's files.[27] Funding to conduct all these operations could not be fully procured; however, Liddy still received a $250,000 budget, earmarked for "two prostitutes, four spies in the Democratic camps and a series of surreptitious break-ins."[28] One history-making operation took place on May 26, 1972, when Liddy's team moved into the Watergate to place electronic surveillance devices in the Democratic National Committee's headquarters and the offices of Democratic politicians. By May 28, the team had entered the office of the Democratic headquarters, photographed documents, and planted bugs. On June 17 of the same year, the burglars returned to replace a faulty listening device in the office of Larry O'Brien, the head of the Democratic National Committee. The June 17 break-in was discovered by Watergate security, and Liddy's agents were arrested. Shortly after, Liddy began a massive cover-up, which involved the destruction of numerous documents. He admitted nothing when finally charged and before he was sent to prison in 1973 to serve a twenty-year sentence.

On the day that James McCord presented a letter to sentencing judge John Sirica containing what were at the time explosive revelations that the Watergate cover-up reached higher into the Nixon White House than was publicly realized, Liddy twice told Judge Sirica that he had "nothing to say" to the court before his sentencing.[29] Liddy later took the Fifth Amendment twenty times before a Watergate jury and refused to answer even when presented with immunity against further prosecution.[30]

Liddy continued to maintain complete public silence until the publication of a letter to his wife in *Harper's* in October 1974. The letter, published under the title "Gordon Liddy: A Patriot Speaks," ran roughly seven pages but did not once mention Watergate.[31] Instead, Liddy provided a dissertation on the American people's "passion for euphemism" and inability to deal with truth, the way "advocacy journalism seeks to shape events rather than to report on them," the "exaltation of [the] young" despite their lack of experience and wisdom, and the shortcomings of education and the need for Americans to develop their competitive spirit in order to thrive in a world where only the strongest survive.[32]

Liddy appeared on the television news program *60 Minutes* in January 1975. He proclaimed Watergate "basic politics," made disparaging remarks about the "stool pigeons" who served in the Nixon administration and later furnished evidence against it, and claimed not to take offense at Nixon's characterization of him as "a little bit nuts."[33] Liddy said, "Power exists to be used," and stated:

> [I]f Watergate is at [sic] it's alleged to be, it was an intelligence-gathering operation of one group of persons who were seeking power, or to retain power, against another who were seeking to acquire power. That's all it was.[34]

On April 12, 1977, President Carter reduced Liddy's sentence from twenty years to eight, rendering him eligible for parole in September of that year. He had served fifty-two months. Liddy's next mission was to host a radio show, where his lack of remorse over the Watergate affair would be an almost weekly topic of discussion. When asked if he had any regrets regarding his involvement in the botched burglary, his standard response was: "I only regret that it failed."[35]

Later, Liddy used his talk-radio show to severely disparage the institutions for which he once worked: the presidency, the White House, and federal law enforcement agencies. Though Liddy is a convicted felon and is therefore prohibited from owning or using a gun, he reported on his show that he used drawings of Bill and Hillary Clinton for target practice.[36] "I thought it might improve my aim," he reasoned.[37] Liddy also has repeatedly suggested that his listeners would do best, when confronted by hostile Bureau of Alcohol, Tobacco, and Firearms agents, to shoot them in the head because they wear protective vests. Liddy later clarified that he was talking only about self-defense. He continued, however, to declare that many listeners would not be skilled enough to hit someone's head, so they should shoot twice to the torso. If the shooter still comes up short, Liddy suggested a groin shot.[38]

It seems safe to conclude that Liddy neither showed remorse nor restructured his life. He is as belligerent as he was decades ago and seems to believe he was sentenced to twenty years in prison for what were actually loyal acts of a White House staffer—politics as usual. He is blameless and the blame lies with those who prosecuted him.

Reagan Administration Officials: One Set Proud of Misdeeds; One, Ambivalent

Two sets of men from the Reagan era are considered in this study. Oliver North and Robert McFarlane both were involved in what became known as the Iran-contra affair. The affair grew out of the Reagan administration's efforts to supply arms to parties in Iran considered moderates with the expectation that these Iranians would influence Muslims in Lebanon to release American hostages. The proceeds of these arms sales were used surreptitiously to support the anti-Sandinista contras, rebels in Nicaragua, despite congressional prohibitions on contra aid. It would soon be revealed that Lieutenant Colonel Oliver North was a crucial part of the operations. In the years that passed since these events, North has proudly portrayed himself as a defender of freedom who tried to fight Communism (in Nicaragua) and win the release of American hostages in Lebanon. McFarlane has been more critical of himself and his role in the Iran-contra affair.

Two more Reagan aides who ran into legal difficulties were Lyn Nofziger and Michael Deaver, both of whom encountered problems with lobbying laws, after they left public service. Nofziger was convicted of violating these laws, although his conviction was later overturned. Deaver was convicted of perjury for his responses to inquiries concerning lobbying activity. Nofziger remained defiant; Deaver claimed that abuse of alcohol caused his inaccurate memory.

Oliver North

In Nicaragua in the summer of 1979, the government of longtime American ally Anastasio Somoza Debayle was driven out of office and replaced by a junta dominated by the Cuban-backed Sandinistas. The Sandinistas were avowed Communists and gradually tightened their control over Nicaragua, despite the efforts of the Carter administration to moderate the Sandinistas' revolutionary tendencies. As part of his program, Carter secured passage of an aid package to Nicaragua that Congress passed subject to certification that the new government was not supporting terrorism.[39] Carter also "signed a top secret finding authorizing the CIA to provide political support to opponents of the Sandinistas" through a "standard political-action program to boost the democratic alternative to the Sandinistas—to develop alternatives to parties and people thought to be close to the Soviet Union and its line."[40]

While Carter sought to work diplomatically with the Sandinistas, Reagan ran in 1980 on a platform that "deplore[d] the Marxist Sandinista takeover of Nicaragua and the Marxist attempts to destabilize El Salvador, Guatemala and Honduras," opposed "assistance to any Marxist government in this hemisphere," specifically mentioning Nicaragua, and promised "we will support the Nicaraguan people to establish a free and independent government."[41] Despite the campaign rhetoric, the Reagan administration moved slowly before settling on a confrontational policy in dealing with Nicaragua. The new administration continued and expanded certain covert measures begun under Carter and terminated Carter's aid program while pursuing negotiations with the Sandinistas from August through October 1981. Finally, beginning in December, the United States began financial and technical support of a paramilitary group of anti-Sandinista rebels known as the contras.[42]

Despite these efforts, the contras neither garnered extensive popular support nor performed well militarily. Reagan wanted to continue the aid effort, but Congress took action to curtail the operation and eventually end it out of concern that the involvement might escalate into "another Vietnam."[43] Between September 27, 1982 and October 17, 1986, Congress passed a series of amendments to appropriations bills collectively referred to as the Boland Amendments. These initially limited the funding that U.S. government agencies could provide to the contra rebels in Nicaragua and eventually cut off all aid.[44] According to the 1984 Boland Amendment, no funds appropriated by Congress for the Central Intelligence Agency, "or any other department, agency, or entity of the United States involved in intelligence activities" could be "obligated or expended for the purpose or which would have the effect of supporting . . . military or paramilitary operations in Nicaragua" by any nation or group.[45]

Early in the summer of 1985, several news articles surfaced that linked National Security Council member Lieutenant Colonel Oliver North to efforts to help raise funds for the contras and to give them tactical military advice, in violation of the Boland Amendments. These news reports prompted the House Intelligence Committee to write the White House in August 1985, asking specific questions about North's relationship to the contras.[46] The memoranda, written by Representatives Michael Barnes and Lee Hamilton, requested all information and documents "pertaining to any contact between Lt. Col. North and Nicaraguan rebel leaders as of enactment of the Boland Amendment in October, 1984."[47] North replied to the inquiry with three letters to Congress, indicating that he was "involved neither in fundraising for, nor in providing military advice to, the Nicaraguan Contras."[48] When Congress made a second inquiry into North's activities, North met with his superior, national security adviser Robert McFarlane, to plan an appropriate response. Subsequently, McFarlane met personally with more than a dozen congressmen and their aides in an attempt to deflect mounting suspicions.[49] McFarlane assured the members of Congress with whom he met that "there was no intent to circumvent restrictions Congress placed on aid to the Nicaraguan Resistance."[50] North, he emphasized, was trustworthy and had never been involved in any illicit fundraising activities: "I can't believe everything everyone says, but I do believe Ollie."[51]

The clandestine U.S. military efforts in Nicaragua were exposed in the fall of 1986. On October 5, 1986, Sandinista forces in Nicaragua shot down a cargo plane and captured Eugene Hasenfus, a former U.S. Marine cargo handler. It was later discovered that Hasenfus had been hired to fly secret arms supplies to the contras.[52] The next month, a Beirut magazine, *Al-Shiraa*, reported that the Reagan administration had surreptitiously "given weapons to Iran in hope of winning freedom for Americans held by Iranian allies in Lebanon."[53] Considering that the U.S. government had repeatedly pledged not to deal with terrorists, this was an embarrassing revelation.

On August 6, 1986, North testified before the House Select Committee on Intelligence that he did "not in any way . . . [or] at any time violate the principles or legal requirements of the Boland Amendment."[54] Yet later that same day, North handled a crisis involving the unauthorized use of a C-123 cargo plane by Felix Rodriguez, who managed the contra resupply effort for North.[55] He also had a phone conversation with Assistant Secretary of State Elliott Abrams about a solicitation of funds for the contras that Abrams was to make to the Sultan of Brunei.[56]

On November 21, 1986, both the Senate and House Intelligence Committees held hearings to investigate the brewing controversy. The allegations included charges of selling Hawk missiles and antitank weapons, as well as the shredding of relevant documents at the White House. In preparation for these trials, North contributed to a false chronology of Iran-related events and began destroying records of the secret mission; although he denied using the term "shredding party," he "recalled telling McFarlane that all key documents had . . . been destroyed."[57] On November 23, North announced to then-Attorney General Edwin Meese that neither the National Security Council nor the Central Intelligence Agency was involved in the much talked-about scandal:

> [Attorney General Meese] directed North's attention to the section of the memorandum describing how the "residuals" [profits left over from the arms sales to Iran] would go to the Nicaraguan Resistance. North appeared to be "visibly surprised". . . North said the CIA did not handle the "residuals" and, though some in the CIA may have suspected a diversion, he did not think anyone at the CIA knew. If North's testimony at the public hearings was truthful, then these statements, too, were lies.[58]

North went on to claim that it was the Israelis who determined what was sent to the rebels, referring to a suggestion by the Israeli government that supposedly initiated the sale of arms to Iran.[59] The United States, he alleged, was merely replenishing the Israeli supplies after the sales were made. The following excerpt from the Congressional Iran-contra hearings in 1987 refers to a Presidential Finding written for the Reagan administration by North:

> Mr. Nields: At the bottom of the first page, it says, "Since the Israeli sales are

technically a violation of our Arms Export Control Act embargo for Iran, a Presidential Covert Action Finding is required in order for us to allow the Israeli sales to proceed and for our subsequent replenishment sales."
Mr. North: Correct.
Mr. Nields: So, the earlier Finding contemplated sales by the Israelis and replenishments by the United States?
Mr. North: Correct.[60]

During the congressional inquiry, North "destroyed documents . . . [and] also altered documents relating to the National Security Council staff's Contra support operation."[61] North also arranged for his secretary, Fawn Hall, to transport documents out of the office by hiding them in her underclothes.[62] In the subsequent congressional hearings, Hall testified that "never before had there been such an organized program of document destruction or such a large volume of documents destroyed."[63]

The scandal finally came to a head in the spring of 1989. North faced sixteen charges, including lying to Congress, destroying official documents, conspiring to defraud the IRS by raising tax-exempt donations to arm the resistance movement, and misusing funds for the rebels. The prosecution threatened conspiracy charges. Far from confessing and taking his lumps, North's defense threatened to subpoena President Reagan and Vice President Bush and use highly classified information to show that North's activities were "widely known and approved at the highest levels of government."[64] North stated that he was "led to believe . . . that the Pres[ident] had authorized what [he] was doing."[65]

The potential negative ramifications of exploring this line of inquiry seem to have been too threatening for independent prosecutor Lawrence Walsh.[66] He dismissed the most serious criminal charges against North and reduced the number of charges from sixteen to twelve, citing the need to protect the confidentiality of secret government documents.

North was convicted in May 1989 of only three of the twelve charges. He did plead guilty to the charges of lying to Congress and was sentenced to two years probation. His convictions involved: (1) aiding and abetting an effort to obstruct a congressional inquiry (the false chronology in November 1986), (2) destroying and falsifying National Security Council documents, and (3) accepting an illegal gratuity (he allowed a private contractor to build a security fence around his house).

Despite these convictions, and the fact that he admitted committing several of the crimes with which he was charged,[67] North displayed very little if any remorse, declaring that he was "not ashamed" of anything in his personal or professional conduct.[68]

In a prepared statement delivered to Congress prior to his being questioned about his conduct during the Iran-contra hearings, North expressed no regrets.[69] To the contrary, he credited President Reagan with "advancing the cause of world peace by strengthening our country, by acting to restore and sustain democracy throughout the world, and by having the courage to take decisive action when needed."[70] He questioned the fairness of the investigative process, arguing that Congress "was both player and umpire."[71] Indeed, North argued that a large part of the fault for the affair lay with Congress, which had vacillated in its support of the contras, supporting aid initially but then cutting it off part way through the Reagan administration.[72] He also charged that the open forum of the congressional hearings "revealed great matters of secrecy" and threatened to hobble the execution of foreign policy.[73] During a 1988 commencement speech, North continued to argue that prosecutors and Congress were in the wrong, telling the audience that criminal charges against him "are not a brand—they are a badge of honor."[74]

In explaining his record of lying to Congress, North declared, "I didn't think it was right, but I didn't think it was against the law."[75] He explained that as far as he was concerned the moral blame lay with Congress because it was "immoral" for the legislature to cut off funds to the contra resistance forces from 1984 to 1986, after having provided CIA support for several years.[76] "Plain and simple, the Congress is to blame because of the fickle, vacillating, unpredictable, 'on again/off again' policy toward the Nicaraguan Democratic Resistance."[77]

North also shifted the blame onto his coworkers, pointing the finger at his superior, McFarlane, who North said should have refused to answer questions instead of lying about them, and who North alleged was responsible for drafting the written denials that were offered to Congress.[78] "I just simply do not believe I wrote this letter. Those words are written in Mr. McFarlane's handwriting."[79] He claimed he was "taught how to run a covert operation," and that the agreed-upon strategy was to "stick as close to the truth without telling them all they wanted to know."[80] North said that he was merely following orders. "I was authorized to do everything I did," he stated in a *Time* interview in April 1989.[81] He maintained, however, that he never considered backing out of the secret effort:[82] "I thought using the Ayatollah [Khomeini]'s money to support the Nicaraguan Resistance was a right idea . . . I still do. I don't think it was wrong. I think it was a neat idea and I . . . advocated [it] and we did it."[83]

North, who pronounced charges against him a "badge of honor,"[84] explained his actions by noting, "I have been accused of helping the brave young men and women of the Nicaraguan Resistance in their struggle for the very liberties we claim as a birthright. I have been accused of trying to rescue American hostages . . . and trying to prevent other terrorist attacks."[85] In explaining his predicament, North said, "Certainly, I did not choose to be caught in the middle of a bitter political dispute between the Congress and the president over the conduct of foreign policy. Nor did I ever dream that I would have to endure the largest investigation in the history of this country."[86]

North's convictions were reversed in July 1990, not because of new evidence that exonerated him or because a mistake in judgment was uncovered, but on the grounds that his televised congressional testimony, given under limited immunity, tainted the subsequent criminal proceedings.[87]

North found forgiveness, or gave it to himself, by relying on a higher authority. North told an interviewer, "Am I open to challenge? Yes. Am I forgiven? Yes. Maybe not by the *Washington Post*, but I know where I'm going, and it's not because of anything that I've done. . . . It's all because God cared enough to send his Son to die for me." North concluded, "I know that I am forgiven."[88] People who believe that he did not face sufficient reckoning for his misdeeds, he argued, are either "jealous, angry and bitter," or merely "just flat remember things differently."[89]

North's unrepentant conduct seems to have found some encouragement in the political support that he received from those who saw him as a courageous patriot seeking to defend freedom against Communism, who had been unduly blamed when Congress attempted to usurp control of foreign policy from the executive branch. This became especially clear when North was selected to make the commencement address at Liberty University in Lynchburg, Virginia, in May 1988. Sixty people protested the speech, but Reverend Jerry Falwell, founder of Liberty, "announced that his national petition drive to obtain a presidential pardon for North has drawn more than 600,000 signatures."[90] In his introduction of North, Falwell likened the former National Security Council staffer to Jesus, saying, "We serve a Savior who was indicted and convicted and crucified."[91] Also reported was a "Draft North for U.S. Senate Committee" with an eye toward the 1988 election for a seat from Virginia; the chairman said North "hasn't been telling us to stop, and that's an encouraging sign."[92]

Throughout his legal troubles and into his 1994 campaign for the U.S. Senate, public opinion polls showed that a substantial percentage of Americans approved of his conduct, or at least did not fault him for it. Gallup polling in May 1989, when North was convicted, found that 47 percent of American adults agreed that North was "a patriot and a hero," while 53 percent disagreed or did not know. Fifty-five percent agreed that North "did not act for personal gain or profit" compared to 45 percent who disagreed or did not know.[93] Another Gallup poll from the same period found that 14 percent regarded North as "a hero and patriot," 69 percent saw him as "well-meaning but misguided," and only 11 percent saw him as "a liar and a criminal."[94] Four years later, a poll found that 62 percent believed "Oliver North acted for the benefit of the nation based on orders from his superiors"; this was more than double the 26 percent who believed that "Oliver North lied to Congress and served his own interests instead of the nation."[95]

In short, far from repenting in any form, North charged the institutions that charged him with wrongdoing and found considerable public support for his stance.

Robert McFarlane

Robert McFarlane served as national security adviser for the Reagan administration from October 1983 to December 1985. He held office during the first years of the

Gorbachev regime, and considers his work on Soviet-American relations his principal achievement.[96] His suicide attempt on February 9, 1987, following the revelations about his role in the Iran-contra affair, indicates that he is infinitely less proud of the political misdeeds than his subordinate North.

McFarlane's memoir, entitled *Special Trust*, reports that in July 1985, David Kimche of the Israeli Foreign Ministry proposed a scheme to assassinate the Ayatollah Ruhollah Khomeini of Iran. Although not interested in that venture, McFarlane was intrigued by Kimche's broader idea of making peaceful gestures toward dissident, moderate groups in Iran, organizations that might be in a position to arrange for the release of American hostages in Lebanon.[97] The idea of making a "gesture" quickly evolved into a request for sophisticated American weapons. As the plan further stipulated, the profits from these arms sales would be used to fund entities in Nicaragua that opposed the Sandinista government. McFarlane reports that President Reagan approved this initiative despite the restrictions in the 1984 Boland Amendment, which, as discussed, stipulated that "no funds appropriated by Congress" for any governmental department or agency could be "obligated or expended for the purpose or which would have the effect of supporting" military or paramilitary operations in Nicaragua."[98]

When reports of illegal activities leaked to the press, inquiries were made by both the House Intelligence Committee and the House Foreign Affairs Committee. In response to these inquiries, McFarlane wrote letters to on September 5 and September 12, 1985. His letters to the House Intelligence Committee contained the following statements:

> I can state with deep personal conviction that at no time did I or any member of the NSC staff violate the letter or spirit of the law. . . . We did not solicit funds or other support for the military or paramilitary activities either from the Americans or third parties.
> Lt. Col. North did not use his influence to facilitate the movement of supplies to the resistance. . . . There is no official or unofficial relationship with any member of the NSC staff regarding fund raising for the Nicaraguan democratic opposition. . . .[99]

His letter further revealed the following:

> Throughout, we have scrupulously abided by the spirit and the letter of the law. None of us has solicited funds, facilitated contacts for prospective potential donors, or otherwise organized or coordinated the military or paramilitary efforts of the resistance. . . . There has not been, nor will there be, any such activities by the NSC staff.[100]

In May 1986, McFarlane, however, took a secret flight with North to Tehran. Their objective was to arrange for the trade of three planeloads of arms and Hawk missile parts for all the American hostages remaining in Lebanon. Although McFarlane's trip made no progress in terms of the hostage swap, it gave *Al-Shiraa* plenty to write about, blowing the cover on the operation.

Congress again launched an inquiry. On December 6, 1986, McFarlane testified before the House Foreign Affairs Committee that he was unaware of any nationals from a third country who were involved in financing the Nicaraguan contras. "The concrete character of that is beyond my ken."[101] When asked about his alleged solicitation of contributions to the Contras from foreign countries and his knowledge of such activity by others, he responded, "I did not solicit any country at any time to make contributions to the Contras. I have seen the reports that various countries have . . . and I have no idea of the extent of that or anything else."[102] This was a statement McFarlane later acknowledged to be misleading. When asked in the 1987 Iran-contra hearings whether he in fact "had a hand in obtaining contributions totaling approximately $32 million" from a contributing foreign country, he responded, "Yes."[103]

Two months later, on February 9, 1987, McFarlane tried to kill himself by consuming a large quantity of Valium. In preparation, he had penned letters of apology to his lawyer, the chairs of the House and Senate intelligence committees, and the editorial page editor of the *Washington Post*.[104] These apologies survived his suicide attempt.

McFarlane was also the most forthright of witnesses to testify before Congress during the Iran-contra investigation. In his introductory statement before the joint hearings, McFarlane said, "There is enough blame to go around in all these matters under investigation. I have been and remain willing to shoulder my part of it."[105] He further stated, "This has been and remains for me a matter of remorse, even anguish, and for many reasons."[106] McFarlane testified, "Although it is painful for me to appear here and to revisit these events, I do so in recognition of a duty and in the hope that it will promote understanding and help in finding a remedy."[107]

After questioning McFarlane, Arthur L. Liman, the Senate Iran-contra committee's chief counsel, said, "McFarlane deserves credit as the one figure to acknowledge that what happened was wrong," and further that McFarlane "felt guilty for having set North in motion."[108] Liman stated that he thought McFarlane had suffered personally during his testimony, and that "Bud McFarlane, who tried to obey both the President and his duty to the truth, has become like a man without a country."[109] Commenting on the tentative possibility of McFarlane's reintegration in public life, Senator Sam Nunn said, "He let his friends know there was remorse, and his friends remain his friends."[110]

While McFarlane went much further on the road to repentance than North, who set no foot on that road, McFarlane had a tendency to explain away his failings while apologizing for them, somehow combining being the victim and the predator. In his memoir, McFarlane implies that he had been misled by North's apparent honesty and patriotism, and that this belief "colored his testimony" in the Senate hearings.[111] "I was determined to help, not hurt, North," he remembers. McFarlane, however, later found during North's trial that the ex-Marine was not the obedient, self-described "pawn among giants"; in fact, he was "devious, self-serving [and] self-aggrandizing," willing to falsely implicate McFarlane in the contra dealings.[112]

McFarlane also argued that his actions were far less reprehensible than those of other high officials in Washington who never received a punishment for their misdeeds. "I could not imagine that even in the most extreme interpretation, what I had done could possibly measure up to the actions of men who had gone before me, men like Lyndon Johnson and Henry Kissinger, who had never been charged with any violations of law or the public trust."[113]

Making a clean break seems to be exceedingly difficult. McFarlane, though, did accept some of the blame and show remorse. Although in the book that followed his trial he tried to put the onus to some extent on others and the circumstances, he neither attacked the institutions that his first acts offended nor tried to make a name for himself or a career based on self-righteous denials of what happened.

Lyn Nofziger

The 1978 Ethics in Government Act was designed to prevent people who ended their federal government employment from using their influence and relationships with government officials for one year.[114] Lobbying of their former agency by certain former federal employees is prohibited by the law for one year if the agency already has "a direct and substantial interest" in the subject of the lobbying effort.[115] In 1982, Reagan aide Lyn Nofziger was reported to have violated this law.

Nofziger left his position as a White House aide in January 1982 to open a consulting firm.[116] On April 8, 1982, Nofziger sent a memo to presidential counselor Edwin Meese III. In it, he suggested that Meese enlist the help of top administration officials—including the president—to persuade the Army to bestow a no-bid contract upon a New York firm, Wedtech Corp. The contract would offer Wedtech $32 million to build 13,000 small gasoline engines for the Army. The Army had opposed granting the contract on the ground Wedtech was not experienced in the area of building combustion engines and was demanding a high price. Nofziger, however, was insistent, emphasizing that "it would be a blunder not to award that contract to Wedtech."[117] Following his receipt of Nofziger's first letter, Meese held a meeting on May 19, 1982, to persuade the Army to award the contract to Wedtech. Following his second letter, sent on May 28, the contract was awarded.

The May 28 letter, in which Nofziger asked another White House aide to help secure a letter of intent from the Army and thus empower Wedtech to secure funds, signaled the beginning of Nofziger's troubles. Wedtech had come under investigation by federal and state authorities for payments of cash and stock to politically connected consultants and law firms. In the process of this investigation, Nofziger's incriminating letter "urging [Meese] or even the president to help Wedtech secure the $32 million deal" was uncovered.[118]

Also in the summer of 1982, Nofziger's consulting firm was paid $100,000 by the

Marine Engineers Beneficial Association, which recruited Nofziger to use his influence to put civilians on Navy ships. Then in September, Nofziger courted two National Security Council staffers in an unsuccessful bid for the continued funding of the A-10 antitank plane, an endorsement opposed by the Pentagon on grounds that the A-10 was an outdated vehicle. One of Nofziger's memos reasoned, "Why not help our friends?"[119]

In the case against him, Nofziger was accused of "sending a memorandum . . . [to] Meese's deputy . . . to enlist support for putting civilian sailors on Navy vessels, an idea advocated by the Marine Engineers Beneficial Association."[120] The official charge for the A-10 lobbying was that he "improperly lobbied aides of the National Security Council in September 1982 on behalf of the . . . makers of the A-10 antitank aircraft."[121] Of the four felony charges, Nofziger was convicted of three. For abusing influence in the White House, Nofziger was sentenced to ninety days in jail and the maximum fine of $30,000. Throughout his trial, Nofziger never wavered from a position of vociferous denial. He made the following statement to the news media about White House underhandedness: "I'm not part of the administration nor was I when these charges were brought. It tells more about the inability of Congress to write a fair law than it does about the administration."[122] Of the Ethics in Government Act, he said, "It's a lousy law. It doesn't apply to Congress. It doesn't apply to the judiciary. It doesn't apply to those below a certain salary level. . . . It's like running a stop sign."[123] And most succinctly, he said, "I feel I am innocent. I don't think I have done anything wrong."[124]

Nofziger stood before the judge and declared, "While I know that there are those in this courtroom who believe that I should be sent to prison unless I come here today and plead guilty, express remorse and ask forgiveness, I cannot do that if I am to be true to myself and to those hundreds of people all over the country who have supported me because they believe that I am an honorable man."[125] He elaborated, "I cannot show remorse because I do not believe that I am guilty of the offenses of which I am charged."[126] After his sentence was announced, he said, "I suppose, if I had been contrite, I might have avoided a prison term, but I am not going to be contrite when I don't think I have done anything."[127]

Nofziger went a step further; he attacked the legitimacy of the law under which he was sentenced. As he himself wrote, "I had not made things any easier for the judge. I had refused to admit guilt. I had called the law under which I was convicted a 'lousy law.' I had refused to suggest punishment."[128]

Nofziger's convictions were overturned in June 1988 on appeal because the New York Court of Appeals held that the prosecutors had failed to demonstrate that Nofziger knew his lobbying actions were in violation of the Ethics in Government Act. To prosecute a former federal employee under the Ethics in Government Act, it must be proven that the defendant "willfully and knowingly" violated the Act's provisions.[129] The court held that "under the section of the Ethics in Government Act under which Nofziger was convicted, the government was required to prove that he had knowledge of all of the facts making his conduct criminal."[130]

Against the widespread belief that his case was reversed on a technicality, Nofziger stated, "I thought I was innocent in the beginning. I still think I'm innocent."[131] Nofziger never wavered. No remorse, restitution, or change in course.

Michael Deaver

Another of Reagan's top administrators who ran afoul of a governmental ethics act was Michael Deaver, former White House deputy chief of staff and longtime friend of Ronald and Nancy Reagan. Deaver worked for President Reagan for over twenty years, beginning when Reagan was governor of California, and ending when Deaver departed from his four-year term as deputy chief of staff in 1985 to start his own lobbying business.

Five months after leaving the White House, well within the one-year prohibition, a South Korean trade envoy attended a personal meeting in the Oval Office with President Reagan. As it happened, Deaver's consulting firm had been in the process of negotiating a lobbying contract with South Korea. News of Deaver's client trickled into the press, and investigators thought it too much a coincidence that Deaver's firm was conducting these negotiations. In fact, South Korea was paying Deaver's business $475,000 per year.[132] When this and other suspicious administration contacts were discovered, congressional investigators requested a special prosecutor. Deaver, far from trying to make amends, said that he welcomed the examination.[133] Initial evidence led investigators to believe that Deaver had exploited personal connections to the federal government in violation of the law. Instead of being charged for illegal lobbying activity, Deaver was charged with—and convicted of—perjury.

The alternate charges arose out of the investigative proceedings themselves. In 1986, Deaver was required to testify before a House subcommittee and a federal grand jury about several incidents in which he was believed to have been involved. He was first questioned regarding his role in arranging the Korean trade envoy meeting. Then, one month later, he had to respond to claims that he had lobbied government officials on behalf of Trans World Airlines, and that he had advocated the retention of a federal tax policy favorable to mainland manufacturers with factories in Puerto Rico. He was also questioned about making contacts on behalf of clients such as Boeing and Philip Morris.

Deaver's responses to many of the questions asked before these committees were later held worthy of an indictment by a federal grand jury, as evidenced in the following transcript:

> [1. The following refers to a request from the South Korean Ambassador, Kim Kihwan, to meet with the President of the United States:]
> Mr. Deaver: The request was in process already through normal diplomatic channels.
> Mr. Raabe: The request from whom?

Mr. Deaver: The request from the Korean Government.
Mr. Raabe: Did you do anything to facilitate that request?
Mr. Deaver: No, sir.
[The grand jury later came to the following conclusion regarding his statement that he "did not do anything" to facilitate the request of Ambassador Kim to meet with the President:]
Defendant then and there well knew, in that, among other things, at the very time he was negotiating a contract for his firm to represent the Government of the Republic of Korea (through the International Cultural Society of Korea) for an annual fee of $475,000, defendant DEAVER suggested that a personal visit be arranged to deliver a letter concerning trade issues from the President of Korea to the President of the United States. . . .[134]

[2. Deaver was suspected, during the congressional hearing, of lobbying advisors to the president on behalf of the Republic of Korea. He told the panel, however, that he had not done so. The grand jury in his perjury trial stated that this earlier response was false.]
Mr. Raabe: [W]ould it be helpful to search your memory further?
Mr. Deaver: Those [previously named instances of contacts with White House advisers] are the only two that I can recall. Once we had established that we could deal with certain members of the NSC and certain members of the OMB, and we didn't check any further on those areas, and I didn't ever talk to anybody in the West Wing of the White House.
[The grand jury ruled regarding this testimony that:]
The [above] answers were false, as defendant then and there well knew, in that, among others, defendant DEAVER had personally contacted [a number of White House senior staff].[135]

Independent counsel Whitney North Seymour, Jr., who had been appointed to investigate the lobbying violations, interpreted Deaver's responses as gestures intended to protect not only a lucrative business, which brought in $3.2 million in fees in its first year alone, but also his friends.[136] Seymour originally wanted to charge Deaver with lobbying infractions, but his efforts to investigate those infractions were obstructed by what he perceived as deceit under oath. Subsequently, Seymour charged Deaver with five counts of perjury concerning his previous testimony.

Deaver tried to use his alcoholism to justify many of his initial replies to the investigative juries. He suggested that alcoholism had so blurred his memory that he was "probably telling the truth" when he said he could not remember, and that his drinking problem was "the worst demon" that he had to face. However, Deaver's lawyers chose to offer no defense at all.[137] Attorney Herbert J. Miller assumed that the prosecution's case was too weak to warrant a defense, and so none of the 200 witnesses on Miller's tentative list, including Deaver himself, was called to testify.[138]

Several White House officials, whom Deaver claimed were uninvolved with his lobbying activities, came forward to give the details of their contacts with Deaver. After the trial, jurors said that there was a clear "paper trail" indicating that Deaver had indeed contacted the officials.[139] Deaver was convicted on the first three charges of perjury and acquitted of the second two. Though he faced a possible fifteen years in prison, Deaver was sentenced to no jail time, a $100,000 fine, three years probation, and 1,500 hours of community service.[140]

One may argue that Deaver had to defend his acts in the courtroom because of fear of the legal consquences of his admitting that he conducted himself inappropriately; however, he was also unrepentant in fora other than the courtroom. In an interview shortly after his perjury conviction, he continued to blame his behavior on a lapse in judgment due to alcoholism.

> Q. Can you say now whether you think that your judgment was affected by the alcoholism which you were suffering at the times that all of this took place?
> MR. DEAVER: Alcoholism is a disease that affects many parts of your body and your emotions, and certainly your judgment. Yes, I do.
> Q: Mike, did it affect your memory? If you had testified, what would you have said about your memory?
> MR. DEAVER: Well, all I can do is tell you that, to this day, I don't recall making some of those phone calls when I was in the hospital sedated. I'm sorry, I just don't remember.[141]

Deaver concluded by stating that his "was a very fair sentence, if I'd been guilty."[142]

Deaver thus joins a long list of people who have blamed some external demon for their conduct rather than assuming responsibility. But unlike Nofziger, he did not add insult to injury by attacking the law.

Atwater, Packwood, and Barry: Uncertain Penitents

The three men considered in this section vary in their ill-considered actions. Lee Atwater, the Republican political operative who managed George Bush's 1988 presidential campaign, earned criticism for undermining the civil society through his negative campaign tactics. Atwater began apologizing to his former targets when he was diagnosed with terminal cancer, shortly before he died, which made some wonder if he would have expressed the same regrets if he could have expected to continue in his profession. Senator Bob Packwood faced numerous allegations of making unwanted sexual advances, which led to his resignation from the Senate. Packwood, who explained that abuse of alcohol impaired his judgment and contributed to his misdeeds, made efforts at repentance that seemed to some observers primarily a bid to keep his Senate seat. Marion Barry was the mayor of Washington, D.C., before a conviction on a drug-related charge led to his temporary departure from public office. Barry claimed that addictions to drugs, alcohol, and sex fueled his problems. Mixing repentance and defiance, Barry's return to grace in some voters' eyes climaxed with his reelection to the Washington mayor's office in 1994. Some questioned the sincerity of his repentance, given that it helped him to regain his post and also wondered if he truly restructured his life, ending his womanizing and substance abuse.

Lee Atwater

Lee Atwater is remembered as one of the most aggressive political consultants and campaigners of recent history. As George Bush's presidential campaign manager in 1988, Atwater earned a reputation for being savvy, driven, and effective. Yet in this and previous political races, Atwater also earned a reputation for being cruel.

During the 1980 congressional campaign of the South Carolina Republican incumbent Floyd Spence, Atwater had supporters call white suburban voters to inform them that the Democratic nominee, Tom Turnipseed, was a member of the NAACP. According to Turnipseed, Atwater also circulated copies of a letter from Senator Strom Thurmond warning voters that the democratic candidate would "disarm America and turn it over to the liberals and Communists."[143] After discovering that Turnipseed had undergone electroshock treatments for depression as an adolescent, Atwater used this information as part of his negative campaign. When Turnipseed accused Atwater of misconduct, Atwater answered that he would "not respond to allegations made by someone who was hooked up to jumper cables."[144] Turnipseed lost the election.

While working for George Bush, Atwater said of presidential competitor Michael Dukakis that he "would strip the bark off the little bastard." At an Atlanta Republican meeting, he suggested that he would make Willie Horton Dukakis's "running mate," referring to the convicted murderer who, on a weekend furlough from prison as part of a program approved by Dukakis, raped a Maryland woman. According to press reports, Atwater boasted: "If I can make Willie Horton a household name, we'll win the election."[145] This was Atwater's way of labeling Dukakis soft on crime. This move is considered one of the factors that decided the election against Dukakis. Various other tactics that have been attributed to Atwater are not discussed here. Atwater fairly concluded "While I didn't invent 'negative politics,' I am one of its most ardent practitioners."[146]

Atwater was diagnosed with an inoperable malignant brain tumor in 1990 and subsequently became a born-again Christian. "I have found Jesus Christ. It's that simple."[147] He no longer craved the relish he took from antagonizing his political opponents. "For the first time in my life, I don't hate somebody," he claimed. "[There's] just no point in fighting and feuding."[148] Those close to Atwater reported that he was pondering his "eternal soul" and becoming more spiritual as he prepared for his death.[149] He sought reconciliation with others. He wrote to Turnipseed, "It is very important to me that I let you know that out of everything that has happened in my career, one of the low points remains the so called 'jumper cable' episode."[150] Atwater also apologized for the two statements about Dukakis, "the first for its naked cruelty, the second because it makes me sound racist, which I am not."[151]

Atwater's acts and apologies appeared not to have made a major impression on the public. A national poll of registered voters taken in late autumn 1989 found a majority, 57 percent, either did not recognize his name or could not rate their impressions of him. Twenty-three percent had a very or somewhat favorable impression of Atwater and 18 percent had a somewhat or very unfavorable view of him.[152]

While Atwater showed remorse, not everyone accepted it on face value, given that it was forthcoming only on his deathbed.

Bob Packwood

At the apogee of his political career, Senator Bob Packwood had cultivated a reputation as being sensitive to, and supportive of, women's issues in Congress. He also held one of the strongest records in Congress of hiring and supporting women, and he was a defender of abortion rights.[153] In November 1992, just days after Packwood's narrow reelection, the *Washington Post* published allegations of sexual harassment against Packwood. The *Post* claimed that Packwood had a twenty-year habit of arranging to be alone with women, fondling or kissing them against their will, and making other unwelcome sexual advances. According to the newspaper, Packwood was "a powerful but troubled man who forced himself on women [and] hustled favors [for them] from lobbyist friends."[154] At the time, the *Washington Post* had contacted at least ten women who were willing to give specific accounts of incidents with Packwood.

By May 1994, twenty-two allegations of sexual misconduct were filed with the Senate Ethics Committee.[155] Charges against Packwood ranged from harassment to outright assault, from coworkers to baby-sitters. The transcript of the Senate Select Committee on Ethics investigative hearing provides the following examples:

> It is therefore Resolved:
> [T]hat the Committee makes the following determinations regarding the matters set forth above:
> . . . (1) That in 1990, in his Senate office in Washington, D.C., Senator Packwood grabbed a staff member by the shoulders and kissed her on the lips;
> (2) That in 1985, at a function in Bend, Oregon, Senator Packwood fondled a campaign worker as they danced. . .;
>
> . . . .
> (18) That in 1969, in his Senate office in Portland, Oregon, Senator Packwood grabbed a staff worker, stood on her feet, grabbed her hair, forcibly pulled her head back, and kissed her on the mouth, forcing his tongue into her mouth. Senator Packwood also reached under her skirt and grabbed at her undergarments.[156]

Initially Packwood and his staff simply denied the validity of the accusations, but expressed regrets nevertheless.[157] "They mentioned charges I'd never heard. They mentioned names I had never heard. And I thought to myself, 'I could not have done those things, I did not do those things.' I denied it to myself because I did not believe it, and I denied it to my friends."[158] In an early statement Packwood said, "I never consciously intended to offend any women. . . . I therefore offer my deepest apologies to all those involved and to the people of Oregon," yet his spokesman was quick to clarify, "The press release should not be construed as a confession of guilt. . . . I think he is saying that there are things in the allegations that concern him."[159] Packwood promised to "restructure, drastically and totally, my attitude and my professional relationships."[160]

When the allegations showed no signs of subsiding, Packwood shifted his position away from denial, now saying, "I do not remember," and "I do not recall." Packwood said, "I'm apologizing for the conduct that it was alleged that I did,"[161] though he declined to specify for what he was apologizing. He also blamed alcoholism for his conduct. Although Packwood did concede that "alcohol at best can only be a partial explanation, not an excuse,"[162] many of his public statements were dominated by an alcoholism theme.

Packwood's political situation worsened when investigators demanded his diary, which contained references to his "Christian duty" to sleep with a particular woman who had been without sex for a while, and to the "22 staff members I'd made love to and probably 75 others I've had relations with."[163] He admitted that he had altered copies of his diary, which could have been considered an effort to obstruct the proceedings of the Ethics Committee. When it became obvious that Packwood would either have to resign or face severe reprimand, he resigned on the eve of Senate action against him.[164]

Prior to his resignation, Packwood reminded women of his devotion to their political concerns. One report of Packwood's performance quotes him remembering "those lonely and solitary hours in the late Seventies and early Eighties, defending *Roe v. Wade*, trying to prevent its reversal or dismemberment."[165] He also attempted to minimize the credibility of charges against him. During an appearance on *This Week With David Brinkley*, Packwood complained that "one woman says that I looked at her in a way that offended her."[166] He sought to dodge reporter Sam Donaldson's questions about specific instances in which women said he had grabbed them. Finally, he claimed that he did not grab or assault any women, although "I have admitted, in the past, that I kissed some of the women."[167]

Packwood also contrasted feminists' reaction to allegations against him with their reaction to Paula Jones's complaint against President Bill Clinton. He told the panel on *This Week*, "The thing that intrigues me most is the way women's groups look for a way to absolutely excoriate me and look for some way to attempt to exonerate the president."[168] Earlier in that show, he had said:

> I noticed in the *New York Times* today, some of the women's groups were distinguishing between Clarence Thomas and Anita Hill and the president and they said, "Well, Clarence Thomas was a direct supervisor of Anita Hill, whereas President Clinton was hardly a direct supervisor of Paula Jones." And

they make that distinction, yet none of them have ever, ever made any distinction with me in that most of the allegations, they come from people that did not work for me at all.[169]

Another double standard about which Packwood complained was the Ethics Committee's refusal to identify specific charges against him, and its ability to act as both prosecutor and judge in dealings with him. Packwood spoke at some length about this in the Senate on November 1, 1993, when complaining about the purposes for which his diaries had been subpoenaed. He told his colleagues:

> If the Senate wants to get to a situation where you can be charged with something—something—and then because you are charged with something the Ethics Committee, to which you will have no rights to argue your position procedurally, your lawyers will never see them; they will hear only from their counsel—to be charged with something and then have the committee say we want to see everything and when we see everything, if something comes to our attention that should charge you with, we will charge you with that, too, that is where we are.[170]

Concerning the double standard, leaks to the media about the possibility that Packwood had committed criminal acts, and the committee's desire to examine his diaries, he said:

> What do you think any bar association or judges would do to a district attorney who says, "I think the defendant is guilty of criminal conduct," and puts out a press release to this end. That district attorney would be the equivalent of disbarred or censured by the judge.
> What do you think would be the judge's attitude if the district attorney went to the judge and said, "I think the defendant is guilty of criminal conduct. I want a general search warrant."
> Do you not think the judge would say, "Mr. District Attorney, be a little more specific. What are you looking for?" "I do not think I will say it. I just think I wish to search all of his diaries to see what is in them. There is this one incident"—again, I keep coming back to the incident that the chairman has referred to as criminal, possibly criminal, and apparently it is this incident on which the general warrant to search all of my diaries is based.
> And Senator Daschle says double standard. Do you think that on that kind of a statement, a common citizen would be subject to a search of all of his papers? Not in a court in this land would you be subject to that kind of a search.
> So if we are going to talk about double standards, let us be very careful what we are talking about. Nor is a Senator going to be treated better than any other citizens. But given these circumstances and almost exactly these facts and the statement by a district attorney that the defendant is guilty of criminal conduct, puts it out in the press before there has ever been a trial, there is not a citizen in this country that would be subject to produce papers that this subpoena is asking me to produce.[171]

Packwood sometimes did strike a repentant position, stating, "The important point is that my actions were unwelcome and insensitive. These women were offended, appropriately so, and I am truly sorry." He also said, "What I did was not just stupid and boorish. My actions were just plain wrong and there's no better word for it."[172] In his public statements, however, he attempted to distance himself from the alleged acts, both by asserting that they were out of character for him and claiming lapses of memory. As late as March 1994, he claimed that he could only remember eight of the over twenty women accusers. On *Larry King Live*, Packwood apologized for "whatever it was I did, even if I couldn't remember."[173] Packwood argued, "My most vocal detractor . . . is a woman whom I handily defeated in the 1974 Senate election. Several of the accusers . . . contributed to my 1992 opponent's campaign. Most are Democrats."[174]

In his resignation speech, Packwood stressed factors other than his ill-considered acts. He proclaimed, "I am aware of the dishonor that has befallen me in the last 3 years, and I do not want to visit further that dishonor on the Senate. I respect this institution and my colleagues too much for that."[175] He added, "It is my duty to resign. It is the honorable thing to do for this country, for the Senate."[176]

After resigning, he explained to Barbara Walters that he was not led to the decision by "a mountain of evidence" against him; rather, "it was very clear that the Senate was going to go through, if I chose to contest it, a brutal battle and I love the place, I love the Senate, respect it and I didn't want to drag them through that and I was ready to move on and you put all those factors together and I decided to go ahead and resign."[177]

In his resignation speech, Packwood continued to imply that somehow his past acts on behalf of women on the Senate floor recompensed or at least mitigated the charges against him. For instance, he insists "Abortion, early on was a lonely fight. I remember in 1970, 1971, when I was introducing the first national abortion legislation, I could get no cosponsor in the Senate. . . . Those were lonely days. That is not a fight that is even yet secure."[178]

Packwood also tried to put his much publicized diaries in a favorable light in the wake of his resignation. While much media attention focused on the lurid contents, Packwood emphasized "in this diary here are personal meetings with Nixon about—personal, one-to-one on Watergate and Judge Haynesworth and Ronald Reagan about you—when I said, 'You can't build the party on white Anglo-Saxon males who are over 40. There aren't enough of us.'"[179]

Packwood did express regrets and apologized, while denying or being evasive about many of the facts, even after these no longer could be used against him as evidence by the Senate, because he already had resigned. He also blamed factors beyond his control, especially alcoholism. One might question whether his punishment—being forced to resign from the Senate, ending his life as a public servant—was disproportionate to his violations. He did not come completely clean, though, for whatever he did do.

Marion Barry

One would think that District of Columbia mayor Marion Barry was paying close attention when his longtime friend Charles Lewis, former personnel specialist for the federal government, was indicted on three counts of cocaine possession and seven counts of lying about drug use on April 13, 1989. In August 1989, Lewis told investigators that he not only sold cocaine to the mayor, but that he also witnessed the mayor's use of the drug on December 22, 1988.[180]

Barry was nearing the end of his third term as mayor and planned on seeking reelection. The Lewis statements were not Barry's first brush with law enforcement regarding his possible drug use. There had been an inquiry in response to previous allegations made by convicted cocaine dealer Karen K. Johnson in 1987, although a formal report was never filed.

The mayor took an aggressive stance against these suspicions, saying that he had "never used any illegal drugs."[181] He stated that it would be "idiocy" for any politician to abuse drugs around other people, and "I've never been accused of being an idiot."[182] On the whole, Barry dismissed the charges as "too implausible for anyone to believe," because "anybody who knows anything about America knows any mayor who really wants to get dope can get it without going on the streets."[183]

The situation changed in January 1990, when a police videotape emerged. On the tape, played before government officials and home television viewers alike, was the video image of Mayor Marion Barry in room 727 of the Vista International Hotel. He was attempting to coax former model Rasheeda Moore into bed, and taking long drags on a pipe that was stuffed with crack. When the federal agents burst onto the scene, the video captured Barry's exclamation, "Got me set up! Ain't that a bitch?"[184]

During the trial that ensued, evidence of his abuse of both drugs and alcohol came to light, as exemplified by the following questioning of Moore, Barry's companion at the time of his arrest:

> Ms. Roberts [for the prosecution]: What did [Barry] say about what he would not allow the hospital to do?
> Ms. Moore: Blood tests, he would not allow the hospital to take blood tests.
> Ms. Roberts: What else was said in those conversations concerning narcotics?
> Ms. Moore: Jeff indicated to me that they had smoked something, cocaine laced with something.
> [With regard to his drinking problem:]
> Mr. Mance [for the defense]: How would you characterize Mr. Barry in terms of alcohol consumption? Was he a regular drinker?
> Ms. Moore: He drank a lot. . . .
> Mr. Mance: And did this usually precede his consumption of drugs?

Ms. Moore: Well, the first thing he would do when he came in would be pour himself a drink, usually a drink, usually a shot of cognac. And then . . . yes.[185]

Barry was convicted of one misdemeanor charge; the jury was deadlocked on the remaining thirteen.

Allegations of alcoholism also surfaced, this time not as an excuse but as an accusation. The mayor's wife, Effi Barry, stated that he had had a drinking problem "from the first day of our marriage." Living with him during his bout with alcoholism, she stated, was "probably the worst experience anyone could possibly go through. . . . Over the years, there were many incidents that occurred that brought great embarrassment, pain, bewilderment, frustration and just anger, as a result of his inability to control his drinking habit."[186]

Barry's reputation as a womanizer also gained additional attention at the time. Lewis testified to having witnessed Barry and Moore together—and using drugs—on a trip to the U.S. Virgin Islands, where Barry was overseeing an employee exchange program. District of Columbia employee James McWilliams testified that Barry and Moore became so amorous on a boat trip that he felt the need to avert his gaze.[187] Still, as late as September 1989, Barry responded affirmatively to questions about whether he was faithful to his wife: "Yes, I am. I've been married to her for 11 years and I love her." (When pressed, he did remark, "Uh, we've all made our share of mistakes and I've made mine and I ask you, the voter, to forgive me for doing that.")[188]

Gradually Barry did accept his guilt. In a letter to the sentencing judge, he wrote that he was "a recovering alcoholic and a drug addict,"[189] acknowledging the pain his public criminality had caused. He told the judge that he wanted "to take full responsibility" for his actions, which were "out of character" for him.[190] On October 26, 1990, he told the court that for the previous 279 days he had avoided alcohol, cocaine, Xanax (an antidepressant), and Valium, to all of which he admitted being addicted.[191] (He claimed that it was his ten-year-old son, who grabbed a bottle out of his hands as he poured a drink, who inspired him to enter his recovery.) Barry explained that he had "an insidious disease that afflicts millions of Americans. Admitting to my illness was the first major step toward recovery."[192] He wrote that he wanted to use his newfound "experience to help, perhaps even save, others."[193] He asked the judge to consider his progress in battling his addiction and his record of public service, and concluded, "I ask the court for leniency in its decision on my sentence. As society redefines its approach to and solutions for the disease of addiction, I respectfully ask the court to decide that the best way for me to be punished for my crime is through service to the community."[194]

On his 468th day of being drug and alcohol free, Barry appeared on the *Sally Jessy Raphael Show* to declare that a craving for sex drove him to drink and abuse drugs, but that he now avoids this temptation. According to Barry, he no longer calls 900 numbers, watches adult movies, reads pornographic magazines, or goes to places where he can get women's phone numbers.[195]

After his sentencing and his defeat in his bid for an at-large city council seat, Barry gave an interview to a Washington-based magazine describing his addictions to alcohol, drugs, and sex. In the article, Barry conceded that he was "ashamed and disappointed" in himself because of decisions he made, explaining that "I've spent a great deal of time working on the character defects that I've developed over the years, the dishonesty, denial, egocentricity, selfishness, the people-pleasing grandiosity."[196]

Like other public figures before him, Barry had a hard time coming to terms with his conviction. The day after his drug-possession conviction, Barry told an audience, "The government has examined my conduct; now it must examine *its* conduct."[197] In an appearance on the *Donahue* television talk program while he was running for an at-large city council seat after he completed his six-month jail sentence, Barry complained about his sentence, arguing against "the unfairness of it all. I'm willing to pay the price of any actions that I've done—any deeds or misdeeds—as long as they are fair."[198] Several months later, after his defeat in his bid for a city council seat, Barry criticized federal drug czar William Bennett for his approach to dealing with drug addicts. Barry argued:

> Bill Bennett has joined the parade of people who are using me as an excuse for our nation's failure to deal adequately with a problem that is an illness that affects millions and at the same time is a multibillion-dollar trade that is spawning violence in every major urban area of the nation . . . the Bennetts of the world must understand . . . that people who become addicted to drugs or alcohol are sick people who need treatment, not incarceration.[199]

Barry also blamed the ego involved in politics for his indiscretions. He explained, "My ego made me think they like me for *me*. With many of the women I went to bed with—I really thought I was the only one. The ego is a bitch! The male ego is worse. And when drugs and alcohol enter the picture, it gets totally out of hand."[200] He elaborated further:

> When I was in power, people around me would say, "Mr. Mayor, you're successful, you've done so much" and I began to believe it. Meetings started when I wanted them to, and phone conversations ended when I was finished talking. I began to feel seven feet tall. I didn't know I was miserable.
>
> As the job got tougher, I kept stuffing down the apprehension and disappointments, tried to push them down. I'd come home and have something on my mind and say, "O.K., I'll deal with that tomorrow." I tried to drown it at first with alcohol, eventually cocaine—and womanizing.[201]

Barry claimed that dependencies were only part of the problem when he took the FBI's bait and followed Rasheeda Moore into the Vista Hotel. He wrote that "the FBI got the right person to cooperate with them when they enlisted Rasheeda. She could talk me into anything. I know people wonder why I went into the Vista when I knew the FBI was following my every footstep. Again, my judgment was impaired, and I'm not trying to excuse it, but my situation was exacerbated by my drinking and drugging."[202]

Barry put even his lack of a moral compass on others, stating that his upbringing by a single mother, a lack of "biological information" and the absence of teaching about "values—nobody taught me about values, about how to relate to women outside of their being sexual objects."[203]

Barry has since married Cora Masters, and no claims of extramarital affairs have been made. He offered to take random drug tests during his most recent—and successful—run for mayor of the District. In April 1996, Barry took a surprise leave of absence for "spiritual and physical renewal" when he noticed "telltale signs of spiritual relapse and physical exhaustion."[204] Though some were skeptical about Barry's puzzling press release, no rumors or evidence of a relapse into drug use surfaced.[205] Addiction specialists praised Barry's self-awareness and said that his course of action was "the ideal, prophylactic treatment approach."[206] Barry's leave of absence lasted for two weeks, after which time he returned to the District to resume his daily duties.

While some consider Barry an old-time mayor and a poor manager of the city, continued snickering about his personal conduct and suspicions that he privately continues in his old ways have no visible foundation. They are a reflection of the difficulties faced by a person who does express remorse, does penance (being driven out of public office and serving a jail sentence), and restructures his life.

Conclusion

To return to Etzioni's observation, of the nine public figures studied only two repented rather fully. This chapter started with Colson and ended with Barry, both of whom showed remorse, did penance, and restructured their lives. Although questions have been raised about the full authenticity of the repentance of both, and both expressed occasional ambivalence about their guilt, these questions seem not to be legitimate. These are human beings, and so should not be held to a standard of perfection. Despite some verbal asides, they have met the standards of repentance.

The other seven are basically of two kinds. Some, including North, Nofziger, and Deaver, are hard-core recalcitrants. These public figures expressed no remorse. They added insult to injury by attacking the legitimacy of their convictions, the laws by which they were judged, and the institutions that judged them. Packwood's case is more complex and nuanced; he might be considered an ambivalent penitent. Atwater started as a hard-core recalcitrant and changed when faced with his own mortality.

It should be noted that a line was deliberately not drawn between violations of laws and those of mores. The issue here is moral conduct, and it matters less if the values that have been offended are ensconced only in mores or also in laws. For the same reasons, this chapter made little of the fact that three of the convictions were overturned.

Spiritual motivations also play some role, although it is not easy to correlate spirituality with repentance. Born-again Christianity contributed to the repentance exhibited by Colson and Atwater, yet North's Christianity has apparently only strengthened his defiant position. Indeed, some of North's strongest supporters are Evangelical Christians who believe that the moral requirements of opposing Communism in the Western hemisphere outweighed any duty to comply with congressional restrictions or subsequent attempts to sort out any wrongdoing. Barry has evoked spiritual components of his determination to shed his past involvement with alcohol, drug use, and womanizing.

Public reaction cuts both ways. North is treated as a hero by many, and such stature has probably reinforced his unrepentant stance. Barry gained politically from his repentance and might have been reinforced by these gains. Colson was celebrated, whereas protests against Packwood in his home state might have encouraged him to resign. Not enough is known about the others to advance this line of sociological analysis. Clearly, though, repentance, which morally is unrelated to gains and losses in public support, can be encouraged and retarded by the community.

Perhaps human beings will be forever tempted to blame some demon—alcohol or drugs—for their wrongdoings. The less society accepts such excuses, in court and in the community, the more people will be encouraged to take responsibility for their acts. Transgressors may, then, not only acknowledge their misdeeds more readily, but truly apologize for them, make amends, take their punishment, and above all restructure their lives.

Notes

1. Amitai Etzioni, "Say 'I'm Sorry' Like a Man," *New York Times*, 23 March 1988. For a definition of repentance and its significance as a civic concept, see Amitai Etzioni, "Introduction," in *Repentance: A Comparative Perspective*, ed. Amitai Etzioni and David E. Carney (Lanham, MD.: Rowman & Littlefield, 1997).

2. Larry Witham, "Moral Solutions," *Washington Times*, 12 May 1993, E1.

3. Witham, "Moral Solutions," E2.

4. Witham, "Moral Solutions," E2.

5. Their publication led to concern that further leaks might undermine the administration's ability to conduct foreign policy; Henry Kissinger later reported, "The massive hemorrhage of state secrets was bound to raise doubts about our reliability in the minds of other governments, friend and foe, and indeed about the stability of our political system." Henry Kissinger, *The White House Years* (Boston: Little, Brown, 1979), 730.

6. Sam J. Ervin, Jr., *The Whole Truth: The Watergate Conspiracy* (New York:

Random House, 1980), 194.

7. Witham, "Moral Solutions," E2.

8. Witham, "Moral Solutions," E2.

9. Fred Strasser, "The Long Repentance of Chuck Colson," *National Law Journal,* 17 December 1990, 5.

10. Strasser, "The Long Repentance of Chuck Colson," 5.

11. Strasser, "The Long Repentance of Chuck Colson," 22.

12. Alasdair Palmer, "From Buck House to White House," *The Spectator*, 15 May 1993, 20.

13. Palmer, "From Buck House to White House," 20.

14. Charles W. Colson, "Nixon: Was loyalty really his 'fatal flaw'?" *USA Today*, 27 April 1994, 10A.

15. Charles W. Colson, "I Shall Be Cooperating With the Special Prosecutor," *Washington Post*, 22 June 1974, A8.

16. Colson, "I Shall Be Cooperating," A8.

17. Colson, "I Shall Be Cooperating," A8.

18. Colson, "I Shall Be Cooperating," A8.

19. Colson, "I Shall Be Cooperating," A8.

20. Colson, "I Shall Be Cooperating," A8.

21. Palmer, "From Buck House to White House," 20.

22. Palmer, "From Buck House to White House," 20.

23. "Watergate or Something Like It Was Inevitable: An Interview with Charles Colson," *Christianity Today*, 12 March 1976, 6.

24. "Watergate or Something Like It Was Inevitable," 6.

25. George Lardner, "Buchanan Outlined Plan to Harass Democrats in '72, Memo Shows," *Washington Post*, 4 March 1996, A7.

26. Lardner, "Buchanan Outlined Plan," A7.

27. Clark Brooks, "Lest we forget, Watergate saga retold," *San Diego Union-Tribune*, 15 September 1994, E1.

28. Lardner, "Buchanan Outlined Plan," A7.

29. Lawrence Meyer, "McCord Ties Others to Plot; Liddy Jailed," *Washington Post*, 24 March 1973, A1, A10.

30. See Bob Woodward and Carl Bernstein, "McCord Charges Backed: Source Calls Allegation 'Disturbing,'" *Washington Post*, 27 March 1973, A10; Bob Woodward and Carl Bernstein, "Nixon Orders Staff to Testify on Watergate: McCord Differs From Mitchell's Testimony," *Washington Post*, 31 March 1973, A1; and Peter Osnos, "Liddy Silent Before Watergate Jury," *Washington Post*, 31 March 1973, A10.

31. G. Gordon Liddy, "Gordon Liddy: A Patriot Speaks," *Harper's*, October 1974, 45-51.

32. Liddy, "Gordon Liddy: A Patriot Speaks."

33. "Liddy Calls Watergate 'Basic' Politics," *Washington Post*, 8 January 1975,

A8.

34. "Liddy Calls Watergate 'Basic' Politics," A8.

35. "In the News," *Wall Street Journal*, 18 June 1992, A1.

36. Howard Kurtz, "Gordon Liddy on Shooting from the Lip," *Washington Post*, 26 April 1995, C1.

37. Kurtz, "Gordon Liddy on Shooting from the Lip," C1.

38. Kurtz, "Gordon Liddy on Shooting from the Lip," C1.

39. This provision placed Carter in a quandary in September 1980 when he had to face the issue of certification. Failure to certify "would lay bare the failure of his year-long policy of cooptation toward Managua and reveal the Sandinistas' cooperation with the Soviet Union, Cuba, and the El Salvadoran Communist party in the campaign then underway to overthrow the government of El Salvador." Despite "mounting evidence in the press of the Nicaraguan government's involvement in El Salvador," Carter decided to certify that the Sandinistas were not involved in such activities, reasoning that while "weapons were being transshipped—the evidence was not conclusive that the government of Nicaragua was responsible." See Richard C. Thornton, *The Carter Years: Toward a New Global Order* (New York: Paragon House, 1991), 513-4.

40. Bob Woodward, *VEIL: The Secret Wars of the CIA 1981-1987* (New York: Pocket Books, 1988), 111-2.

41. Quoted in Alan Riding, "Central Americans Split on U.S. Voting," *New York Times*, 4 August 1980, 3.

42. This initial support began pursuant to a classified "finding" about the need for such support, which the administration reported to Congress in compliance with applicable law. See Nina M. Serafino and Maureen Taft-Morales, "Contra Aid: Summary and Chronology of Major Congressional Action 1981-1989," CRS Report for Congress, Congressional Research Service, 1 November 1989.

43. Tip O'Neill and William Novak, *Man of the House: The Life and Political Memoirs of Speaker Tip O'Neill* (New York: Random House, 1987), 371. O'Neill was particularly concerned that the new administration wanted to get into a war in Central America; he later reported that he was afraid that Americans would look back on military action in Grenada "as a dress rehearsal for our invasion of Nicaragua," 367.

44. One of the initial aims of contra aid was to interdict the flow of arms to Communist guerrillas in El Salvador (which had no Caribbean coast and could not be supplied by Cuba directly). The Boland Amendment, initially prohibiting attempts to overthrow the Sandinistas, was passed by a vote of 411-0, a full year after the administration began supporting the contras. At the same time, the House rejected by a vote of 13-27 a proposed Harkin amendment that would have forbade all military aid for the contras. See Serafino and Taft-Morales, "Contra Aid." The unanimity of support for the Boland Amendment suggests the administration was satisfied that it could operate its contra aid program within the requirements of the

law. Over time, the prohibitions of the Boland Amendment were tightened. None of the Boland Amendments mentioned the National Security Council by name in the list of agencies prohibited from aiding the contras, a fact that led some administration supporters to argue that the council was not subject to the amendment's restrictions.

45. Amendment to the Intelligence Authorization Act for Fiscal Year 1983, 98th Cong., H.R. 2760, July 28, 1983. See Section 801(a).

46. Nicholas M. Horrock and Glen Elsasser, "North convicted on 3 counts, Jury acquits ex-Marine on 9 charges," *Chicago Tribune*, 5 May 1989, C1

47. Joint Hearings before the Senate Select Committee on Secret Military Assistance to Iran and the Nicaraguan Opposition, 100-2, at 546 (Barnes letter); *Hearings*, 100-2, at 559 (Hamilton Letter).

48. Joint Hearings before the Senate Select Committee, 5.

49. *Report of the Congressional Committees Investigating the Iran-Contra Affair*, 17 November 1987, 141.

50. Senate Intelligence Committee News Release, 5 September 1985.

51. Senate Intelligence Committee News Release.

52. Senate Intelligence Committee News Release.

53. Horrock and Elsasser, "North convicted on 3 counts," C1.

54. Peter Kornbluh, "Oliver Twisted: A Day in the Former Life of a Would-Be Senator," *Mother Jones*, May/June 1994, 11.

55. Kornbluh, "Oliver Twisted," 11.

56. Kornbluh, "Oliver Twisted," 11.

57. *Report of the Congressional Committees* 10-11, 305. Cf. North Test., *Hearings*, 100-7, Part I, 7 July 1987, at 28-33.

58. *Report of the Congressional Committees*, 314.

59. *Report of the Congressional Committees*, 271, 313. Cf., North Test., *Hearings*, 100-7, Part I, 8 July 1987, at 106-8.

60. *Report of the Congressional Committees*, 98.

61. *Report of the Congressional Committees*, 286.

62. *Report of the Congressional Committees*, 10, 318. Cf., Fawn Hall Test., *Hearings*, 100-5, 8 June 1987, 508-10. See also Robert C. McFarlane's testimony concerning "shredding parties" in "Joint Hearings before the House Select Committee to Investigate Covert Arms Transactions with Iran and Senate Select Committee on Secret Military Assistance To Iran and The Nicaraguan Opposition," 100-2, 11 May 1987, 71.

63. *Report of the Congressional Committees*, 307.

64. Stephen Engelberg, "Prosecutor Asks for Dismissal of Key Charges Against North: Disclosure of Secrets Feared," *New York Times*, 6 January 1989, A1.

65. Engelberg, "Prosecutor Asks for Dismissal," A1.

66. Engelberg, "Prosecutor Asks for Dismissal," A17.

67. When asked during the congressional hearing whether he was "avoiding

telling the truth for the military purposes of the Contras," North answered: "Very clearly." Quoted in Mary Belcher, "Prosecutor, North spar over 'lying,'" *Washington Times*, 12 April 1989, A1.

68. *Hearings*, Part I, 192.

69. *Hearings*, Part III, 1636-46.

70. *Hearings*, 1636.

71. *Hearings*, 1636.

72. *Hearings*, 1641-44.

73. *Hearings*, 1644-45.

74. "North Labels Iran-Contra Charges 'Badge of Honor': Vilified and Slandered, He Asserts," *Los Angeles Times*, 2 May 1988, 1.

75. Belcher, "Prosecutor, North spar," A8.

76. Belcher, "Prosecutor, North spar," A1.

77. *Hearings*, Part I, 191.

78. Belcher, "Prosecutor, North spar," A8.

79. "North blames McFarlane for letter falsely denying Contra aid," *San Diego Union-Tribune*, 12 April 1989, A3.

80. "North blames McFarlane," A3.

81. Ed Magnuson, "Pawn Among Giants," *Time*, 17 April 1989, 22.

82. Belcher, "Prosecutor, North spar," A8.

83. *Hearings*, 100-7, Part I, 109.

84. "North Labels Iran-Contra Charges 'Badge of Honor.'"

85. "North Labels Iran-Contra Charges 'Badge of Honor.'"

86. David M. Poole, "North brandishes 'badge of honor,'" *Roanoke Times & World-News*, 3 May 1988, A6.

87. Ethan Bronner, "North's conviction remains nullified," *Boston Globe*, 29 May 1991, A1.

88. "Interview—Oliver North: 'I Know That I'm Forgiven,'" *Christianity Today*, 25 November 1991, 44.

89. Lynn Rosellini, "Oliver North's New Crusade," *U.S. News & World Report*, 6 June 1994, 33.

90. Poole, "North brandishes 'badge of honor,'" A6.

91. "North Says Criminal Charges Against Him Are 'an Honor,'" *New York Times*, 3 May 1988, B7.

92. Poole, "North brandishes 'badge of honor.'"

93. Unless otherwise indicated, all polling data unless otherwise indicated is obtained via LEXIS from Roper Center, Public Opinion Online. Gallup Organization conducted a telephone poll of 500 adults nationally on May 5, 1989, for *Newsweek*. Polling data on North as a patriot is found at accession no. 0048536. Polling data on North acting for personal gain or profit is found at accession no. 0048535.

94. Additionally, 6 percent said they didn't know. Gallup Organization telephone poll of 1,239 adults nationally between May 4 and May 7, 1989. Accession no.

0026246.

95. Additionally, 4 percent were neutral and 8 percent unsure. The Tarrance Group & Mellman, Lazarus & Lake telephone poll of 882 registered voters nationally conducted between April 16 and April 18, 1994. Accession no. 0216302.

Additional polls show a fairly consistent picture. A May 1989 poll found that 59 percent of adults reported very or mostly favorable opinions compared to 28 percent that were mostly or very unfavorable. Gallup poll of 1,239 adults nationally taken between May 4 and May 7, 1989, asking opinion of North found 22 percent very favorable, 37 percent mostly favorable, 18 percent mostly unfavorable, 10 percent very unfavorable, 1 percent never heard of him, and 12 percent can't rate. Accession 0026244.

A poll in October 1994 found respondents reported 32 percent favorable impressions of North, as opposed to 47 percent unfavorable. Yankelovich Partners poll of 800 adults nationally sponsored by *Time* and CNN conducted between October 11 and October 12, 1994, asked if impressions of North are generally favorable or generally unfavorable; 16 percent of respondents reported they were not familiar with North and 5 percent were not sure. Accession no. 0223306.

A poll in July 1994 found 24 percent favorable and 27 percent not favorable. CBS News and *New York Times* poll of 1,339 adults nationally conducted between July 14 and July 17, 1994, asked respondents their opinion of North; 30 percent of respondents were undecided, 18 percent had not heard enough, and 1 percent refused to answer. Accession no. 0219243.

A poll released in September 1994 found 43 percent very or mostly favorable, while 36 percent were mostly or very unfavorable. Princeton Survey Research Associates poll sponsored by *Newsweek*; 1,202 adults nationally were polled between August 26 and September 1, 1994, on their overall opinion of Oliver North and 9 percent answered very favorable, 34 percent mostly favorable, 22 percent mostly unfavorable, 14 percent very unfavorable, 5 percent never heard of him, 16 percent had heard of him but could not rate him, and fewer than 0.5 percent refused to answer. Accession no. 0228332.

A poll from September 1994 found overall opinions of North were 47 percent very or mostly favorable as opposed to 43 percent mostly very unfavorable. Princeton Survey Research Associates poll of 3,800 adults nationally sponsored by the *Times-Mirror* with interviews between July 13 and July 27, 1994, and some reinterviews between September 9 and September 11, 1994, asked overall opinion of Oliver North. Respondents reported 14 percent very favorable, 33 percent mostly favorable, 33 percent mostly favorable, 26 percent mostly unfavorable, 17 percent very unfavorable, 4 percent never heard of North, 6 percent could not rate. Accession no. 0222507.

96. *New York Times Book Review*, 13 November 1994.

97. *New York Times Book Review*, 13 November 1994.

98. Amendment to the Intelligence Authorization Act for Fiscal Year 1983, 98th

Cong., H.R. 2760, 28 July 1983. See Section 801(a).

99. Rita Ciolli, "McFarlane: I Lied; Guilty of Deceiving Congress about Secret Aid to Contras," *Newsday*, 12 March 1988, 5.

100. Ciolli, "McFarlane: I Lied," *Newsday*, 3 March 1988.

101. Cf. Robert C. McFarlane, Testimony, Joint Hearings Before the House Select Committee to Investigate Covert Arms Transactions with Iran and Senate Select Committee on Secret Military Assistance to Iran and the Nicaraguan Opposition, 100-2, 11 May 1987, at 86.

102. McFarlane, Testimony, 86.

103. McFarlane, Testimony, 86.

104. Brock Brower, "Bud McFarlane: Semper Fi," *New York Times*, 22 January 1989, A21.

105. McFarlane, Testimony, 2.

106. McFarlane, Testimony, 2.

107. McFarlane, Testimony, 2.

108. Brower, "Bud McFarlane," A21.

109. Brower, "Bud McFarlane," A21.

110. Brower, "Bud McFarlane," A21.

111. Robert C. McFarlane with Zofia Smardz, *Special Trust* (New York: Cadell & Davies, 1994), 112.

112. McFarlane with Smardz, *Special Trust*, 362.

113. McFarlane with Smardz, *Special Trust*, 357.

114. Tribune Wire Services, "Nofziger Convicted of Illegal Lobbying: Ex-Reagan Aide Found Guilty in Wedtech Case," *San Diego Union-Tribune*, 11 February 1988, A6.

115. Tribune Wire Services, "Nofziger Convicted of Illegal Lobbying," A1.

116. George Lardner, Jr., "Nofziger Convicted of Illegal Lobbying: Ex-Reagan Aide Attacks 'Lousy' Law," *Washington Post*, 12 February 1988, A1.

117. Harris Collingwood, "Where Lying Was Business as Usual," *Business Week*, 20 November 1989, 16.

118. Tribune Wire Services, "Nofziger Convicted of Illegal Lobbying," A1.

119. Christopher Drew, "Jury Convicts Nofziger: Reagan's Ex-Aide Guilty of Influence Peddling," *Chicago Tribune*, 12 February 1988, C1.

120. Martin Tolchin, "Nofziger Wins Court Reversal of Conviction," *New York Times*, 28 June 1989, A5.

121. Tolchin, "Nofziger Wins Court Reversal," A5.

122. Tribune Wire Services, "Nofziger Convicted of Illegal Lobbying," A1.

123. Lardner, "Nofziger Convicted of Illegal Lobbying," A1.

124. "Nofziger Convicted in Lobbying: Former Reagan Aide Is Convicted of 3 of 4 Felonies," *San Diego Union-Tribune*, 12 February 1988, A1.

125. Paul Houston and Eric Lichtblau, "Unrepentant Nofziger Gets 90 Days, Is Fined $30,000," *Los Angeles Times,* 9 April 1988, A1.

126. Houston and Lichtblau, "Unrepentant Nofziger Gets 90 Days," A1.

127. Houston and Lichtblau, "Unrepentant Nofziger Gets 90 Days," A1.

128. Lyn Nofziger, *Nofziger* (Washington, DC: Regnery Gateway, 1992), 353.

129. Collingwood, "Where Lying Was Business as Usual," 16.

130. George Lardner, Jr., "Nofziger's Convictions Overturned," *Washington Post,* 28 June 1989, A1.

131. Jay Mallin, "I'm Innocent: Nofziger conviction overturned," *Washington Times,* 28 June 1989, A1.

132. Robert L. Jackson, "Jury Convicts Deaver of Three Perjury Counts: Ex-White House Aide Faces Up to 15 Years in Prison, Plus Fines," *Los Angeles Times,* 17 December 1987, A1.

133. Ben A. Franklin, "Deaver Found Guilty of Lying 3 Times Under Oath," *New York Times,* 17 December 1987, A1.

134. "The Deaver Indictment," *Legal Times,* 23 March 1987, 16.

135. "The Deaver Indictment," 20.

136. Franklin, "Deaver Found Guilty," A7.

137. Robert L. Jackson, "Deaver Fined, Gets 3 Years Probation: Ex-Reagan Aide to Pay $100,000 in Perjury Case, Do Community Service," *Los Angeles Times,* 24 September 1988, A1.

138. Bill McAllister, "Deaver Is Found Guilty of Lying About Lobbying: Former Reagan Aide Acquitted on 2 Counts," *Washington Post,* 17 December 1987, A1.

139. McAllister, "Deaver is Found Guilty," A1.

140. Jackson, "Deaver Fined," A1.

141. "Q&A with Michael Deaver, former White House aide in front of U.S. District Court following his sentencing," *Federal News Service,* 23 September 1988.

142. Jackson, "Deaver Fined," A7.

143. Tom Turnipseed, "What Lee Atwater Learned," *Washington Post,* 16 April 1991, A19.

144. John W. Mashek, "Ailing GOP Chief Regrets Statements on Dukakis in 1988," *Boston Globe,* 31 January 1991, A2.

145. Associated Press, "Atwater Apologizes for '88 Remark about Dukakis," *Washington Post,* 13 January 1991, A6.

146. Associated Press, "Atwater Apologizes," A6.

147. Lee Bandy, "GOP 'Bad Boy' Atwater Says He's Found Jesus," *Chicago Tribune,* 3 November 1990, A1.

148. Lee Bandy, "Religion changes 'Bad Boy' of politics: GOP's ailing Lee Atwater says he's through fighting," *Orange County Register,* 3 November 1990, A6.

149. Rowland Evans and Robert Novak, "Atwater Without Apologies," *Washington Post,* 5 April 1990, A1.

150. Turnipseed, "What Lee Atwater Learned," A19.

151. Maschek, "Ailing GOP Chief," A7.

152. Hamilton & Staff poll of 1,503 registered voters nationally conducted for the American Medical Political Action Committee between November 29 and December 14, 1989, asking impressions of Lee Atwater, found 3 percent very favorable, 20 percent somewhat favorable, 2 percent a little of both, 11 percent somewhat unfavorable, 7 percent very unfavorable, 57 percent don't recognize or can't rate. Accession no. 0075309.

153. Clifford Krauss, "Drinking Might Have Prompted Sexual Advances, Senator Says," *New York Times*, 28 November 1992, A9.

154. Guy Gugliotta and John E. Yang, "Exhaustive, Damning Documents," *Washington Post*, 8 September 1995, A1.

155. Gugliotta and Yang, "Exhaustive, Damning Documents," A9.

156. Senate Select Committee on Ethics, *Documents related to the investigation of Senator Robert Packwood*, S. Prt. 104-30, Vol. 1 of 10, 3-4.

157. Florence Graves and Charles E. Shepard, "Packwood Accused of Sexual Advances; Alleged Behavior Pattern Counters Image," *Washington Post*, 22 November 1992, A1.

158. Martin Tolchin, "Packwood Offers Apology Without Saying for What," *New York Times*, 11 December 1992, A24.

159. Krauss, "Drinking Might Have Prompted Sexual Advances," A9.

160. "Packwood Offers Apology," *New York Times*, 11 December 1992, A24.

161. "Packwood Offers Apology," A24.

162. Kevin Sack, "It's Not Me That's Guilty, My Addiction Just Took Over," *New York Times*, 6 December 1992, 4.

163. Gugliotta and Yang, "Exhaustive, Damning Documents," A1.

164. Phil Kuntz, "Senate Panel Urges Expulsion for Packwood," *Wall Street Journal*, 7 October 1995, A16.

165. Kate O'Beirne, "Bread & Circuses: Senator Bob Packwood's Public and Private Stance on Women," *National Review*, October 1995.

166. *This Week With David Brinkley*, Transcript #654, 8 May 1994.

167. *This Week With David Brinkley*, Transcript #654.

168. *This Week With David Brinkley*, Transcript #654.

169. *This Week With David Brinkley*, Transcript #654.

170. *Congressional Record*, 1 November 1993, S14737.

171. *Congressional Record*, S14748-S14749.

172. William J. Eaton, "Packwood Apologizes, Vows Not to Resign," *Los Angeles Times*, 11 December 1992, A4.

173. Helen Dewar, "Packwood Defends Conduct, Apologizes on Television Show," *The Washington Post*, 1 April 1994, A12

174. Bob Packwood, "Bill and Me," *Wall Street Journal*, 13 May 1994.

175. *Congressional Record*, 7 September 1995, S 12796.

176. *Congressional Record*, S 12797.

177. *20/20*, 8 September 1995, Transcript #1536-2.

178. *Congressional Record*, 7 September 1995, S 12796.

179. *20/20*, 8 September 1995, Transcript #1536-2.

180. "The Barry Verdict: Mistrial," *Washington Times*, 11 August 1990, A8.

181. B. Drummons Ayres, Jr., "Washington Mayor Assails U.S. Officials on Reports of Drug Use," *New York Times*, 1 September 1989, A12.

182. Sharon LaFraniere, "Barry Lashes Out Against Allegations of Using Drugs," *Washington Post*, 16 September 1989, B1.

183. LaFraniere, "Barry Lashes Out," B1.

184. David Remnick, "The Situationist," *The New Yorker*, 5 September 1994, 87-8.

185. These are highlights reprinted from the Barry trial in the *Washington Times*. In cross-examination of Moore, Barry's defense attorney Robert Mance was attempting to demonstrate that Barry's alcohol abuse clouded his thinking and led to his drug abuse. Quoted "Southerland tells of buying Barry cocaine," *Washington Times*, 12 July 1990, B4.

186. "Interview with Effi Barry," *United Press International News Service*, 21 February 1990, BC cycle.

187. Remnick, "The Situationist."

188. Sharon, "Barry Lashes Out."

189. Sharon, "Barry Lashes Out."

190. Michael York and Tracy Thompson, "Barry Sentenced to 6 Months in Prison," *Washington Post*, 27 October 1990, A1.

191. York and Thompson, "Barry Sentenced to 6 Months in Prison," 372.

192. Quotes from Barry's letter are found at "I Ask the Court for Leniency in Its Decision on My Sentence," *Washington Post*, 26 October 1990, A12.

193. Barry, "I Ask the Court for Leniency," A12.

194. Barry, "I Ask the Court for Leniency," A12.

195. Michael Specter, "Marion Barry, Airing His Vices," *Washington Post*, 14 May 1991.

196. Jacqueline Trescott, "Barry and the Addictions of Power," *Washington Post*, 1 April 1991, D8.

197. William Raspberry, "Barry's Saturday Speech," *Washington Post*, 13 August 1990, A11.

198. Michael Abramowicz and Renee Sanchez, "Barry Basks in Glow of 'Donahue,'" *Washington Post*, 1 November 1990, B4.

199. "Barry: Bennett Using Him as a Scapegoat," *Washington Post*, 10 November 1990, B7.

200. Trescott, "Barry and the Addictions of Power," D8.

201. Trescott, "Barry and the Addictions of Power," D1.

202. Trescott, "Barry and the Addictions of Power," D8.

203. Trescott, "Barry and the Addictions of Power," D8.

204. Yolanda Woodlee and Cindy Loose, "A Weary Barry Finds Little Rest," *Washington Post*, 30 April 1996.

205. Barry's wife, Cora Masters Barry, sought to dispel any speculation by reporting that Barry had not begun using drugs or alcohol again.

206. Amy Argetsinger, "Addiction Specialists Hail Mayor's Move," *Washington Post*, 30 April 1996.

Chapter Seven

Rx: Redemption

Stanley Platman

Despite its ubiquity in religious doctrine and practice, the concept of redemption has rarely been a major factor in American secular life. If a citizen commits a felony, for instance, he or she is not always allowed to reestablish such rights as voting or the ability to hold certain occupations or to possess many kinds of weapons—abrogations that place such people distinctly apart from (indeed, below) the status of other Americans. It is rare that transgressors are presented with a clear and distinct path to redemption—a list of steps and milestones that can be completed, with the expectation that the citizen would be returned to full secular status when they are finished.

The rest of this book argues that the presence of a carrot-and-stick approach to redemption can be a valuable facet of American civil culture. If those who have transgressed are presented with a distinct plan to clearing their name and reputation, they would presumably have an incentive to remain on the straight and narrow. The idea is that this status would not be achieved on the cheap—the activities of a transgressor on the way to redemption would be subject to rigorous verification, so that his or her honesty and credibility could be assured. (For one thing, redemption that is granted too easily would encourage antisocial behavior in the first place, which is obviously not desirable.) Thus, this chapter argues that a clear system of incentives—rather than an adhoc system that lacks an explicit contract between the community and its transgressors—would serve the public good by investing violators in the law-abiding mainstream and helping keep them there.

Certain professions, depending on the state, do offer practitioners a procedure for regaining their status after committing a work-related violation. For instance, an attorney's disbarment may sometimes be reversed if certain conditions are subsequently met. Typically, such redemptions are set in motion once a practitioner has already been identified to the public, and to his or her peers and clients, as having transgressed. But for the past decade or more, many members of the medical community have been perfecting a different model, one in which drug- and alcohol-abusing physicians are allowed one big chance to straighten out their lives before their abuse even becomes public, in the hopes that they will take the opportunity to straighten themselves out.

Instead of being reported to a disciplinary board—which does exist, and punishes noncompliant physicians severely—the vast majority of substance-abusing doctors under this system are referred to a committee that acts simultaneously as their advocate and their monitor, all in an effort to cure the impaired physicians rather than punish them. Doctors who work within this rigorous system to cure themselves will be rewarded with a minimum disruption to their medical practice. It is almost as if they were privately counseled and absolved by a priest who has the ability to monitor their subsequent actions and blow the whistle if they fail to stay clean.

As this chapter will discuss later, such a system is inherently delicate because it must simultaneously balance the sometimes opposing needs of doctors and patients. That is, since these programs as a rule do not tell patients about the misbehaviors of doctors who are treating them (because continuing to practice often helps a doctor's recovery), substance abuse counselors running the program must make hard decisions about which doctors remain sufficiently unimpaired from their substance abuse to be allowed to continue treating patients.

Yet despite such challenges, these physician rehabilitation programs are worth a closer look for two key reasons. First, program administrators report that patients have rarely been harmed by doctors who were allowed to continue practice after being identified as having a substance abuse problem. Second, the results of such programs—as measured by the percentage of doctors who have emerged from them clean and practicing first-rate medicine—indicate a startling success.

A good example is the Physician Rehabilitation Program of the Medical and Chirurgical Faculty of Maryland (known as Med Chi), a program that will be the focus of this chapter. Initially, in the late 1970s, the program was informal. But once officials began doing outreach, the number of referrals tripled, from 50 to 60 in the late 1980s to 146 in 1992-93, before falling back to about 125 to 130 during the late 1990s. A 1992 longitudinal study that went back to the program's creation found an 89 percent success rate for cases of chemical dependency, according to the program's director, Michael Llufrio. When mental health factors were included, the rate dropped slightly to 86 percent. In 1996, the program had a 3.5 percent relapse rate. (The longitudinal "failure" figures include physicians who never managed to go straight at all, not just those who succeeded and later relapsed.)

To supporters, these findings indicate the power of a program that levels honestly with its transgressors and forces them to take their predicament seriously—with both serious penalties for continued violations and tangible rewards for genuine compliance. Such programs may not work for every profession or in every community. But their apparent success in Maryland demands closer investigation. The purpose of this chapter is to describe how such programs work, in order to gauge what their broader value might be.

The Problem and Its Detection

For better or for worse, the medical community will always have problem doctors. As the *British Medical Journal* has pointed out, "Think how surprised we would be by a community of 130,000 people (the number of doctors in Britain) where nobody committed terrible crimes, went mad, misused drugs, slacked on the job, became corrupt, lost competence, or exploited their position. Such a community cannot be imagined. And yet doctors often behave as if they are surprised by the existence of problem doctors. We choose to turn the other way rather than understand and develop ways of responding."[1]

Reliable analyses attribute at least three-fourths of physician impairment cases to substance abuse and addiction; these can also be "primary," or "secondary" to underlying psychopathologies or physical illnesses.[2] A 1973 article by the American Medical Association's Council on Mental Health[3] suggested that as many as 3.2 percent of physicians suffer from alcoholism, 2 percent from drug abuse, and 1.3 percent from other mental disorders. But later studies have placed these figured dramatically higher—as high as 12 to 16 percent.[4]

At the outset, substance abuse is not always harmful to a physician's quality of care, but can become so if it continues untreated. The impairment potential of licit drugs used legally or illegally has been well recognized and has been found to be a reason for both changing performance and hospital admission.[5] But physicians with substance-abuse problems are not always recognized by their peers, even if they work in a hospital and must collaborate with many other professionals under quality assurance regimes. The following are some of the telltale signs: changes in behavior, failures in responsibility, small errors, missing drugs, alcohol on the breath, missed appointments, not returning phone calls, absenteeism, malpractice cases, and friction with staff and peers.

In Maryland's program, identification of potential substance abusers begins after a report is received from a physician, patients, family, office or institutional staff—or even anonymously. Michael Llufrio, the Maryland program's director, notes that hospitals are not required by law to report suspected substance-abusing doctors to his committee, though some do so voluntarily. Rather, he says, referrals are most often made by the physician himself or herself, with referrals from physician colleagues ranking second. Complaints from peers, he says, are generally not about a physician's practice of medicine being impaired; they are generally about reports of doctors seeming depressed or missing work time or smelling of alcohol.

Only infrequently does substance abuse causes actual medical impairment in

Maryland, Llufrio says, possibly because the state's carrot-and-stick approach encourages doctors to undergo rehabilitation before their problem becomes that serious. The most serious cases—in which doctors are blatantly disruptive to their environment—are typically forwarded to the disciplinary board directly, rather than offering a chance at quiet redemption. But these cases are rare—fewer than one in ten of all substance-abuse cases, according to Llufrio's figures.

The Intervention Process

Upon receipt of a report, the physician rehabilitation committee will make several discreet inquiries to multiple sources so that their information may be verified. At this point, problems may arise—for instance, the committee may get a report from the spouse of the physician, who states that he or she may not talk to the physician for fear of the response. Alternatively, if no problem is found to be evident, the case is either dropped from active status or held open for continued observation.

However, if the initial report appears to be substantiated, the physician is contacted and informed, with a request to meet the committee's members and staff. This phase is known as intervention. The committee will include a team of drug counselors; in all, it can take several hours of interviews. The philosophy of the initial evaluation is one of helpfulness and honest communication. It is not intended to be an inquisition, although often it is assisted by allowing encounters involving many individuals associated with the physician. The physician who is suspected of abuse may attend this initial evaluation alone or with family, significant others, or a lawyer.

"We collect our information from a variety of sources," Llufrio explains. "We get reports from the treatment person, whether in- or outpatient. There's a monitor—a committee member, myself, or my staff. We meet monthly to start with. Also you may have a therapist. We conduct monitoring, which can be draconian. We take urine and breathalyzer samples, three to four times a week, winding down over time to a couple times a year. We also get reports from vocational monitors—people who have an opportunity to observe them at work. It can be a chief of service, a practice partner, the medical director of the HMO. It can be an office manager if they're a solo practitioner. The physician always knows who it is; they have to sign a release."

At the outset, of course, some physicians are reluctant to admit how impaired they are. But many come to realize—after repeated contact with addiction professionals—just how important their endeavor is. One physician recalled that when he first met with the committee:

> I still did not really believe that I had a problem. I felt angry at all the things they forced me to do: see a counselor who specialized in drug rehabilitation, see a psychiatrist, go to regular twelve-step meetings and get a sponsor, report to a monitor, and submit to random urine screens one to two times a week. . . . I went along at first, simply because I had no choice, As time went by, I started to realize that I did have a serious problem with substance abuse, and that everything that

physician rehab required was for my own good. I found my life turning around; I felt much happier than I had been since childhood, more at ease, more confident, and much more in control than I had ever been. I also began to understand that my counselors were on my side.[6]

Sometimes this process can be contentious; one physician who eventually recovered from his addiction recalled that when the committee called him in, "I called them liars and asked them how much money they planned to make by keeping me in their program. They told me money was not a factor, and I blustered more."[7] With the vast majority, however, it is often immediately evident that although the individual is having serious problems, he or she is anxious to be helped and enter into treatment.

Monitoring and Enforcement

At this point, the physician will be referred for treatment—or, indeed, may have already voluntarily entered treatment by himself or herself. In either case, the physician is asked to sign a customized contract and a monitor, usually a committee member, is assigned to the case. The contract typically lasts for five years, with built-in penalties for relapse or noncompliance. "You either agree to the contract or not," in the words of one recovering alcoholic we will call Joel. "But if you don't agree to it, they sure as heck would have you reported. It's a stick-and-carrot method. You know you're under the gun."

Contracts are variable, depending on the individual needs of the doctor. In severe cases, physicians will be hospitalized immediately, which naturally prevents them—in the short term, at least—from practicing medicine and potentially endangering patients. In somewhat less severe cases, the physician can be given a few weeks to close their office and then enter hospitalization for, say, three months.

But like most doctors who come before the committee, Joel was not deemed to be in imminent danger of harming patients, so he was allowed to continue his medical practice as his treatment progressed. He was assigned to meet with a counselor, at first once every two weeks, though this frequency was eventually lowered as his counselor confirmed that he was making substantial progress. In addition, Joel was placed in once-a-week group therapy sessions for addicts and recovering alcoholics. Since he was already seeing a psychotherapist, Joel agreed to continue doing so as part of his contract. And he pledged to attend Alcoholics Anonymous meetings, at first a minimum of three a week, and preferably more, plus an end-of-the-month written summary of his reactions to the most significant topics.

Joel was also placed on a random urine screening regimen. The frequency and invasiveness of urine screening varies depending on the patient's condition. The physician-patient is required to call a phone number every day to find out if his or her number has been drawn. If it's their day, patients must go to a lab for the sample to be taken. The frequency of screenings per month varies; in Joel's case, it was three to five, but "problem" cases can go higher. "I think they were gentler with me because I turned myself in voluntarily."

Llufrio said that Joel was "probably fairly moderate in his degree of resistance, but he may have had a fair amount of denial initially. There's a wide variation in the degree of denial—people may comply with the letter of the law, but not the spirit. They'll say, 'I can't drink now, and I'll put in my five years, but then I'll do what I want.' They will play the game. Some of them will be honest; some never really buy it, but those are rare. Sometimes they'll finish five years and come back voluntarily. Mostly you're looking at a long-term process. Some of these people have spent years and decades getting into the condition where they are now. It really takes a toll, physically, mentally, and emotionally."

In the most serious cases, counselors may order the use of antabuse, a drug that creates a toxic reaction when alcohol is ingested; it's capable of making the patient severely nauseated. The patients may administer it themselves, but as a way of enforcement, the random urine screenings check for it. "In my case they recommended it, but I objected," Joel says, citing its side effects, which include ulcerations of the skin, queasiness, dizziness, and, in the long term, the potential for neurological damage. Because the rest of his regimen was verifiable, and his case was not deemed to be so severe as to warrant forcing him to take antabuse, his counselor agreed to back off from ordering it. Joel says that this flexibility deepened the trust between him and his counselor, and he kept his treatment steady enough that his counselor never forced it on him involuntarily.

Contracts such as these typically run one year and are reevaluated at the end of those twelve months. "One of the things about Med Chi and the physician rehabilitation committee is that they act like they're on your team, and they're not there to punish you," Joel says. "They only punish you if you don't cooperate, and even then it's not just arbitrary. I didn't want to take antabuse. I said I was offended by the idea, that I came here voluntarily, so give me a break. They said fine, and that was reevaluated every time I came in."

The contracts are in force even when patients are on vacation—indeed, especially when on vacation, since the temptations of alcohol and drugs are often higher in such circumstances. "They would really lean on you," Joel says. "They'd say, 'Look, you're really taking some very serious risks here, so let's try to reduce those risks by taking antabuse.' They have the right to say you'll have to go to a lab and get screened. I've heard of cases where somebody's on a ski trip and they'll have to drive thirty miles to the closest lab."

There are built-in steps for dealing with relapses—the counselors will augment a physician's treatment first, then at the second relapse, he or she is reported to the disciplinary board. "If you have a breach," Joel adds, "you rewrite the contract. If the breach is only a slip that's very minor—maybe you just got a little drunk—or whether it's a binge, they have penalties suited to each case. These guys are very professional. They know a drunk when they see one. They can always say that if you don't do something, they'll turn you over to the board."

In Joel's case, he did have one slip, which he reported to the committee; they rewrote the contract. He also told his counselor about a depression he was going through at one point, and they adjusted his regimen to cope with that situation most effectively. A key to his recovery, according to Joel, is that the medical disciplinary board "still doesn't know I exist," he says. "I first turned myself in January 1995, and I'm still on contract, which is typical. For a good case like mine, a contract is required for five years. At end of the five years, I won't be on contract anymore, though I'm always welcome to call. My counselor has gotten me through some very tough moments, and I would not hesitate to call him if I was in a bad state."

Llufrio agrees that the counselor's role is pivotal. "I've been doing this for twenty years," he says, "and I know I have to be a bit cynical about everyone I deal with. It's not that I don't allow them the opportunity to change, but at the same time, I have to pace myself. There are a few people who are simply very good—they're basically sociopaths who are very good at playing the game. It absolutely does happen, though it's a small percentage. Generally, for any alcoholic, life can be difficult. You have to build a defense mechanism, and they use it in an unhealthy way. Everybody else needs to do that for their emotional health, but for the alcoholic it's over the fence. Some people can't give up relying on their defense mechanisms."

Successes and Failures

On the one hand, the results of substance abuse treatment have been viewed by the medical profession and the public as generally poor.[8] Recidivism can indeed be high where individuals of low socioeconomic status have little follow-up or continuity of care; in these cases, acute detoxification is often the primary method, which can do little more than temporarily reduce the individual's tolerance over the short haul. But addiction treatment, if done correctly, has been shown to work generally; an article in the *Journal of the American Medical Association*[9] reinforces the value of combining mandatory inpatient rehabilitation with follow-up in Alcoholics Anonymous, rather than using compulsory AA or other treatments by themselves.

More to the point, the treatment of physicians and other health professionals has had even more positive outcomes than that for the general public—usually in the 75 percent range[10] and even as high as 85 percent, which is a remarkable rate of success for any chronic, relapsing disorder. A two-year follow-up of physicians at the Mayo Clinic in 1984, for instance, showed a success rate of 83 percent for physicians, compared to 62 percent in nonphysicians.[11]

"Some people who are exceedingly sick will have a huge battle and never get well, because of cumulative physical damage," Llufrio says. "But for others, you'll do an intervention and they'll have a moment of clarity and will get into a strong recovery pattern." On a personal level, Llufrio says, "a lot of the success has to do with how internalized the person is and the responsibility they take for their past. If their finger is pointed away from them—why they got into the situation they got into—then chances are not good. You look for at least partial responsibility. A good recovery requires a good inward look. If not, they're not getting it, they're not focusing on their character defects. It takes recognizing that a change within is more valuable than the outside world."

Part of what keeps physicians clean is the reinforcement from Alcoholics Anonymous meetings. "We ask them to attend twelve-step fellowship meetings—four or five a week at the beginning is typical," Llufrio says. "We don't get slips signed, but we do ask them to fill out a form with a narrative—who, what, where it was, followed by a few sentences about how the topics discussed applied to you. We feel that anyone can make a list of dates and facts, but after a while if you see the same narrative, you start to suspect things."

Successful results for physicians are also due to a number of special factors, including: fear of losing one's livelihood; the need to get their license back for employment; higher socioeconomic status; a better support system; a contingency contract with an entity that has the clout to jeopardize one's future; mandatory urine testing; monitoring by peers; financial support; long-term follow-up; a close relationship with the medical society's impairment committee and the state's licensing authority; and the availability of supervised employment opportunities.

Of these, the most significant factor keeping doctors clean may be the fact that they are usually allowed to continue practicing medicine during their recovery. In Maryland's program, the percentage of people who continue to work is very high—more than 80 percent. (The rest either need inpatient care, have their license suspended, or simply volunteer to withdraw from their practice.)

"I needed to work because I thought I could continue safely without my status as a recovering alcoholic interfering with my judgment," Joel says. "When your whole life is medicine, as it is with most doctors, it's not a 9-to-5 job. It's seventy hours a week. That's a big vacuum. It's also financially significant to continue to work. I have three kids in private school and a mortgage. If I don't work, I don't eat. So that becomes fundamental to the success of the recovery."

As one recovered Maryland physician added, "My name never got in the paper. My license did not get taken away. My family did not reject me. . . . I have enjoyed over two and a half years of continuous sobriety and drug-free life, and continue to do all the legwork to maintain my recovery program."[12]

Balancing Risks and Roles

For hospital administrators and fellow physicians, handling substance abuse among doctors is tricky. That is because the two main goals can often be in direct opposition: ensuring safe and competent patient care and demonstrating concern for the welfare of the sick physician and his or her family. For Llufrio and his colleagues, giving the go-ahead for a possibly impaired doctor is a judgment call—but one that, in practice, has rarely turned out to be detrimental to patients.

"Sometimes you bargain someone down to intensive outpatient care rather than inpatient care, then they relapse, and you say to yourself, 'Gee, I should have gone with inpatient care,'" he says. "But you have to look at what areas of a person's life have been affected. Medicine is usually the area most protected and least impacted by a substance abuse problem. It is what they identify with most; it's who they are, not just what they do. You have to go by the severity of symptoms—cognitive damage, or how the referral came. If the concerns are raised by their work peers, you have to take it seriously. If the nature of the concerns are not incompetence, but maybe a breakdown of their abilities, maybe it's time to step in."

The committee will also act as an advocate for physicians seeking employment or under threat of punishment from the Board of Quality Assurance. The committee—after judging how well the physician has done in his or her treatment program—may advocate for the restoration of the right to practice medicine in the state. It also puts its money where its mouth is: Maryland was the first state medical society to loan physicians funds for treatment if their impairment depleted their finances. Over the committee's history, more than 80 percent of these funds have been repaid—one indicator of the excellent clinical outcomes for most physicians entering treatment under the committee's auspices.

This advocacy role has made many recovering physicians express overwhelming gratitude for the committee's role in their struggle. "Only committee members visited me at the rehabilitation center," wrote one. "Even my family did not visit. On weekends and at inopportune times for them, I'm sure, members came to inquire about my health, to share their experiences, and to offer the support I was not getting elsewhere. Upon returning to the outside world (if I may again use that phrase) the committee helped me find a place to live. In fact, I lived with a member of the committee and his family for an extended period of time. The committee supported my efforts to rehabilitate myself in the profession, to recommit as a person in the world, and to bring light to my self-worth. They offered any help, reassurance, and care I needed, the likes of which I cannot fully express in words or feelings. They and their families literally opened their homes to me, fed me, took care of me, and offered me a circle of friendship I will never forget. To a great extent, these friendships still exist after many years. I consider these people and their families to be part of my family. . . . I will never be able to thank them enough for what they did for me."

Stigma and Redemption

To their benefit, most doctors who manage to conquer their addictions do regain—or indeed, because of the privacy rules, simply retain—their preaddiction status in the community, Llufrio says. But privacy remains crucial for recovering physicians. Despite some progress in public attitudes, substance abuse remains stigmatized in this country. As a result, keeping knowledge of one's condition private is still a powerful motivator. "Some are fairly open with large groups," Llufrio says. "Others have a very strong recovery for twelve years or more yet maintain only a small base of people they'll talk to. Solo practitioners might not be concerned about losing a thriving pracice, but people in HMOs and hospitals, where politics are a big deal, tend to be more circumspect."

Nor do many doctors tell their patients about their problems, at least in the short term. "We don't recommend that they do it," Llufrio says. "Some of them feel so good about what they're doing—seeing themselves taking steps they never thought they could—that they want to tell perfect strangers in the elevator all about it. Normally, of course, we don't talk to people in elevators at all. If the patients are told, some of them handle it well, and others find new doctors."

Instead, Llufrio continues, "we ask that the physician get a more realistic picture. If he or she wants to tell people, they should do it a year or two down the road. There is a process in the twelve-step programs about making amends, but it's not up front. It's usually a couple years into recovery. Making direct amends to the people you've harmed—that's the ninth step. For most people, the first four steps take up the first year. Then you get to the rest later. Individual amends at first go to your family, your colleagues, and it could be patients, too."

This time spent attending Alcoholics Anonymous or Narcotics Anonymous meetings adds an undercurrent of spirituality to the matter of treatment—and redemption. The Twelve Steps of Alcoholics Anonymous[13] describe both the spiritual basis as well as the necessary actions that form the backbone of recovery. They require a willingness to change and become a healthy human being who can live harmoniously with others. They are:

1. We admitted we were powerless over alcohol; that our lives have become unmanageable.
2. We came to believe that a Power greater than ourselves could restore us to sanity.
3. We made a decision to turn our will and our lives over to the care of God as we understood Him.
4. We made a searching and fearless moral inventory of ourselves.
5. We admitted to God, to ourselves, and to another human being the exact nature of our wrongs.
6. We were entirely ready to have God remove all these defects of character.
7. We humbly asked Him to remove our shortcomings.
8. We made a list of all persons we had harmed, and became willing to make amends to them all.
9. We made direct amends to such people wherever possible, except when to do so would injure them or others.
10. We continued to take personal inventory and when we were wrong promptly admitted it.
11. We sought through prayer and meditation to improve our conscious contact with God as we understood Him, praying only for knowledge of His will for us and the power to carry that out.
12. Having had a spiritual experience (awakening) as the result of these steps,

we tried to carry this message to alcoholics, and to practice these principles in all our affairs.

The concept of making amends is a basic principle in AA. As Step Nine asserts, alcoholics are to make "direct amends. . . wherever possible" to all the people who have been harmed by their drinking. Also noted in Step Ten is the review of the inventory of our assets and liabilities. It is not that members of AA must spend most of their waking hours drearily rehashing their sins of omission or commission; they simply need the recognition that "a great many of us have never really acquired the habit of accurate self-appraisal."

These spiritual aspects of AA are unequivocally reflective of the concepts of repentance. Repentance is defined in the *Random House Dictionary of the English Language*[14] as:

1. A deep sorrow, compunction, or contrition for a past sin, wrongdoing, or the like. 2. Regret for any past action.

It is important to note that even if there is a need for an apology, it is not one offered automatically or unfeelingly but one that is earned over a long period of time. If the physician should fail during this payback period, it is likely that he or she will never return to practice.

Recently, there have been a number op-ed articles discussing the rise in "no-fault apologies," such as Baptist denominations' apologizing to the descendants of American slaves, or the governmental apologies for experimentation on unaware humans. Bar organizations publish lists of lawyers, organizations send "people to Coventry," and licensing boards for physicians publish the names of "bad" doctors, even on the Internet. Drunk drivers have to put special license plates on their cars, convicted shoplifters must take out advertisements in their local newspapers, and men in cities around the country who are convicted of soliciting prostitutes are identified on newspapers, radio shows and billboards. These various writers have noted that this epidemic of apologies is the logical outgrowth of the culture of confession by so many famous and infamous people who have bared their souls on national television.

But Maryland's program seems to avoid the worst of these pitfalls by mandating a trust-but-verify approach. As a counselor, Llufrio says, "you can't assume that everything you're told is the truth. Some are lies, some has to do with denial and self-delusion. It's important to speak with family members, partners, people who know them in various walks of life. The physician may not be totally honest. You need people experienced in dealing with addicts and alcoholics. You need to have funding in place. You need a solid core of people working on it; we work with volunteer physicians who are very dedicated. You need them behind you."

Though the medical disciplinary apparatus remains one step removed in Maryland, the broader medical society's demand for regular recertification remains another powerful check on violators, since full disclosure of substance abuse is required—while covering it up is grounds for fraud charges, for which penalties can be quite serious.

"Doctors are continually having to renew their credentials," Llufrio says. "When they're recovering, the hospital will want a letter from us, and I need to see them to do that. They can't just say they were recovering two years ago and let that get them by. The state's general renewal comes every other year. They'll ask whether, in the past two years, you have had a [drunk driving arrest] or lots of other things. When you check 'yes,' they generally refer it to us. In some cases we say he's been with us for eighteen months, and we send them a copy of the contract. But it's not made public."

Certainly the humane treatment at Med Chi's physician rehabilitation committee seems to provide an incentive for impaired physicians to turn themselves in, creating a conduit of trust that runs both ways. "This kind of program would be extremely valuable for other professions," Llufrio says. "One of the reasons physicians recover so well is that we provide support and monitoring. The average person is on their own. Doctors often do it because they choose to. If we can insist on people going through the motions, maybe they'll do it."

The system, Joel adds, is "very humane. At Med Chi, they are sensitive to the fact that this is an agency set up by physicians themselves to monitor physicians so they can take care of themselves. This is a real good thing. You have value. You've spent a lot of your life becoming a physician, but you're an addict; you have a disease, but that does not make you into a lousy physician. Some diseases overwhelm you, and you have to be treated. But when you're not overwhelmed—when you're in recovery—they let you be who you are, which is a physician. That's how it should be. You'll be an alcoholic for the rest of your life; that never changes. But I haven't had a drink in years now, and I have no desire to do so, either. So that's what the program gives me—it gives me back my profession and my life."

Appendix A

"And then I woke up, and I was a doctor. Thank you."
A Personal Testimony

Here is one case among the many overseen by Maryland's physician rehabilitation program:

My husband still teases me about saying this in my sleep several years ago. My eleven years of recovery have in many ways been a process of waking up after trying, with alcohol and drugs, to dampen the anxiety inherent in living my life authentically.

Recovery has given me the courage to confront the person I am and to become the person I was meant to be.

Born in Brooklyn, growing up on Long Island, I lived in the classic upwardly mobile, though dysfunctional, Jewish family. The prevailing message of my childhood said that no matter what I achieved, I wasn't quite perfect enough. I might be the smartest in my class, but I also must be the most beautiful and most popular. To become a doctor was okay; to marry a doctor would be preferable.

I always felt a bit different from the other girls in my neighborhood, most of whom were being groomed for "princesshood." I found solace in the burgeoning women's movement of the late sixties, but simultaneously got my first job at age fifteen in a drugstore. With the drug culture gaining momentum, I experimented with Seconals and Quaaludes—pharmacologically solid alcohol. I believe my initial reaction to drugs and alcohol was qualitively different from my friends' reactions; I experienced feeling normal. The inner tensions that had come to characterize my daily life were numbed. Life as it was never was quite enough, so I spent the next four years chemically augmenting my existence with pills.

In my second year of college, I awoke with a vision of myself as a cynical, old man with bulbous nose and twisted grimace. I knew that my soul was dying. In 1972, I took my first of several geographical cures, and transferred to a prestigious Ivy League university that had just become coeducational. I consulted a psychiatrist on campus about my drug problem. She diagnosed a problem with "coping mechanisms," and for the next two years we had weekly discussions concerning this.

I stopped doing drugs, but was soon drinking alcoholically. The occasional oblivion of an alcohol induced blackout punctuated the constant work, work, work. I led a dual existence; I graduated second in a class of "a thousand male leaders," but otherwise felt isolated except for my two year affair with an alcoholic psychology professor. To all the world, my professors and classmates, I appeared to be the girl who had everything. But I was running as fast as I could and continued to do so for the next twelve years.

After deciding I needed something more tangible than what my psychology degree offered, I gained acceptance to the top medical schools in the country, giving me instant external validation and an eight-year reprieve from self discovery! Medical school is a great enabler of the progressing alcoholic, for people assume that anyone who got there must basically have his or her act together. As my drinking escalated from sporadic to nightly, I started to occasionally overstep my tolerance and switched from hard liquor to wine only. With minor transgressions excused, I succeeded at medical school in the day, and looked for Mr. Goodbar at night. If anybody noticed that my life was becoming unmanageable, they attributed it to eccentricity, and besides, with one month rotations, no one got to know me too well.

I was falling uphill, and began a highly competitive internship on the west coast. After a twenty-four hour shift, I would stop at the local liquor store, pick up three bottles of Andre champagne, and head for the beach to black out, pass out, and start all over again the next day.

I took two years off from residency to work as a house physician at the local hospital. My drinking intensified, and though I sometimes didn't make it to the supermarket, I always had a gallon of Gallo wine in the refrigerator. After three months traveling in Europe, where Europeans often asked me why I drank so much, I again gained entrance at a prestigious hospital to complete my training.

At this point, I could no longer accurately predict when a single drink would put me into a blackout or ten drinks would fail to give me the sought after buzz; my days of drinking were numbered. I couldn't understand why I felt so jittery; why I couldn't sleep; or when I did, why I awoke with a sense of impending doom; or why my hands shook when I sutured a laceration. A glass or two of wine made this go away, made me seen to function better.

In my fourth month of residency, on my way to the hospital for an evening shift in the ER, I heard a spot on the radio from the Impaired Physicians Committee. I remembered this the next day when my residency director informed me that someone in the hospital reported smelling alcohol on my breath. I went into the next room and called the Committee; the following day, I attended my first Baltimore physicians AA meeting. I was touched by the laughter I heard, and realized that my life contained little laughter anymore. I had been trying to chemically expand my world, but it collapsed inward instead, rendering it a small and dark place.

I wish I could say it was a simple as that, but even though my recovering colleagues told me "one day at a time," I knew they meant I would not drink again. I could not fathom a life without alcohol. Maybe they didn't understand that I needed to have a drink, that it was the only time I felt okay. So I tried controlled drinking for three months, until one day, unexpectedly my fellow resident called in sick and I, hungover, was left to manage the surgical intensive care unit by myself for twenty-four hours. I started to take recovery seriously after that. Pain pushes until passion pulls.

At age thirty-one, I started to explore the self I had anesthetized since age fifteen. I discovered that I was enough, and to recognize the self I tried to annihilate as my guide to a peaceful coexistence with the universe. I discovered a sense of God in my life that I had never gleaned from my culturally Judaic heritage. I discovered that I could not afford to betray myself; otherwise, the urge to dissipate the dissonance was rekindled. I have started to experience gratitude, which has little to do with material wealth and everything to do with the space from which I approach life. My QOD dose of AA helps mitigate my inherent perfectionism and authoritarianism and goes much further in bringing me the sought after peace than my Q4hH shot of wine.

Today, I have a large and successful practice because I practice good medicine and truly listen to what my patients say. I have a husband of integrity and humor—even if he is a lawyer. We have a two-year-old son who I delivered at age forty. I believe God made me physiologically younger than my years because He knew I would have much catching up to do. Most of all, today, I have choices. As I sit here on vacation, gazing out on the Caribbean Sea, with a possible relocation to the Virgin Islands in my future, I thank God for the recovery that has given me the courage to change.

—Anonymous[15]

Notes

The interview with the patient whose pseudonym is Joel was conducted in August 1997. Interviews with Michael Llufrio, program director of the Physician Rehabilitation Program, were conducted in October and November 1997.

1. Editorial, "All doctors are problem doctors," *British Medical Journal*, 22 March 1997.

2. *Report of the Inspector General on Medical Malpractice and Impairment* (Washington, DC: Department of Health and Human Services, 1986).

3. AMA Council on Mental Health, "The Sick Physician: Impairment by Psychiatric Disorder including Alcoholism and Drug Dependencies," *JAMA* 233 (1973): 684-867.

4. G. D. Talbott and E. B. Benson, "Impaired Physicians: The Dilemma of Identification," *Postgrad Medicine* 56 (1980): 68.

5. G. Oster et al., "Benzodiazepine Tranquilizers and the Risk of Accidental Injury," *American Journal of Public Health* 80 (1990): 1467-70. Also, B. Hemmelgarn, S. Suissa, A. Huang et al., "Benzodiazepines Use and the Risk of Motor Vehicle Crash in the Elderly," *JAMA* 278 (July 1997): 27-31.

6. "My story," *Treatment Talk, Straight Forward* 7 (Winter 1996): 1.

7. "Medical Education: Not a Guide to Life," *Treatment Talk, Straight Forward* 1, April 1991.

8. D. R. Gerstein and H. J. Harwood "Treating Drug Problems, Volume I," *Institute of Medicine* (Washington, DC: National Academy Press, 1990).

9. D. C. Walsh et al., "A Randomized Trial of Treatment Options for Alcohol-Abusing Workers," *JAMA* 325 (September 1991): 775-82.

10. James H. Shore, "The Oregon Experience with Impaired Physicians on Probation," *JAMA* 257 (1987): 2931-4.

11. R. M. Morse et al., "Prognosis of Physicians Treated for Alcoholism and Drug Dependence," *JAMA* 251 (1984): 743-746.

12. "Everything I Ever Needed to Know About Recovery," *Treatment Talk, Straight Forward* 1 (September 1991).

13. "Twelve Steps and Twelve Traditions" (New York: Alcoholics Anonymous World Services, 1981).

14. *The Random House Dictionary of the English Language* (New York: Random House, 1967).

15. "And then I woke up, and I was a doctor. Thank you," *Treatment Talk, Straight Forward* 4 (Fall 1995): 1-2.

Index

About the Contributors

Gordon Bazemore

Gordon Bazemore is currently an Associate Professor of Criminal Justice at Florida Atlantic University. His primary research interests include juvenile justice, youth policy, community policing, corrections, and victims' issues, and he is the author of numerous journal articles, book chapters, and monographs on these topics. He is the editor of *Restoring Juvenile Justice: Changing the Context of the Youth Crime Response*, forthcoming in 1999.

David Carney

David E. Carney is a third-year law student at the College of William and Mary School of Law. He currently holds an editorial position on the *William and Mary Law Review*. Prior to law school he worked as a research associate for the Institute for Communitarian Policy Studies. He is the editor of *To Promote the General Welfare: A Communitarian Legal Reader*, forthcoming (1999), and coeditor with Amitai Etzioni of *Repentance: A Comparative Perspective*.

Amitai Etzioni

Dr. Amitai Etzioni is University Professor at George Washington University and the Director of the Communitarian Network in Washington, D.C. He is the author of numerous books, the most recent of which include *The New Golden Rule* and *The Spirit of Community*.

Estelle Frankel

Estelle Frankel, M.S., M.F.C.C., is a therapist in private practice in Berkeley, California, specializing in the interface between psychology and spirituality. She has been an instructor at numerous colleges in Israel and in the United States, including Lehrhaus Judaica (Stanford and University of California at Berkeley campuses) since 1978.

Patrick Glynn

Patrick Glynn is the associate director of the George Washington University Institute for Communitarian Policy Studies. His new book, *God—The Evidence*, was released in 1997.

John O. Haley

John O. Haley is the Garvey, Schubert & Barer Professor of Law and Professor of International Studies at the University of Washington. He is also Director of the Asian Law Program. Recent publications include *Restorative Justice: International Perspectives*.

Jeffrey L. Harrison
Jeffrey Harrison is the Chesterfield Smith Professor of Law at the University of Florida. He holds a Ph.D. in Economics and Business Administration from the University of Florida and a J.D. from the University of North Carolina. He has held positions at the University of North Carolina, the University of Texas, the University of Houston, and Leiden University. He writes in the fields of antitrust law, business regulation, and socioeconomics.

Stanley Platman
Stanley Platman, M.D., serves as Chairperson for the Physician Rehabilitation Committee of the Medical and Chirurgical Faculty of Maryland. He is a clinical professor of psychiatry at the University of Maryland and is the author of over seventy papers and chapters.